Compiled by Steve Levin
For his Father and Family
And also for the public to enjoy
To honour
His Grandfather
Eric Godfery Levin
From his memoirs and historical accounts
PER ARDUA

The Stokers Creed

Keep the sprayers open wide,
DO NOT touch the valves at the side.
Keep a pressure on the pump
And up your bally steam will jump.
If the smoke is black and thick
Open up your fans a bit.
If the smoke is thin and white,
Check the temperature is right.
If these instructions you will follow,
You'll make a balls up, I bet a dollar.

Thank you to the following people;

Jenny Levin my wife for putting up with me
during the writing and editing process.

Eric Levin my father for all the help
with my Grandfathers memoirs and photo's.

Susan Ewin, daughter of T/S.LT Donald Lefever
for the information from her father who is 90
and in the early stages of dementia.

Coastal Forces Veterans and its members
Especially: CFV admin team,
Ted Else
Brain Holmes
And Rupert Head

World Naval Ships Forum member
Jack W1208

CHAPTER ONE

START OF CAREER

At last I have found time to write up my grandfathers exploits when he served in the Royal Navy. I will be writing this in his perspective as he left my father about a dozen pages of his memories before he went in to ill health just before he died. Enlisting 13/July/1938 at an age of 25 I completed basic training at HM Dockyard Chatham, HMS Pembroke. Just after passing my course I had to have an appendix operation and some recovery time. Prior to being drafting to the Mediterranean on board HMS Malaya. I was embarked in transit on HM Troopship Nevasa from Southampton to Malta. On board her was the 2nd Battalion Kings Own Regiment they were on route to Haifa, Palestine Sept 1938.
 *Reference picture's 1, 2

It was a touching and poignant moment leaving the safety of England. With our hearts in our mouths with trepidation, it was the first time for many a lad to have left the country of their home. Many soon to be nearly drowned in vomit! I suppose I was lucky as life aboard ship was never difficult for me. I loved the adventure and was lucky I never got seasick.

It was generally not a pleasant experience embarking on a troopship destination unknown to many on board. Until the duty rumours had reached them of where we were going. Life on board varied greatly, a new experience to most, especially washing in salt water!

There were so many troops on board the Nevasa her fresh water was saved for drinking and cooking. Fortunately most of us on board had been able to acquire some salt water soap the night before from the canteen at the docks. Even so it was still difficult to lather up for a decent shave. Cleaning your teeth had to be done using your mugs with a little drinking water in them. Washing and rinsing off had to be done in the cold salt water. There were no beds for us junior ranks the senior non commissioned officers got mattresses to bed down. But of course the officers got the cabins with beds junior officers had to share the bigger rooms and the senior officers got the single man rooms. Us junior ranks were given hammocks and a single blanket all of us Navy in transit could put up our hammocks. But the Army lads found it hard and spent the entire trip sleeping on the deck. Not very comfortable and most of the time wet with seawater and vomit.

The ships Crew continually tried to get us involved in "Crown and Anchor" dice games usually for cigarettes. At times it was pelting down with rain, and the heavy gales rocking the ship to and fro. With her going plunging up and down over the waves and side to side most of the troops were seasick. The stink of sea sickness spread around the decks all the hand basins were full all the fire buckets were full and the decks were slimy with vomit. The emptying of stomachs stench was getting etched into our memories. All I can remember were pale soldiers entering the mess grumbling and groaning, grabbing some essential scoff.

Then they raced across the deck trying not to slide over on the slime. Out they went through the opposite door to chuck up over the side holding onto the rail hopefully not into the wind. Common sense prevailed eventually especially when the ship was rolling and pitching with the weather. The most sickness prone survived on canned food from ration packs and dry bread. What a way to go to war green as a frog or paler than a sheet and puking all the way.

Ten days later we arrived at Malta. I was billeted at HMS St Angelo previously Fort St Angelo. A large fortification in Birgu it was one of the base's of Operations for the Navy in the Med. My stay was only for 24 hours not enough time to get drunk or see the sights. Then it was time to board my first assignment.

HMS MALAYA

HMS Malaya was a Queen Elizabeth-class battleship of the British Royal Navy, built by Sir W. G. Armstrong Whitworth and Company at High Walker and launched in March 1915. She was named in honour of the Federated Malay States in British Malaya, whose government paid for her construction. See pictures 3, 4.
She and her sister ships were the last real battle wagon dreadnaught battleships in the Navy. Before military idealists changed their views that they were to big a target for enemy aircraft.
 She was commissioned on the 1st Feb 1916.
Her displacement was 33,020 tonnes and she could pack a punch.

3.

Length: 645 ft 9 in (196.82 m), Beam 90 ft 6 in (27.58 m), Draught: 29 ft 10 in (9.09 m)
Propulsion: Parsons direct drive steam turbines 24 boilers With 4 propeller shafts 56,500 hp Top speeds of 25 knots, Range 4,400 miles, Crew Complement 1,124 to 1,300

Armament when she was built; 8 × BL 15-inch Mk I guns, (4 x 2) 16 × single BL 6-inch Mk XII guns, 2 × single QF 3-inch 20cwt anti-aircraft guns, 4 × single 3-pdr (47 mm) saluting guns, 4 × 21-inch (530 mm) submerged torpedo tubes.

After her 1934-1936 refits she had more weapons added; 8x single six-inch guns, 8x double 4-inch Mk XVI anti-aircraft guns.

The following day I joined HMS Malaya I was assigned to Mess 42. I was happy to join in with the usual friendly banter that was the usual welcome to any new member to the mess. It was then down to acquainting one-self as part of the ships crew and get to know the working departments.

The mess deck was your home. You had your meals there, you slept there and you wrote your letters there. We all were issued a locker in which you stored your belongings / kit. All the lockers were around the outside of the mess with cushions on top to serve as seats or beds to get a nap between shifts. You only used your hammocks if you were going to get a whole night sleep.

4.

There were bars running across the top of the mess to use when you slung your hammocks ready for a rest. In front of the lockers were four tables, two to each side of the mess deck. Bolted to the floor, from which you ate your meals. Space aboard ship was very cramped no real privacy.

Even the heads (toilets) were partly public you could have a chat to your mates over the low partitions. While you sat and did your business. You did all your own clothes washing and all us ratings did our own cooking in duty shifts. All the serving of food and clearing away was done by us and you had to keep your mess spotless.

In the Navy the day was divided into watches /divisions. Each watch was four hours except for one which was divided into two. In order to give an odd number of watches per day so you didn't keep repeating the same routine at the same time all the time every day. It could be monotonous but like everything else you got used to it.

The ship had four Boiler rooms with two admiralty three-drum boilers in each. That makes 24 boilers in total and one large central engine room. The ship had two smaller wing engine rooms these were watch-keeping parts of the ship for experienced time-served hands, out of bounds for us newbie's. All the engine rooms had Parsons direct drive steam turbines. So to the boiler rooms I was destined, one had to become very knowledgeable of everything appertaining to the boiler rooms etc. Whether working in various roles as boiler cleaning party, uptake parties, or double-bottom and bilge parties etc.

5.

We hardly ever had to work with coal or a shovel. We had 3,300 tons of oil on board and a reserve of 100 tons of coal we handled the oil fuel valves to feed the furnaces. Not a particularly dirty job just bloody warm at times. On every watch there was a Petty officer who handled the steam valves. Also there was an Artificer whose job was to check and run the generator to make sure we had emergency lighting if it was needed.

Nothing was ever missed out. One had to serve one's time in all these departments of the boiler room complex. Before finally you achieved enough experience. You had to be lucky and skilled to be chosen to move from the sanctity of the boiler rooms. You could move to another section like the; auxiliary machinery spaces; i.e. CO_2 Room, dynamo generator room and hydraulic room. These departments were where you did watch keeping it was a bit of a cushy job. But you still had along with this cleaning and painting and all the other duties within these areas. Also the daily routine duties like preparing the meals and cleanliness of the mess etc.

One also had to take into account all morning divisions and evening divisions that accounted for the running of the ships regulations. However when one became accustomed to the routine it became natural to ones everyday life. So there was very little spare time, even to write home. Every one of the ships crew had a make and mend half day at one time in the rota. You can make up your own mind what you want to do with your time off. Like writing home, sewing, darning your socks or reading what ever you liked.

That's what life is all about on board a ship. Everyday we all got a tot of rum the entire junior ranks had it watered down I think that's where the term "grog" (meaning week bear) came from. Petty officers and chief petty officers were allowed to have neat rum and many of them would keep a flask or some other container to save for later but junior ranks was not allowed to do that.

October 1938
On operations we patrolled the Palestine coast in a bid to stop gunrunning. We must have searched as many as 140-150 vessels a week various sizes. Most of the vessels were Arab type dhows or little llaut open fishing boats. Sometimes sea mines were deployed off the ship we had to carefully row them ashore in the long boats. They were used with time delay fuses to destroy houses or weapons caches that had been found. Sometimes the charges laid were so large that neighbouring houses came down they made the earth shake like an earth quake. Many a piece of flying debris hit watching bystanders that's what you call flying shrapnel. We also used the ships spotlights along the coast to blind the locals turning the dark of night instantly to daylight. We used them when there was trouble ashore to aid shore parties and to disperse the Arab snipers.

November
We got called away from the Palestine coast to sail to Schurma Turkey. Most of the ships company disembarked to travel by train up to Constantinople.

We were representing the Royal Navy at the funeral ceremonial for their beloved leader Mustafa Kamil Attaturk. To display the respect felt by Great Britain's government to Turkey and its people. There were quite a lot of other country's navies also present. It was a very big occasion for the country of Turkey and their people. Of course, respect for all countries in the world at that time was paramount. Then it was back to Malta but not for long though.

December 1938- March 1939
We went back to operations in Palestine. First stop landing a Royal marine contingent at Haifa. To reinforce the British Army forces in containing trouble. Also to evacuate GOC Sir John Dill having a price put on his head by Palestine Arabs. We lost one Royal Marine in the conflict at Haifa.

At the request of the Army the ship landed platoons of mixed crew and marines. We were put ashore to help protect Haifa in support of the local police. We were doing patrols and dispersing riotous mobs. I heard one of the marine's tell another crew member. "Keep your boots tied on while onshore the Arabs (Ab-Dabs) will steal anything that's not tied down". During our stay the Captain told us that in all the incidents on shore they had recorded; 50 fires, 25 bombings, 20 stonings or stabbings and 4 shootings. At least most of us were safe when we were aboard the ship off the coast.

April 1939
All the ships in the Mediterranean fleet sailed for Gibraltar. We were to join the home fleet for the annual "Spring Manoeuvres". This took place in the Western Approaches in the Atlantic. The ships crew did a lot of anti-aircraft practice loading and firing the 4-inch ack-ack guns and gunnery drills.
*Reference picture 5.

The ships 4-inch anti-aircraft guns practiced their shooting firing on an unmanned plane called the Queen Bee. It's flown by radio control or if you like remotely controlled. Designed in 1935, the DH 82B was a converted De Havilland Tiger Moth. It derived from the civilian De Havilland Gipsy Moth plane. Modern Remote operated aircraft have adopted the name "Drone" to pay homage to the first of their kind the "Queen Bee".

Depth charge drills and 15-inch turret drills and firing also were practiced. Then it was do it all over again with anti-gas drills and equipment. There was a lot of ship manoeuvring into and out of formations. This was a lot of work for us in the boiler rooms. Changing speed and pressure and the amount of fuel oil needed. It lasted the duration of 3-4 weeks. Everyone did well and had got it right in the end, only a few minor hiccups. It was pats on the back for all the crew from the officers and an extra tot of rum. When there was any down time during the Manoeuvres. We were kept busy involved in PT on deck or resting and reading.

While the marine's did not rest instead they did stick fighting and bayonet practice that's the keen leather necks for you.

May 1939

All the forces on manoeuvres got their orders to disperse to their particular stations etc. During our way to return to Malta we visited places on the French and Italian Rivera's "showing the flag". Up until we had orders to return towards Spain. To blockade any ships participating in aiding Franco's Civil War. After a week or so of this the Admiralty had finally decided which ships should stay in that area. We were relieved of that duty to carry on with our "showing the flag". We cruised along the coast of: Villefranche, Nice, Monte Carlo and Mentone.

There were visits to quite a number of exquisite places a bit of sight seeing and R&R. One visit stands out very much in my memory. We visited the scent-manufacturing centre in Grasse up in the French Alps. It's world famous as the centre of the French perfume industry and is known as the world's perfume capital.

By the time we all left there, one could smell the perfume on us a mile off. They simply bathed us with the stuff there is nothing more off putting than a bunch of rugged hairy sailors smelling like a whore's hand bag. One of our last ports of call was Venice where the American actor and film director Douglas Fairbanks, senior and his close friend Noel Coward came aboard. It was only a flying visit for afternoon tea with the Captain and officers. *Reference picture 6.

10.

22nd May
The Germany/ Nazi's sign "Pact of Steel" with Italy to unite together militarily.

  On completion of our Spring Cruise as they called it, it was back to Malta where we got a few runs ashore. Costing 2/6p which paid for bottles of Xanger's beer (blue label), a big eat of local cuisine, the pictures (cinema), a bed for the night, with port and lemon on awakening and a continental breakfast. We still had some change to buy a coffee royale before returning aboard ship in the morning. Whilst trying not to fall off the gangplank still suffering from the night before. Nobody wants a dunk in the sea unexpected but we all did occasionally.

1st September
Nazi Germany invades Poland.

2nd September
All the Mediterranean fleet met up again at Alexandria for the annual regatta. Last year's winner of the "Cock of the Med" (which was Top prize for most wins in the regatta) was HMS Barham. Also known as the Merry Barham as the crew always got into trouble with other ships crews. With the challenge to out drink the amount of beer consumed ashore. It usually resulted in drunken punch-ups whilst waiting for the boats to take the crews back aboard their ships.

However due to the Italians and their leader Mussolini aligning to the Germany. Their invasion of Albania made trouble for us and it became more trying on runs ashore for the crew's. It was a little too much to ask the crews to be more diplomatic and sensible whilst still getting drunk. With Great Britain, France, Australia and New Zealand declaring war on Germany the fleet had to show some restraint. And the crews had to behave on runs ashore due to the League of Nations conventions. But many fracases escaped the notice of the police and shore patrols.

5th September
United States proclaims its neutrality.

9th September.
The then C in C of the Mediterranean Fleet was Admiral Sir Dudley Pound. He was presenting the awards for the annual regatta on the final day. This was the day before war was officially declared. After honours were exchanged it became apparent. HMS Malaya had won all the trophies. Thus we became the last "Cock of the Med" before all out war. I was a member of the Stoker's rowing team and we won all our races helping towards the overall win. The trophy was a large silver cockerel standing about two feet tall on a plinth. Nobody knows what happened to the trophy over the war years it went missing. The navy couldn't confirm where it went or even if it existed after the war. Since then the Navy has reinstated the trophy but now it is a lot smaller.
*Reference picture's 7. 8.

10th September 1939
Canada declares war on Germany; Battle of the Atlantic begins.

11th September
We sailed from Alexandria to carry out a big gunnery exercise. The fleet comprised of sister Battleships: Warspite and Barham. With Cruisers: Devonshire, Sussex, Arethusa and Penelope. Also Destroyers: Afridi, Gurkha, Mohawk and Sikh. As 1st battle squadron there was a lot of to-in and fro- in to different places engaging different targets of various sizes.

9th October
We sailed from Alexandria to carry out exercises in company with; HMS Glorious (aircraft carrier), Battleships: Warspite and Barham, Cruiser Penelope and Destroyers: Bulldog, Dainty, Daring, Duncan, Gallant, Gipsy and Grafton.

14th October
We were ordered to the Indian Ocean via Suez Canal to join East Indies Command. Because of the activities of German raiders we joined J Force in that theatre of operations. We operated around the areas of the Seychelles, Socotra (An Island off Yemen) and Mombassa in company with HMS Glorious (aircraft carrier), Destroyer Bulldog and Daring for convoy defence.

15th October
Going through the Suez Canal was a bit of a tight squeeze.

16th October
Arrived in Aden waters and carried out anti raider sweeps along convoy corridors. We were always on the look out for the German Panzerschiff / Pocket-Battleship, Admiral Graf Spee. That was reportedly in the area. But we did not know by then she had moved on to other seas, I was looking forward to being in my first big fight with a proper man of war.

16th November
HMS Ramillies Revenge-class Battleship and Destroyer Delight joined us to carry on with the sweeps of the Gulf of Aden. At times British submarine HMS Talisman joined us on patrol. She was later in November of 1941 to be involved with Operation Flipper. * Reference Picture 10. She carried 59 commandos on an audacious mission to kill Rommel. But faulty intelligence did not know he was not at his HQ at Beda Littoria, Libya. But he was in fact vacationing in Italy with his wife Lucie to celebrate his 50th birthday.

December
We were nominated for service in the Atlantic. So we sailed from Aden escorted by Australian destroyers HMAS Vendetta and Waterhen. We went through the Suez Canal on the 11th getting to Malta on the 14th. We had at least a few runs ashore for ambeet/amtot slang for cheap Maltese wine.

14.

December 21ˢᵗ

We then left Malta escorted by Destroyers: Delight, Diana and Watchman. The general buzz went round the ship we were destined for the UK. It was two days before Christmas when we arrived at Gibraltar. An announcement was given that we would celebrate Christmas day with all the trimmings. Everyone enjoyed the festivities until teatime when orders were announced to put to sea immediately. However we were only underway for two hours when the next day's ships orders were put on the Daily Ships Routine Board. "Ship is on course for Halifax, Nova Scotia – Canada". Well you can imagine the talk and subdued state the whole of the ships company below decks were in. However, having recovered from that shock we all thought we would see blighty before long. We endured a very rough crossing over the "POND".

The weather caused tremendous problems. The sea was violent with waves of 30ft plus smashing over the bow. We were rolling as much as 30 degrees to port and starboard. We had to use lifelines when going on deck. These lifelines were tied very firmly to the ships companionways. Anyone going on deck had to fix a rope round their waist it had a loose length of rope with a hook on the end of it. You could hook and attach it to the lifeline. You had to gradually move when the ship was steady and hold firm when rolling. If you didn't stand firm and hold on tight when she rolled. Your feet would leave the deck and at 30 degrees you were left hanging over the side above the sea.

15.

At maximum roll the ship would shudder for a few seconds debating and then if lucky she would decide to come back over. We eventually got there and everything was snow bound. The place was 20ft deep in snow everywhere and even deeper in drifts. It took us more than 6 hours to get carefully moored up to the frozen quay. In the following days a good portion of the ships company were going down with the flu and other cold weather ailments. It took the town of Halifax a week or so to really to accept the ship and her company.

There was one main street (Barrington Street), which ran from their naval dockyard down to the KGV (King George V) Quay. We were limited in the amount of shore leave to only 6 hours in daylight at that time of year. The town was under prohibition, so we could only get alcohol from the Liquor Licensing Authorities. They controlled all the places that sold alcohol, and one had to consume it on their premises. We stayed at anchor for two weeks waiting out gales to blow over at least it was a rest from being at sea. The gales had delayed the convoy's formation that we were to escort to the UK. All the merchants struggled to get there in the winds and waves from their home ports where they loaded with their cargos.

8th January 1940
Rationing begins back home in Britain as the strangle hold of the Battle of the Atlantic intensifies and the support of the troops abroad kicks in.

CHAPTER TWO
CONVOYS

14th January 1940

The weather eased down and the cruisers and destroyers were sent off to round up all the dirty drab ducks of the merchant ships. We were able to sort some resemblance to a convoy with the un- disciplined merchants. It always seemed that they wanted to work alone at their own speed and sod everyone else. Eventually at last everything was in order and all the merchant skippers had been briefed and told what to do off we sailed. With dirty grey black smoke belching from the dirty unkempt boilers of the merchants. It was a big formation of all types of merchant navy ships to come under the command of the Commodore Escorts from Canada. We joined destroyers HMCS Ottawa and Saguenay and it was called convoy HX16.

Ships name & Cargo
Melmore Head- General grain, Esmond -Newsprint, Pacific Ranger- General, Athellaird- Molasses, Athelknight- Fuel Oil, Josepth Seep- Crude Oil, Zeus- Grain, Athelqueen-Molasses, Wearwood -Grain, Manaqui- General, Venetia-Gasoline, Laristan-Crude Oil, British Officer-Gas Oil, Hopemount- Gas-Oil, Fuel, Virgilia-Benzine, Aldington Court-Lumber Grain, Rhea- Crude oil, Imperial Transport-Fuel Oil, Badjestan- Grain, Athelmonarch-Molasses, Volontaire- Cold Fish, Scottish Trader-Grain, W.H.Libby-Crude Oil, Margarita Chandri-Grain. Oil reliance-Gasoline'

Days and days were endured by zig-zagging steering at 5 knots toward the U.K. Some ships were damaged due to being in collision with one another chiefly in the dark hours. As no ships were allowed to carry any lights whatsoever under convoy orders. All the merchants in the convoy would tow a little buoy behind their ships. It was like a little water ski that spouted water up two or three feet high into the air. Other ships would try and keep this in sight so they didn't run into each other.

After seeing the Atlantic in the winter I was glad to be a stoker I was down below decks where it was warm. When our convoy got within range of the escort ships sent from the U.K. We handed control of the convoy over to them. So HMS Malaya and another six destroyers could leave and we proceed to the Clyde for a rest. We later heard Badjestan was so severely damaged in a collision. She grounded ashore off Clanchaig Point, Isle of Arran, all her crew were rescued by HMS Maori. We then left Clyde only after a couple of days to return to Halifax Canada for another convoy task.

30th January
We sailed from Halifax with convoy TC3 we had a lot of company: Aircraft Carrier Enterprise, Battleship Valiant and fourteen of our Destroyers: Faulknor, Fearless, Forsight, Firedrake, Foxhound, Fortune, Fame, Fury, Diana, Daring, Kelvin, Kingston, and Hunter, Also with us were HMCS destroyers: Fraser, Ottawa, Restigouche and ST Laurent.

The convoy comprised of Troopship Liners: Aquitania, Empress of Britain, Monarch of Bermuda, Empress of Australia and Polish Chobry. One of the ships carried 600 Italian prisoners of war, which were going to Britain to work on the farms. On the second day HMS Hunter, HMC Fraser, Ottawa, Restigouche and ST Laurent were detached from the convoy for other tasks. On the fifth day Aircraft Carrier Enterprise was detached from us. From my point of view merchant seamen were frightfully important and it took guts to be on a merchant ship. Because they were so slow and they were transporting sometimes very dangerous cargos. Whilst still being unarmed mostly but for the private ownership of small arms that the crews could get hold off.

Arrived back home at Clyde on the 7th February. Without any serious incidents we then had a bit of a rest and shore leave time to visit the family. Whilst we had leave the ship had degauzing equipment fitted on board. To counteract the magnetic mine menace that was out there on the high seas. Other refits at that time were added like new equipment and upgrading the old equipment. Type Air Warning 286 Radar was fitted at the masthead. An A type Surface Radar 284 was fitted on the Low Angle Director Control Tower. A type of High Angle 285 radar was added on each of the HA DCT's. Some 20 additional 20mm Oerlikon guns were added for Anti-Aircraft defence they could also be used to shoot up enemy vessels that were too close for the big guns. They could always be used to shoot up the cost if we were close enough.

27th February

We had the chance of becoming a floating Fort Knox. The crates of gold bullion we were transporting were just sitting on the dock. After being dumped there by the armoured car security guards, like there was nothing special about them. The Captain had to come down to the dock and count them so he could sign for them. If only he had miss counted and we could have spirited one of the crates away. We then loaded them on to the ship for the crossing the captain placed the Marines on guard over them so no crew members could get light fingered. * Reference picture 11.

We sailed from the Clyde with the tons of gold bullion for transfer to Canada. It was to help with the war deficit owed by England to Canada and the United States. We had the company of armed merchant Cruiser Ascania. We were also escorted by Destroyers: Fame, Faulknor, Forester, Fury and Mohawk.
We arrived at Halifax on the 4th March.

10th March

We set Sail again and joined Destroyers HMCS Saguenay and Skeena escorting convoy HX26. We were only just getting in to the crossing on the second day when Saguenay and Skeena left. This left Malaya as the ocean crossing escort on her own it was a difficult crossing controlling the merchants. We had to make full use of our Swordfish spotter plane and the captains launch all the way over.

<u>HX26 Ships and cargo;</u>

Diplomat-General, Hertford-Frozen, Arina-Gasoline,
Stylianos Chandris- Grain, Nova Scotia, General,
Victoria City- Wheat Lumber, Amberton-Wheat,
Athel Viking-Molasses, Ripley, San Zotico-Fuel Oil, Lumber Wheat,
Voco, Lube Oil, Fowberry Tower-Maize, Nailsea Manor-Grain,
Atland-Pig Iron, Siris-General, Delphinula-Lube Oil,
 Kenbane Head- General, Beaverdale-General, San Fabian-Fuel Oil,
Antonio-Wheat, Persephone-Crude Oil, Statesman-General,
Kurdistan-Wheat, Ahamo-Fuel Oil,Pontypridd- Cerials,
Lorento- General, City of Bagdad- General, San Tiburcio-Fuel Oil,
Troilus-General, British Courage-Fuel Oil, Argyll-Wheat Lumber,
Appledore-Scrap Iron, Rossington Court-Lumber Wheat,
Port Fairy-Refrigerator, Montreal City-General, Solstad-Lube Oil,
Llanishen- Cerials, Argos Hill- General, Marstenen-Canned Goods,

13th March 1940

About 600 miles into the crossing Athel Viking's steering got jammed somehow. She cut into the side of the Liberty Ship SS Rossington Court in the dark hours. Slicing through to the engine room, due to radio silence and a fog nobody noticed she had gone down. Until dawn broke the convoy sailed on unawares and then the convoy realised she was missing. One of the other ships broke away from the convoy with us to see if we could find her or if there were any survivors floating about. The Atlantic was very rough so we could not launch the spotter plane. But by a miracle the other ship found a lifeboat bobbing about full of survivors.

They had learnt from the crew that the other lifeboat on board had been crushed by the collision. But all the crew and officers had managed to squeeze into the one boat and still float just. Our ship later found out the SS Rossington Court abandoned due to the damage she had received from the collision. The crew had transferred to another ship in the convoy letting her drift off to sink. We had to sink her just in case she was a danger to any other shipping.
*Reference picture 12.

The rest of the journey went by uneventful except for when we were three quarters of the way across. One very early morning there was an alarm one of the lookouts from up top shouted U-boat. The U-boat was on the surface five miles off the starboard quarterdeck. We were told it looked like a U-boat shape but it was strange as they were virtually stationary in the water. So the captain gave orders for our swordfish (String-bag) spotter plane to be launched to investigate and attack. Strangely again the U-boat did not dive when our plane took off noisily from the catapult. The pilot of the aircraft must have thought this was his lucky day. For a D.F.C. (Distinguished Flying Cross) was the usual reward when an aircraft sank a U-boat. He must have been delighted when he went in for the kill. He dropped a couple of bombs but they were badly aimed and missed in his excitement so he dropped another stick of four more bombs.

There was a line off great water spouts but strangely one of them was tinted pinkish red and the object in the water rolled on its back it was a bloody whale!

To look out over the convoy and see all those ships in a pattern was an eye opener. Looking like a large checkerboard with a few battlewagons circling it. While our ship was busy zigzagging to keep the speed right down and not get too far ahead of the convoy. So time on convoys consisted mainly of nervous sweating and waiting for anything to happen. Everyone was scared of the unseen menace of the U-Boats and what was waiting for us over the horizon everyone was becoming restless. However there was total discipline and respect for each and every one of us getting on with the jobs at hand and doing our duty.

That's what I really liked in the Navy the respect from the guy next to you. It did not matter if he was higher or below you in rank, it was teamwork in a grand scale. We all understood the higher rank they were the louder they would shout to get the best out of us all. There was always a competition to get faster in your drills and smother in the running of the ship. We all knew when the time came our lives would depend on it. That split second saved in the automatic response to drills, alarms and orders would make the difference.

16th March
Nazi Germany bombs Scarpa Flow naval base.

22nd March
When the convoy reached the north western approaches we
were informed that escort ships had been sent out to meet
us. We detached from HX26 after a fast hand over to the
escort warship's commander and returned to Halifax,
Canada for another convoy.

3rd April
We were nominated for transfer to Mediterranean Fleet but
first we had to escort HX32 back to the U.K. We sailed the
same day at 1800 Hrs and met up with the convoy to
relieve the Canadian Navy. We had 30 merchant ships in
total for the convoy with all sorts of cargo for beleaguered
Britain.

Ships and Cargo;

Parthenia-General, Queen Maud-Wheat Lumber,
Point Bonita-General, British Honour-Fuel Oil,
Hopecrown-General Lumber, Eclipse-Crude Oil,
Rugeley-Wheat Lumber, Benwyvis-Wool, Octavian –Paper
Esmond-Newsprint, Wellington Court-Sugar,
San Alvaro-Gasoline, Balmoralwood-Wheat,
British Prince-General, Carslogie-Timber,
Star of Alexandria-Newsprint, Thistlegarth-Sugar,
Leontious Teryazos-General, Lochmonar-Timber Grain,
Gitano-Copper, Sugar, Minnie De Larrinago-Pig Iron, King
William-Lumber Grain, Weirbank-Timber Grain,
Antonious Chandris- Grain, Athellaird-Molasses,
Kingswood- Flour, British Chancellor-Benzine, Capsa-
Crude Oil, Port Hunter-Butter, Wool, Beaconhill-Gasoline.

A bit about convoys, a convoy covered a large area of the sea, proportionate to the number of ships of which it comprised. A convoy of 31 ships could spread out over 15 square miles; the ships were divided into columns. There was a mile distance between each column and half a mile distance between each ship in line. Ammunition carriers and Oil tankers took position in the centre, as they were the most important to the war effort and had to be protected most. The command ship was at the head of the first column in the middle, with the other ships spread out in a rectangular pattern. The escorts were placed all around the convoy to protect it like circling the wagons around the homesteaders in the cowboy films.

The convoys didn't want to cross the pond in the middle as it was called the "Black Hole". An area where an estimated 100 to 150 German submarines were set up to torpedo anything that moves. It was a free zone for them, as Allied planes protecting the convoys didn't have enough fuel to reach that area. So in the boiler room below decks we didn't get see too much of the action but you get to know the massiveness of the whole thing and remember the noise and commotion.

9th April

Nazi Germany invades Denmark and Norway. With Norway's entry into the war our ship sent a message to the Octavian a Norwegian freighter. To wish their armed forces, good luck and good hunting. Octavian sent back the reply "We will do our best" as all the crew wanted to go home and go on active service.

This convoy's passage passed uneventful. We all started to feel like the enemy's subs and surface raiders were scared. It seemed they didn't want to take on the convoys being escorted by our ship. We were all thinking they had been intimidated by the size of the Malaya. On the 14th Apr we were released from the convoy and we steamed off for Gibraltar. The day after we had been relieved the Port Hunter collided with Queen Maud at 250°/51m near Bishops rock. She was diverted to Southampton for repairs

19th April 1940
We arrived at Gibraltar and all the crew were glad for some shore leave. Even if it was only a few hours a day it was a bonus and enough time to get a few beers in. I did get to visit the Rock climbing to the top took some time to look out over the busy shipping channels and docks. We all were trying to avoid the rock-apes the resident monkeys. They love stealing sailor's headdress and anything they can get hold of. We heard some good news from the top brass. That a British mission captured a German U-boat, intact but damaged. They had recovered a partially damaged de-coding machine (Enigma). So the Admiralty was more able to decode Germany's radio traffic. They could now work out how to trace where the U-boats were or at least where their areas of operation. Good news for future convoys if true we thought as they could avoid those areas.

28th April

At 1600 Hrs sailed from Gibraltar we had Battleship Royal Sovereign with us. We were being escorted by Destroyers: Velox, Watchman and HMAS Vendetta and Waterhen. Waves were at 40-60 feet high the ship was leaking like a sieve from the upper works. She was groaning and grumbling like a living thing and getting tossed about like a cork. Some times the Med can be like a millpond smooth and calm but at other times the Med can be a cruel mistress.

29th April

Off Algiers we were joined by a French battle group of 3 Battleships, 4 Cruisers and 3 Destroyers. This put us all on edge I think the British have never really trusted or liked the French since the Battle of Agincourt. There was a lot of shouting ship to ship with lots of our crew holding two fingers up to the French. An old British signal from Agincourt days as the French used to chop off captured long bowmen's fingers so they could not fire any more arrows. So the signal is meant to say sod you I have my fingers.

30th April

Off Bizerte destroyers: HMAS Stuart and Vampire joined the flotilla. Later in the Sicilian Channel we also were joined by Cruiser Orion and Destroyers: Decoy and Defender. I think this was more to keep a watch full eye on the French then for protection.

1st May

Off Malta Destroyers Velox and Watchman detached into Malta Harbour. We carried on with the convoy to Alexandria.

3rd May

Arrived at Alexandria we released the convoy to their anchorage in the safe harbour so they could wait their turn unloading. We deployed with Battleship Royal Sovereign after refuelling. We were to patrol the local area protecting the approaches to Alexandria and provide escort cover for the passage of convoys in the eastern Med.

At this time the Mediterranean had been an Allied "lake". The French Fleet and the Royal Navy dominated the sea. So during this month extensive exercises were carried out. We were anticipating the future outbreak of hostilities with the Italians. The 1st battle Squadron was preparing for more than a few offensive operations against enemy shipping.

10th May

Nazi's invade France, Belgium, Luxembourg and the Netherlands; Winston Churchill becomes British Prime Minister.

15th May

Holland surrenders to Nazi Germany.

26th May

Evacuation of Allied troops from Dunkirk begins and undoubtedly the heroes of this were all the civilians in their small boats coming to the troops rescue. The Navy just could not handle the immediate need for so many ships at such short notice with all the other operations happening around the world. The sight of the small ships armada crossing the channel must have been a sight to behold and extremely welcome by the beleaguered troops waiting on the beaches.

28th May

Belgium surrenders to Nazi Germany.

10th June

Norway surrenders to the Nazi Germany.

11th June

Italy declared war on Britain and France at 0001 Hrs changing the threat in the Med excessively toward the Axis Power.

12th June

At 0230 Hrs We sailed from Alexandria with Battleship Warspite and Air Craft Carrier Eagle. We also had a screen of protective Destroyers around us consisting of; Dainty, Hasty, Ilex, Janus, Juno, Nubian and HMAS Stuart, Vampire and Voyager. Our task was to carry out a sweep and clearance of the Mediterranean Sea.

Showing off our almighty power along the African coast to try and demoralize the enemy. We were joined later throughout the day by order of appearance;
Cruisers: Caledon, Calypso.
Destroyers: Mohawk, Havock, Hereward, Hostile, Hyperion and Imperial.
Then at 1953 Hrs HMAS Stuart, Vampire and Voyager detached from the fleet but were replaced by Destroyer Diamond joining us.

14th June
The whole fleet returned to Alexandria for run up exercises. We got the news that Nazi German troops had entered Paris. There was the possibility of the Germans taking control of the French fleet at Mers-El-Kebir, on the coast of French Algeria. Our government ordered them attacked after they had ignored terms of surrender. This resulted in the attack by force H from Gibraltar on the 3rd June. This attack caused 1,297 deaths of French sailors and the sinking of one French battleship and damaging five other ships. In my opinion it's only the Froggies Oh well what a shame at least that sorted out the threat there.

22nd June
The French sign an armistice with Nazi Germany and its consequence changed the threat in the Med considerably. The French Fleet at Alexandria became a potential threat to our fleet in Axis hands.

4th July

We took part in negotiations with the French fleet in Alexandria. Admiral Cunningham gave them the same terms that they had received at Mers-El-Kebir.

1. Join us and fight the Germans.
2. Be escorted to a British port.
3. Have your ships disarm at Oran under British supervision.
4. Scuttle the ships where they are, but with a promise no force would be used against men who had worked so well with the British fleet.

The French Admiral agreed on the 7th to disarm his fleet and stay in port. They stayed until the French eventually joined the allies in arms against the Germans.

CHAPTER THREE
AIR WAR

7th July 1940
At around 2330 Hrs we sailed in company with
Battleship's: Royal Sovereign and Warspite alongside
Aircraft Carrier Eagle. We had a Destroyer screen from:
Dainty, Defender, Hasty, Hyperion, Ilex, Imperial, Janus,
Juno, Garland and HMAS Vampire and Voyager. We were
assigned as Task Force C. We were to provide cover for the
transit of two convoys MF1 and MS1 from Malta to
Alexandria. To extract empty merchant ships instead of
returning empty they were being put to good use. They
were evacuating British civilians and dependants also some
Maltese civilians.

8th July
0600 Hrs HMS Imperial left us to return to Alexandria with
a burst steam pipe. But unknown to us two Italian planes
Cant Z506 (tri-engine floatplane) or Heron were nearby.
They spotted our fleet and were shadowing us for nearly
four hours. Until their land based bombers could attack us.
We suffered from at least 70-120 planes coming in to attack
in waves. I believe they had serious intentions to sink us
all. We didn't know a lot below decks just any increase of
speed to add more fuel to the boilers or decrease and when
to make smoke or not.

Of course you could feel the old girl listing to one side after a loud thunderous concussive blast went off near us. Luckily for us the Italians operated at high altitudes. During the early stages of the war they didn't learn low-level dive-bombing was more accurate but risky off the Germans till later. The Italians dropped scores of bombs that day at us it was a real nightmare wave after wave of bombers. From twelve thousand feet up of course there aim was a bit off because of cloud cover and wind affecting the flight path of the bombs. We suffered only slight damage from bomb splinters. The fire control of the heavy 4-inch flak guns was temporarily incapacitated but repaired in double quick time.

HMS Gloucester town class light cruiser took a major hit to the bridge. This Killed the captain, six officers and eleven ratings, also wounding three other officers and six ratings. As a result of this the ship could not be steered from the bridge for a short time it was uncontrolled. Until an officer used his brain and took charge from the aft secondary steering position. Despite the damage she took to her bridge and the forward fire control being destroyed. She still fought on bravely staying with the fleet at full steam. That is what I call great endurance and seamanship.

8th July
 At 1400Hrs a Sunderland reported that an Italian fleet of two Battleships, six Cruisers and seven Destroyers was 100 miles North West of Benghazi. They were sailing north to Taranto so we altered course and gave chase.

We were going to try and cut them off from their home port base. Our Cruiser group was spread out in front of our Fleet trying to spot them. HMS Warspite spotted the enemy first with her high power optics. We opened fire at a range of 24,000 meters but our fall of shot was short by 2700 meters. We were trying a lucky shot to hit them at our extreme range. After a short guns duel the Italian Battleship Giulio Cesare and the heavy Cruiser Bolzano were hit. The Italian admiral decided to withdraw leaving the fight to aircraft. He also left his destroyers fighting covering his withdrawal.

At 1601Hrs the Italian destroyers generated enough smoke to get their ships under cover. Over the next hour both fleets attempted to make long-range torpedo runs. Both their Destroyer groups and ours had little to no success. Around 1640 Hrs the Italian Air Force made an attack with 126 aircraft. There was some minor damage to us and other ships. Some 50 of the Italian plane's attacked their own ships but missed theirs as well pity.

The battle ended shortly after 1700 Hrs and our fleet returned to Malta for a short refuel stop. Whilst we were there we heard of the great air battles taking place over Britain. The Battle of Britain had begun on the 10th we eventually got back to port in Alexandria on the 15th.

19th July
At 1230 hours we sailed in company with Battleship Ramilies, Aircraft Carrier Eagle. Destroyers Hasty, Hero, Hyperion and Ilex with Australian Cruiser Sydney joined us. We were on a sweep into the Aegean Sea to find two reported Italian Cruisers.

34.

HMAS Sydney was the first to find them off Cape Spada at the North West tip of Crete. Bartolomeo Colleoni was stopped by gunfire and finished off with torpedoes from the Destroyers. The Bande Nere managed to escape and believed to be making for Tobruk.
 * Reference picture 12.

20th
Off Tobruk, Eagle launched an air strike to find and locate the Cruiser Nere. She failed although the Swordfish of 824 Squadron did find and sink Destroyers Nembo and Ostro. Also an Italian freighter was sent to the bottom. We returned to Alexandria getting back the next day.

27th July
0300 Hrs We sailed from Alexandria in company with Battleship's; Warspite and Ramillies and Aircraft Carrier Eagle. We had with us Destroyers; Decoy, Hereward, Hero, Hyperion, Ilex, Imperial, Jervis, Juno, Nubian and Mohawk. We were to escort cover the passage of convoy AS2 /1. South of Crete, Cruisers Neptune and HMAS Sydney joined us later in the day.

28th July
South of Kitherat we met the convoy being escorted by Cruisers; Capetown, Liverpool. With Destroyers: Dainty, Defender, Diamond and HMAS Stuart. All of a sudden the whole fleet was subjected to numerous Italian air attacks. I can really remember this one as a tanker got hit in the convoy.

The tankers cargo of fuel spewed into the ocean and ignited into a hissing, spitting, roaring fireball. As the tanker burned the horrified witnesses on the ships close by could hear the weak cries of the tankers crew stuck behind the inferno. After a short time these too were drowned out by the thunder of the angry fire. Everyone knew there was no helping them from our ships. The convoy rescue ships also saw no point sticking around the crew were beyond any help.

HMS Eagle quickly sent up her fighter planes to defend the convoy. They were Sea Gladiators of 813-fighter Squadron. The Sea Gladiator was a biplane fighter with an enclosed cockpit. They quickly rose to the occasion to break up one of the attacks. Unfortunately one of the fighters flown by LT. Massey pursued the foe too far. With his fuel exhausted he had to put down in the sea next to HMAS Stuart. This proved to be the only Sea Gladiator lost off Eagle in 6 months of operations. The fleet arrived back at Alexandria on the 30th and the convoy proceeded on to Port Said. With escort Cruiser Capetown and Destroyers, Dainty and Diamond.

31st July 1940
At 1420 Hrs we set off with Battleship Ramilillies and Aircraft Carrier Eagle. With Destroyers: Hasty, Hereward, Hero, Hostile, Ilex, Imperial, Jervis and HMAS Vendetta. To carry out gunnery practice once we had completed this we received orders to sail to Gavdos Island off Crete.

36.

We were designated Task Force B. For operation Hurry but shortly after embarking on this we had problems. Salt water had got in the ships condensers so we could not get up to full steam so the whole of Force B returned to Alexandria. They did not want to complete the operation without our fire power present.

13th August 1940
Germany starts a bombing offensive against airfields and factories in England. Lots of the crew start to worry about family and friends working in factories.

15th August
News arrived of intensified air battles and daylight raids over Britain. This caused a rush to get letters off to family members. As the crew were concerned about their safety. This runs the store of paper on ship down so the captain implements a restriction. Every crewmember can only write one letter unless they have their own supply of paper in their kit. I bet the officers don't have this done to them.

16th August
We sailed at 1030 Hrs. Force B was reinstated with Battleship's Ramillies and Warspite with us. We were accompanied by 12 Destroyers and Cruiser Kent. Our task was to go to the Libyan port of Bardia and fort Capuzzo for operation MB2. Our aim was on the 17th at 0700am Hrs to shell Italian troop concentrations and stores.

We were ordered to do as much damage as possible to the material and moral of Italian troops as they prepared for their advance into Egypt. The light Italian coastal batteries did not have the effective range to reach our ships. The three Battleships shelled the Italian positions for 22 minutes. We fired 62 rounds of 15in and 104 rounds of 6in ammunition. We sent up our spotter plane that reported one of the big shells landing directly on Fort Capuzzo. It landed among the troops gathering in the compound. The small Italian fort of Romla, which marks the frontier of Libya, was totally destroyed and no longer exists to this day.
*Reference picture 13.

Then we switched targets to the large concentrations of troops massing for the invasion. Four salvos landed directly on top of them. While the other ships bombardment damaged barracks at Bardia. We were later told from the British military headquarters in Cairo. That the Italians after the bombardment withdrew all its troops from Fort Capuzzo or what was left of it.
                                The fleet slipped out to sea around 0900 Hrs to try and avoid a retaliatory strike from the Italian air force. But only 90 minutes later we came under heavy attack. British fighters from land bases swooped down from the sky surprising the Italians. So much so they jettisoned their bombs after losing 11 planes in the first wave of attack and fled home with their tails between their legs. So the fleet continued its voyage unmolested.

17th August

Hitler declares an all out blockade of the British Isles. This news brings a laugh to many of us and some comments like. "Let him try and stop us returning to Britain in our Battle wagon".

On the 18th we came under attack from another Italian retaliatory strike. The ships guns defended off the attack by throwing up a protective shield of AA fire. They shot down 12 of the Italian aircraft before they had a chance to release their bombs. The remaining aircraft released there bombs to hit nothing except empty sea.

23rd /24th August

News arrived to the ship of the first air raids on Central London. There were a few worried Cockneys on board. Everyone puts aside their own troubles when on duty and gets on with the task in hand. The time to worry was on your down time when you were trying to sleep. If the nightmares let you sleep.

25th/26th August

The news of the first British air raids on Berlin rose everybody's moral "Take that Mr Hitler". Every success for our forces was celebrated on the ship and nine times out of ten we would get an extra shot of grog. Good news from home no matter what form it took was the very best thing for moral on the ship.

30th August

We slipped out of Alexandria nice and quite as a fleet could be. With us were Battleship Warspite and Aircraft Carrier Eagle. We also had Cruisers Orion and HMAS Sydney. We were escorted by eight destroyers: Decoy, Defender, Hereward, Imperial, HMAS Stuart, Vampire, Vendetta, and Voyager. With us was a Polish ship ORP Garland. We were being sent on operation HATS/MB3. The fleet sailed towards the Gulf of Taranto. The objective was to cover the passage of reinforcements for the Mediterranean Fleet and convoy MF2. We were using MF2 as bait so it was being defended weakly. It only had 4 Destroyers to invite the Italian fleet to attack. So we could surprise them with the whole British Mediterranean Fleet.

Early in the morning on the 31st just as the sun was coming up. Returning Cruisers Kent, Gloucester, Liverpool and Destroyers Hasty, Hyperion and Ilex joined us. They came from a sweep of the southern Aegean.

On reaching a point about 100 miles west of Cape Matapan, Greece the Fleet turned south. We then found out the Italian Fleet (4 Battleships, 14 Cruisers and 39 Destroyers) had sailed from Taranto at 0600 Hrs.

At 1554Hrs Kent, Gloucester and Liverpool detached from the Fleet to join convoy MF2. To make it seem as close to normal as possible. But still it was quite light in defence. This was to entice the Italians on.

1700 Hrs

We were around 150 miles west of Crete. When we found out the Italian Fleet was 120 miles North West of us. This made a fleet action very likely to happen. At that point it was believed that the Italian high command knew the whereabouts of the convoy. But they did not know the presence of our Mediterranean Fleet. So it was puzzling why they ordered the Italian Fleet to return to base without engagement. It was a big disappointment to all of us. So at 1815 Hrs the Fleet turned west heading for Malta. Except HMS Decoy that detached from us to join MF2 to bolster its defence.

3rd October

West of Crete the fleet divided again. Our ship carried on with Destroyers Eagle, Dainty, Diamond, Vampire, Vendetta and Wryneck. We proceeded directly back to Alexandria arriving on the 4th at 2100Hrs.

7th September

The Blitz against Britain begins.

8th October

We sailed in the company of Aircraft Carriers; Illustrious and Eagle with Battleships Ramillies, Valiant and Warspite. Cruisers; Ajax, Gloucester, Orion, York, HMAS Sydney was along for the ride. With eleven Destroyers in a defence screening force, Hasty, Havoc, Hereward, Heron, Hyperion, Ilex, Imperial, Janus, Jervis, Juno and Nubian.

We were to provide distant cover for passage to Malta of convoy MF3 from Egypt, ME4 from Malta and AS4 from Greece. We also were to launch an air attack on Leros Greece Operation MB6.

Cruiser Liverpool and Destroyer Diamond joined the Fleet on the 9th At 0254 Hrs. At intervals during the 10th and 11th various units of the Fleet detached refuelled at Malta and returned. But at 1105 Hrs Imperial hit a mine and was badly damaged. She was towed into Malta by Decoy at 1600. MF3 safely arrived at Malta. The Italian fleet was 100 miles southeast and unknown to us. An Italian civil airliner spotted our fleet and reported our location back to their Government.

At 2245 Hrs We sailed leaving Malta for Alexandria with convoy ME4. River gunboat Aphis was one of the unusual ships among the convoy. We were joined by escort Cruisers: Calcutta and Coventry. Destroyers: Wryneck and HMAS Waterhen also joined us. Later in the evening all the refuelling units returned to the Fleet. Unknown to us north east of Malta there were positioned 4 Italian Destroyers, 3 fast and light torpedo boats and 4 MAS boats (heavily armoured torpedo boats). They were just waiting in anticipation for a convoy to leave from Malta. It was just our bad luck that it happened to be our convoy.

12th October
During the return passage to Alexandria at 0200 Hrs the Fleet was 125 miles west of Malta and about 70 miles north of convoy ME4.

Three Italian torpedo boats, Ariel, Airone and Arione attacked our furthest northern ship the Ajax. All of which missed on the first try with torpedoes. After the initial confusion Ajax opened fire at a range of 3600 Meters sinking Ariel and Arione. But she missed the third boat that struck the Ajax with 3 shots of her 3.9-inch guns before being damaged by Ajax.

Immediately 4of the Italian Destroyers came to the aid of the torpedo boats. At 0230 Hrs the Artigliere launched a torpedo attack at Ajax. With a lot of luck Ajax managed to avoid the torpedoes'. Ajax returned fire at the Destroyers managing to damage Aveiere and severely damage Artigliere. But Ajax was hit by gunfire from Artigliere damaging her radar and a twin 4-inch mounted gun turret. The Ajax was running out of flash less gunpowder. This was affecting the vision of her gunners in the black of night. Also the Italian destroyers were making smoke and withdrew behind the smoke screen. So Ajax broke off the action to get to a safe distance.
Later the next day Artigliere was spotted undertow by destroyer Camicia Nere 107 miles west of Malta. Cruisers HMS York with Ajax and 4 Destroyers were sent to engage them. Destroyer Camicia Nere slipped the tow and escaped and the York finished off Artigliere.

14th October
At 1845 Hrs 70 miles Southeast of Crete the Fleet came under Italian air attack.

HMS Liverpool sustained a torpedo hit that blew up one of her fuel storage tanks. Blowing the roof off A turret and the port gun turret fell into the sea. Orion took her undertow and the Fleet headed back to Alexandria to recoup.

On the 15th there were massive air raids on all the major cities across England. This news brought a new all-time low to the moral, hitting everyone aboard the ship.

25th October
We set Sail with aircraft carrier Eagle, cruiser Coventry, escorted by destroyers Janus, Mohawk, Wryneck and HMAS Vampire and Voyager. We were on operation MAQ2 covering a convoy from Port Said to Dardanelles and Piracus. We also would protect HMS Eagle as her aircraft carried out an air attack on the island of Rhodes. The aircraft from Eagle would attack the airfield at Mataza with all intensions of destroying all the enemy aircraft there and damaging the airfield.

26th October
The Fleet sailed to the southern end of the Kasos Strait.

27th October
Swordfish planes from the Eagle carried out an air strike on the airfield at Mataza on the island of Rhodes. The attack went in shortly after dawn and was a partial success.

28th October
We arrived at Alexandria late afternoon and had an overnight stop for taking on stores and to refuel. Italy invades Greece on this day.

29th October
The Fleet sailed for the west of Crete on operation Church. British forces were to set up a base at Suda Bay on the north coast of Crete. Our fleet was to cover the military convoys carrying personnel and stores for the new base.

30th October
The Fleet sailed north until it was 126 miles west of Cape Matapan Greece. We swept the area and got to within 75 miles off the Greek coast. Then turned back and cruised around to the west of Crete. We arrived back at Alexandria on the 2nd November.

CHAPTER FOUR

FORCE X OPERATION MB8 And JUDGEMENT

6th November
The Fleet sailed on operation MB8 it was made up of six
forces totalling: Two Aircraft Carriers, five Battleships, 10
Cruisers, and 30 Destroyers.
It consisted of several six phases:

Operation Coat.
A convoy of reinforcement ships sailed from Britain to
Malta carrying troops and much needed anti-aircraft guns.

Convoy ME3.
From Malta comprised of four merchantmen sailing with
ballast back to Alexandria to re-supply.

Convoy MW3.
From Alexandria this was made up of seven ships, five
merchantmen bound for Malta. Two merchantmen ships
providing stores to the base at Suda Bay.

Convoy AN6.
This convoy consisted of four slow tankers bound for
Greece from Egypt.

Operation Crack

Ark Royal would carry out an air attack on Cagliari, by aircraft, whilst she was en route to Malta from Gibraltar. While this was going on reinforcements for Crete embarked in light Cruisers HMS Ajax and HMAS Sydney. While light Cruiser Orion transported RAF supplies to Greece and an inspection team to make sure Suda Bay was operational.

Operation Judgement.

Aircraft from Illustrious would attack the harbour of Taranto. It was one of the Italian's most important navy ports in the Med.

The Italians were aware of our naval sorties from Malta, Alexandria and Gibraltar by 7th of November. But they were unaware of the size of forces being used and thought it was for normal regular routine convoys. They sent out nine submarines to attack convoy MW3. But they came up empty-handed as the convoy slipped past them. MW3, ME3/Operation Coat and AN6 safely reached their respective ports unmolested.

Light cruisers HMS Ajax, and HMAS Sydney after their part in operation Crack would join Force X. HMS Orion after Convoy MW3 would also re-join Force X. Over the 11/12 of November we would carry out a raid on the Otranto Strait and carry out attacks on convoys in Straits of Taranto.

All the ships of Force X proceeded north during the night of the 11th. They reached a limit of exploitation a line between Bari and Durazzo by 0100 Hrs without incident. They turned to run southward thinking that it was going to be another failed mission.

Twenty minutes later the raiders encountered six darkened enemy ships. Including what they thought were two Destroyers and four merchantmen. The Italian ships passed directly across their front and were making for the Italian mainland. HMS Mohawk opened fire at 0127 Hrs and action became general all around the raiding force. During the hours of darkness the action was confusing. HMAS Sydney attacked the leading freighter at a range of 7 miles setting it on fire and sunk her. Over the next 23 minutes the other three merchant freighters were damaged and Sydney left them burning to sink later.

The La Masa class Destroyer/Torpedo ship Nicola Fabrizi was hit and heavily damaged. She retired heading toward Valona with 11 dead and 12 wounded. The auxiliary cruiser Ramba III fired off 19 salvos hitting nothing and broke off the action unscathed. The Rigia Marina (Italian Navy) suffered in total 36 dead and 42 wounded. All our ships avoided any damage; Sydney narrowly missed a torpedo behind her stern at 0140 Hrs. The firer was unknown but it probably came from Nicola Fabrizi who had two twin torpedo mounts aboard her. She probably fired them off just before she retired out of the fight.

The Aircraft Carrier HMS Illustrious had aboard 16 Fairey Swordfish planes from 815 and 819 Squadrons. She also had attached to her five more from HMS Eagle. So we had 21 aircraft for the attack at 1800 Hrs on the 11th November. Illustrious headed for the launch position protected by her escort of four destroyers, 170 miles south of Taranto. Each plane had to leave out the air gunner and replace him with an extra fuel tank. Now crewed by only the pilot and observer the aviators were briefed and prepared as the force moved into position. Other ships and ours provided a protective covering screen some miles off toward the enemy coast.

The first wave of twelve Swordfish launched just before 2100 Hrs. After a night transit of two hours requiring considerably good navigation skills they arrived on the target area. The defences of Taranto were on full alert already after a Sunderland had strayed too close to Taranto on a recce. Having become separated in cloud, eight aircraft arrived just before 2300 Hrs to begin the attack. Two aircraft were detailed to illuminate the south east of the outer anchorage with flares. Before diving down to bomb the harbours oil storage facilities.

The target area was lit up although the flares from only one aircraft were all that was needed. The flare lights from the two aircraft lit up the entire target area like daylight. Three of the Swordfish in a torpedo run succeeded in striking the Battleship Conte de Cavour. A torpedo blasted a hole in her side below her waterline. One aircraft however was shot down by Italian AA fire its pilot and observer managed to survive and was taken prisoner.

49.

Within moments the second sub-flight of three Swordfish attacked from the north. Dodging the barrage balloons they received heavy anti-aircraft fire from the Italian warships and shore batteries. The second sub-flight launched their torpedoes from less than half a mile away. They successfully hit the Battleship Littorio with two torpedoes. The pilots then dragged their aircraft around into tight turns at wave top height to egress the target area as quickly as possible. The remaining four aircraft, which had become separated en-route, had now caught up; each was armed with six 250lb bombs. The Swordfish now dive bombed warships in the inner harbour and Taranto's seaplane base before departing the target area at approximately 2335 Hrs.

The second phase started badly when one aircraft was delayed in launching after a taxiing accident on deck. A second Swordfish had to abandon the strike and return to illustrious. After its auxiliary fuel tank detached and flooded the cockpit with fuel. The remaining eight Swordfish arrived at Taranto some twenty minutes after the first wave had departed. The cloud that had hampered the first wave was now beginning to clear. The fires caused by the first waves bombing and torpedoing were visible from 60 miles away. The skies were still lit up by the fierce barrage of AA fire from warships and coastal emplacements. The second wave repeated the same initial steps. By lighting the target area with flares from two of the Swordfish planes. That then went on to bomb Taranto's fuel depots.

A torpedo strike from the North West succeeded in scoring one further hit on the Littorio and one on the Caio Duilio. Blowing a large hole in her hull that flooded both of her forward magazines. Another torpedo was fired at the flagship the battleship Vittorio, but it failed to hit. One Swordfish of the second wave was shot down whilst attacking the heavy Cruiser Gorizia. Both pilot and observer were killed instantly when the extra fuel tank got hit and exploded turning the plane into a fireball in the night sky. The second wave's two bombers carried out attacks on ships moored in the Mar Piccolo anchorage. But they found the targets difficult to identify. So one aircraft attacked two Cruisers from 1,500ft and the other aircraft attacked four Destroyers. Two unexploded bombs hit the Cruiser Trento and the Destroyer Libeccio. Near misses also damaged the destroyer Pessagno.
 * Reference pictures 14, 15.

The second strike was over in only ten minutes. AA guns continued to fire afterwards for a further 45 minutes filling the air like fireworks. By 0250 all 18 surviving Swordfish had successfully recovered to Illustrious. The damage inflicted by the 20 Royal Navy biplanes was catastrophic. After severe flooding of the Caio Duillio she beached shortly followed by the Conte de Cavour and the Littorio. Three Battleships had been flooded and abandoned with the loss of 52 men. Fuel and oil depots on the shore were also damaged and consequentially caught fire. The seaplane base was severely damaged along with the loss of two aircraft.

Superficial damage was also caused to several other smaller warships by the dive-bombing. Not only had the Italian fleet lost half of its capital ships in one attack. It also moved its surviving three battleships to Naples for better protection. This placed them out of range of being able to quickly react to operations in the Mediterranean. The Swordfish crews returned to a heroes welcome back on board Illustrious, followed by three rounds of whiskey soda's in the wardroom.

13th November
The whole Feet arrived back at Alexandria. We were all rewarded with shore leave in shifts to celebrate the success of the operations. Yet again I fell off the gangplank coming back on board after a heavy session on shore.
The successful completion of operation Judgement changed the philosophy of Aircraft Carrier operations around the world. The high ranking officers of the military had got the message that an Aircraft Carrier with all her planes could be a major asset and replace the need for so many ships. It was decided the firepower of Ramillies and Malaya was not needed in the Mediterranean. As it seemed a bit of overkill compared to the enemy forces threat they had left. Aircraft could patrol and have control over both the sky's and the sea. So we were going to be released from duty but not until the 24th of December. So it was back to the grindstone.

23rd November

We sailed from Alexandria in company with Battleship Ramillies and Aircraft Carrier Eagle. With Cruisers; Ajax, Orion and HMAS Sydney joined the force. Together with six Destroyers: Dainty, Diamond, Hasty, Havock, Hyperion and Ilex. We were designated Force C for Operation MB9 and Operation Collar. This included protecting a fast three-ship convoy.

24th November

We arrived at Suda Bay at 0800Hrs where cruiser Berwick joined us. Then we carried on to Malta arriving at 0830on the 26th. We refuelled all the ships, which took four days to complete.

We sailed again as soon as we all were ready to Alexandria. We had Warspite and Valiant helping cover the passage of new Cruisers Manchester and Southampton. That had only just arrived in the Mediterranean with Corvettes Peony, Salvia, Gloxinia and Hyacinth.

9th/10th December

British begin a western desert offensive in North Africa against the Italians.

16th December

We departed Alexandria with destroyers Defender and Diamond. Escorting a Malta supply convoy MW5A. Under the title Operation MC2 we arrived at Malta on the 20th at 0400 Hrs. We picked up on route Destroyer's; Nubian and Wryneck no untoward incidents occurred.

On route to join us HMS Hyperion was attacked by Italian Argnauta Class Submarine Serpente. The attack failed although the Italians declared she had sunk the Hyperion it was a propaganda lie. We were only in port eight hours and we set sail again. With destroyers Hereward, Hyperion and Ilex escorting convoy MG1. The convoy was formed up consisting of SS Clan Forbes and SS Clan Fraser they were both British Cargo Steam Ships. Convoy MG1 with our three escort ships were joined by a further two Destroyers; Hasty and Hero shortly after setting sail. The Force headed for the Sicilian Narrows, to R/V with force H.

HMS Malaya transferred to Force H with Aircraft Carrier Ark Royal and Battle Cruiser Renown. We formed up as part of Operation Hide. We were to escort convoys to Gibraltar. Whilst the Two destroyers did Operation Seek an anti-submarine sweep ahead of the convoys.

22nd December 1940
At 0156 Hrs we were 24 miles west of Cape Bon. HMS Hyperion struck an Italian mine and sustained major structural damage. Two attempts by HMS Ilex to tow were unsuccessful. The ships company were taken on board Ilex. Hyperion had to be sunk by Destroyer Janus as she would be a threat to other shipping drifting about. Unexpectedly two of Hyperions crew were not accounted for and reported missing presumed killed in the mine explosion or got thrown overboard to drown.

We arrived at Gibraltar on the 24th at 1000 Hrs whilst in port we had a few air raids. They were after big ships and we were obviously a great target. We also had a near miss as two Italian/Spanish saboteur frogmen managed to get in to the harbour. They swam into the harbour after dark and they had targeted our ship. They had swam under what they thought was our ship and stuck two limpet mines on the hull below the water line.

They thought it was safer to swim to a jetty and give them selves up. Rather than swim back out through the harbours defences. They thought they were soon to put Malaya out of action so they were happy with themselves. Little did they realise until the big bang that in the darkness they had placed their mines on the hull of the merchant ship moored ahead of us " Lucky us".

Over the next week the main diet aboard was rice and peas in all forms boiled, baked and fried really boring. It was the sense of humour of everyone aboard that got us through. The crew members started bowing to each other and talking in a typical Chinese/oriental accent all for a laugh. The ship's crew said the merchant ship sunk by the frogmen was our re-supply ship of food all suffered a bit, who is laughing now?

29th/30th December
There are massive German air raids on London.

7th January 1941

At 0800 Hrs we sailed from Gibraltar in company with Battle Cruiser Renown, Aircraft Carrier Ark Royal and cruiser Sheffield. We were being screened by seven Destroyers; Faulknor, Firedrake, Forester, Fortune, Foxhound, Fury and Jaguar. We were Given the Task Force H name again. We were to cover the passage of convoys to Malta and The Athenian port of Piracus in Greece.

Our four Fleet Destroyers; Duncan, Hasty, Hereward and Hero had just arrived and were reinforcements for the Mediterranean Fleet at Alexandria (Operation Excess). They were given a second task to cover the transit of cruiser Bonaventure she had a number of navy reinforcement personnel on board for the fleet.

9th January

At 0930 Hrs cruisers Gloucester and Southampton and destroyer Ilex joined us from the east. To build up our strength in the convoy's close escort through the Skerki Channel and on to Malta. The channel was a known danger area covered by enemy forces both sea and air. Unknown to us, we were located by Italian air reconnaissance but thankfully Wellington bombers had just bombed Naples. They damaged the Italian battleship Giulio Cesare with three near misses. This caused the only other operational Italian battleship Vittorio Veneto to retreat. Away from our approaching convoy as she was out gunned and out numbered.

At 1320 Hrs the Force came under high-level attack by 10 Italian SM79 aircraft. Eight of the aircraft singled out and attacked Malaya it was very close but still inaccurate. All their bombs fell just ahead of us creating a cacophony of large explosions. Rocking us down to the soles of our boots and echoing throughout the lower decks of the ship but they caused no damage to the hull. FAA Fulmars the carrier born fighters from Ark Royal fended them off and shot down two of the attackers.

At 2200Hrs Force H reversed course and set our bows toward Gibraltar. Force H arrived back at Gibraltar on the 11th at 1930 Hrs. We were dry docked in No.1 dock. So the dockworkers could bream/grave the hull by burning off weed and 'Huch' the dirt and barnacles from the underside of the ship's hull with Hogs a rough flat scrubbing broom. Then they gave the old girl a coat of antifouling paint so the ship would not be slowed down on future operations. This paint had a chemical compound in it to stop barnacles and weed growing

22nd January
A cheer goes up around the ship as news hits us that British and Australian troops have taken Tobruk.

CHAPTER FIVE

DAM ATTACK

31st January
1300 Hrs Force H sailed from Gibraltar on Operation
Picket. To carry out an air attack on San Chiara Ula
hydroelectric power station and the dam on Lake Tirso in
central Sardinia.
 * Reference picture 16.

1st February
HMS Ark Royal, Malaya and the rest of the escort Force
steamed eastward towards the flying off position with a
freshening north-westerly wind. So Malaya moved off the
position 60 miles to the northwest to form a blocking
position and to secure the intended recovery position for
the aircraft.

2nd March
At 0555 Hrs a striking force of eight Swordfish from 810
Naval Air Squadron armed with torpedoes. The torpedoes
had been fitted with contact pistols in the warheads. The
Swordfish reported back to the Ark Royal that the recovery
position would have to be the same as the flying off
position. The wind direction was making the return trip
harder and to make navigation easier. At 0730 Hrs Two
Swordfish were flown off to securely communicate to
Malaya. The intentions were for Ark Royal to stay in the
same position with a signal light.

So they Directed Malaya to rendezvous with Renown at 1000 Hrs. A flight of Fulmars was maintained over the Fleet during the day to provide air cover and warn the Fleet of approaching ships. When the aircraft reached the coast it was still dark with heavy rain. Visibility was reduced so the leader signalled to the others to turn out to sea and wait for light. One aircraft did not see the signal and continued inland and got lost in the cloud. The lone Swordfish failed to locate the target so returned to the Ark with his torpedo.

Testing the cloud cover another of the aircraft tried to get through. They found a gap between the clouds north of a hill on Cape Mannu. They came through the clouds with four miles to go to the dam. He suddenly found that the intelligence reports about the dams' defences being light were wrong. It was heavily defended with batteries on either side of the bridge at the foot of Lake Tirso. Turning away to the north the aircraft came down again to make for the target. But anti aircraft fire was so heavy. The pilot jettisoned his torpedo and made for the coast. No body saw his aircraft ever again.

The Italians announced later that the crew had been captured and were prisoners of war. The remaining six aircraft crossed the coast slightly to the north. They separated to carry out there attacks. Two of them made an early turn south and avoided the heavy batteries. But as they made for the target they still came under anti aircraft fire. Nevertheless both managed to drop their torpedoes and make a good getaway. But on the way out they were unable to observe any results.

59.

The next two aircraft got separated in cloud one came in at 50feet the whole way. Following the river at such a low height it was not spotted and was not fired upon until after he dropped his torpedo. He then turned sharply away to try and avoid further AA fire. He could not see the result of his attack and escaped to the coast all at low level. The other wingman dived through the cloud and came out too high above the target. So he turned right round dived again and came in at 150 feet, nose down with a speed of 145 knots. The gunfire was getting intolerably close to him only missing the crew by a few inches. Shrapnel was ripping through the fuselage so he decided to drop his torpedo then and there. He flew right over the dam with his rear gunner firing at the anti aircraft batteries. They managed to get away without any major damage to his aircraft.

The sixth and seventh aircraft approached from five miles to the dam. Like the others they met heavy anti aircraft fire. But seeing a gap in the clouds they climbed up through the cloud to avoid some of the fire. They came down further through another gap at their top speed right into the heavy anti-aircraft fire. Dropping there torpedoes 150 feet from the dam. They too flew across the dam shooting up the gunners on their AA guns. Then they flew to the coast at their best possible speed.

By 0905 Hrs seven of the striking force had landed on the Ark the result of the attack was unsuccessful. It had been skilfully planned and courageously carried out but to no avail.

The aircraft had to contend with an impossible amount of natural hazards. All through the mission from: rain, hail, severe icing conditions and full cloud cover over the target. Added to that the problems of the anti aircraft gunfire being impossible heavy. A further possible reason for none of the torpedoes reaching the dam was that they might have run into a bank of silt that had built up in front of the dam.

Malta re-joined the Fleet and headed to the northwest. The weather started to get very rough the seas became steeper and steeper pitching the ships about. All ships reduced speed to 15 knots and some of the Destroyers escorting started to report damage in the rough seas. The rest of the operation was cancelled and we was ordered back to Gibraltar arriving on the 4th at 1800Hrs

6TH February 1941
Force H sailed from Gibraltar at 1615 Hrs on Operation Result. (The air attack on Azienda oil refinery at Leghorn also laying sea mines in the port of La Spezia) and Operation Grog (The bombardment of Genoa).
We split up into groups to try and sneak up to within striking distance. We had a calm moonlit passage with a thick mist blanketing the Italian coast. There was no sign that our presence had been detected throughout our approach. We all arrived at a pre-arranged RV location with no incidents.

9th February

At 0400 Hrs HMS Ark Royal and her 3 Destroyers: Duncan, Encounter and Isis. Split off from the rest of the Fleet to go to her launch position. At 5am 70 miles off the coast she launched her striking force of fourteen Swordfish. Each armed with four 250lb bombs and incendiaries and four more Swordfish carrying magnetic mines.

The bombers reached the Azienda oil refinery without being spotted and carried out their attack. With only light defensive anti aircraft fire being returned. One large explosion was seen from the ships off the coast. But subsequent reports said the damage was slight. The minelayers made a gliding approach to Spezia. The town was only partially blacked out due to air attack warnings from the other bombings. They laid their mines successfully in both entrances to the harbour.

At 0600 Hrs Force group one consisting of Malaya, Battle Cruiser Renown and Cruiser Sheffield launched their catapult Swordfish aircraft. They were to act as spotter planes during the bombardment. The bombardment ships were being protected from approaching Italian naval ships. On watch were our eight Destroyer escorts: Firedrake, Jupiter, Jersey, Fury, Foresight, Foxhound and Fearless. The spotter aircraft made an eagerly awaited report at 0711 Hrs "No enemy battleships could be seen". But it is now known that this report was wrong. The Duilio damaged at Taranto was in dry dock there. Genoa was placed on alert after seeing the ships spotter planes at 0715 Hrs. But they did not know of the fleet just over the horizon with their guns trained on the city.

As the zero hour approached a low haze hid the foreshore and as the mountains beyond turned from grey to pink in the rising sun. We turned into position to start the bombardment with Renown and Sheffield. Suddenly an Italian patrol boat challenged us. They signalling to us all in flickering white and green lights "who are sou". We had been spotted. In reply a great spurt of red flame shot from the Renown's side at 0730 Hrs. The first salvo of her 15inch shells screamed towards the distant targets. The range was from ten to fourteen miles, so not much of Genoa could be seen from the ships. Then suddenly we opened fire, the fire from the side of our ship was an almost continuous blast of flame. The concussive blast of the main guns all firing was rocking the ship from side to side. Sheffield joined in with the horrendous out pouring of munitions.

Renown's salvos were quickly directed by the aircraft on to the Ansaldo works, marshalling yards and factories, Sheffield directed her fire at industrial installations. Our guns on Malaya concentrated on targets in the inner harbour including the power station and dry docks. Even so, the Duillio was not hit there was many a close impact. One salvo impacted 15 to 60 meters near to her, close enough to shower the hull in shrapnel. A targeting error by one of our gunnery officers led to an armour piercing round hitting Genoa Cathedral. There was little damage to the building as the shell failed to explode and remains on display there today. All the ships secondary armaments that could reach pounded the waterfront.

This Caused fires and explosions all over the place with smoke billowing out from a fired oil tank. It made spotting from the ships difficult. We then steamed parallel with the coast relying on our spotter aircraft high above the targets. The spotter planes relayed co-ordinates to our gunners and corrections constantly. They had to dodge a vicious hail of anti-aircraft fire whilst still trying to constantly signal directions to our guns.

For fifteen minutes the Italian batteries failed to reply. Two of our inshore destroyers started to make a smoke screen to hamper the coast artillery. Then came a red flash from the shore followed shortly after by a white column of water sprouting up a thousand meters short of us. More shells came from the shore batteries but the Italians aim was so bad and short of us. The escorting destroyers abandoned making the smokescreen. As it was doing more harm than good and they moved closer to us out of danger.

The fleet had fired 273 rounds of 15-inch, 782 rounds of 6-inch, 400 rounds of 4.5-inch as well as numerous other smaller calibre munitions. Add to that we fired on Malaya 148 of the 15-inch rounds, 228 of 6-inch rounds and 200 4.5-inch rounds. All ships ceased fire at 0750 Hrs. The spotter planes soon returned to the ships giving us all a swooping fly past in a victorious manner. The observer's leaning out of their cockpits waving their hands above their heads. The spotter planes were recovered to the Ark Royal for a mechanical service before transferring back to their own ships later. All the other Swordfish apart from one that was reportedly shot down were recovered before 0900 Hrs.

The Ark Royal launched six fighters to maintain air cover for the expected Italian retaliatory air attacks. As we all turned away steaming south at 17 knots. A number of Italian bombers were detected on radar screens. They attempted to close in on our position. But they were met by a terrific barrage of anti-aircraft fire from all the ships. Two were quickly shot down in the first salvo as the six fighters already airborne forayed to meet the rest. The Italian bombers only managed to drop three bombs exploding in the sea half a mile behind Ark Royal. After 1300 Hrs low visibility weather assisted the withdrawal of all forces. Force H reached Gibraltar on the 11th February at 1430 Hrs without further incident.

There can be no doubt the attack came as a surprise to the Italians. As they had made no precautions to guard against a naval incursion into the Gulf of Genoa they had no lookouts or sentry ships. Once more fortune had favoured the bold the bombardment did grave damage in Genoa. The tanker Sant Andrea was hit trying to get in the harbour blocking it. Several steamers in the port harbour were severely damaged by shrapnel. Garibaldi and Duilio in dry dock were holed several times by shrapnel. The Steamer Salpi received several direct hits and sunk. Also a training ship Garaventa sank after being hit numerous times. In total 28 vessels were damaged or sunk. It was a pity 144 civilian's died and 272 wounded as a result of the shelling but that is war and it happens. The moral effect on the Italian people was serious. They thought their Navy and Air Force had let them down.
* Reference pictures 17, 18.

17TH February
Force H set sail to do a quick run with us to meet up with convoy WS6A.

It consisted of twenty-nine ships:
Almanzora, Ascamius, Bellfrophon, Bergensfjord, City of Athena, City of Carinth, City of Hankow, City of Pitsburg, Highland Brigade, Llandaff Castle, Llangibby Castle, Logician, Manchester Citizen, Mahseer, Mataroa, Nova Scotia, Rangitata, Ruahine, Salween, Scythia, Burdwan, Capehorn, Dalesman, Cathaw, Leopoldville, Kina II, Opawa, Port Alma, Thysvele.

We joined the convoy on the 19th off the Azores. As ocean escort and Force H detached and returned to Gibraltar.

28th February 1941
At 0800 Hrs Destroyers, Faulknor and Forester joined us for the day.
          At 1815 Hrs Destroyers, Faulknor and Forester detached from close protection of WS6A. Instead they proceeded ahead of the convoy clearing the way doing submarine sweeps to Freetown. WS6A and all the escorts reached Freetown on the 1st March at 1600 Hrs with out incident.

We immediately topped our fuel off and Faulknor and Forester refuelled. All three of us put to sea again at 1705 Hrs to catch up with convoy SL67 it was large with 55 merchant ships.

Convoy SL67:
Alphard, Anadyr, Ashworth, Banffshire, Baron, Belhaven,
Baron Cawdor, Beaconstreet, Bolton, Castle, British
Captain, British Diligence, Umberleigh, Urbino,
British Hope, British Integrity, British Security, Celtic
Monarch, City of Dunkirk, City of Kimberly, City of Cairo,
City of Nagpur, City of Rangoon, Clan Macbean, Deebank,
Defender, Dunkwa, Friesland, Godfrey B.Holt, Guido,
Harmodius, Harpefjell, Helder, Henrik Ibsen, Hindpool,
Innerroy, King Edwin, Lahore, Llangollen, Martaban,
Mendoza, Nagina, Nardana, Nebraska, Ogmore Castle,
Peisander, Queen Anne, Recorder, Roxane, Sanau, Sire,
Solfonn, Taxiarchis, Tielbank. Tunisia, Turkistan, Winsum.

3rd March
We eventually caught up with the convoy at 1500 Hrs.
With Destroyers: Faulknor and Forester. We were also
joined by AMC (Armed Merchant Cruiser) Cilicia,
Corvette Asphode and Land Armed Trawlers; Kelt,
Spaniard and Turcoman.

4th March
The armed trawlers Kelt, Spaniard and Turcoman detached
to carry out another task.

CHAPTER SIX

U-BOAT TERROR

7th March 1941

British forces arrive in Greece.

German battle cruiser Scharnhorst and Gneisenau sighted
our convoy SL67. But finding Malaya was part of the
escort and having orders from Hitler. "Not to endanger
their ships engaging the British Super Dreadnaughts or any
other heavy unit" they hauled off. Unknown to us and
before being spotted by us they made off. They
rendezvoused with U-Boat 124 and U.105. To make plans
for the U-Boats to attack and try to sink us so the German
heavy's could have a duck shoot. During the afternoon
Malaya refuelled Faulknor, Forester and Asphodel.

All that afternoon and evening we were being hunted
by the two U-Boats stealthily. They had been trying to
intercept us but because of our zigzag patterns they kept on
missing us. That was some feet missing us, as our
formation was so large. With the convoy spread out over
forty miles and slow in progress.

Later having read "Grey Wolf Grey Sea" I got a surprise
how close the U-Boats got to us.

8th March

U-Boat U-124 spotted Malaya at around 0130 Hrs in the
pitch black from her periscope. All of us on board had no
clue she was about and was just carrying out our normal
routines. Our ship was zigzagging around the outside of the
convoy trying to protect it.

The U-Boat came about behind us and surfaced with all her torpedo tubes loaded ready for a surface attack. The U-boat had scarcely settled in behind us when suddenly we hard turned to port and changed speed up a few knots. We had no idea who was on the bridge and what sort of zigzag pattern they had planned and were carrying out. But we later found out the U-Boat captain thought we were making it up as we went along. Another thought was someone on the con was drunk either way we had put him off their attack and made the impression we knew how to throw a U-Boat off.

So U.124 left us to go after some of the ships in the convoy in the pitch black of night. They sneaked right in the middle of the convoy on the surface between the merchants. When suddenly U.105 who had come to the same decision. They attacked a merchant ship from the outside of the convoy at 0251 Hrs sinking Harmodius. All the ships now were suddenly aware of the threat and were sending up star shells. We tried closing up the convoy to make it harder for the U-Boats to pick targets. One of the destroyers chased off U.105 after the initial attack. But because of the position of U.124 in amongst the convoy she was not spotted. Until she had sunk four ships Nardana, Hindpool, Tielbank and the Lahore. Then another of the destroyers spotted her by following one of the torpedo tracks back to her. They chased her into an emergency dive and drove her off with depth charges.

We had heard amid all the noise and excitement a few whirring sounds from outside the ship. As the torpedoes passed us by or went under our ship. Being shut in the bottom of the ship you do not know what is happening above you until afterwards. The only idea you get is from the bridge wanting more steam, to go faster, slower or to stop. It wasn't until we were given a rest and swapped hands that some of us could come on deck to get a cigarette and a breath of air. The fresh air felt good at first until the pungent smell of oil fuel on fire got to you. It was a smell that you can taste and cannot forget for years. We kept the convoy steaming on course with all her escorts. The rescue ships picked up survivors for two hours. It was a horrendous sight seeing ships picked off by a U-boat knowing you could be next. You knew the bridge was trying to avoid the ships on fire with sailors in the water. As well as maintaining the defence of the convoy.

1330 Hrs
Only ten hours after the U-Boat attack we was 130 miles off Cape Blanco. Destroyer Forester was off to the west flank of the convoy. She spotted a brief glimpse of the battle cruiser Scharnhorst and Gneisenau. They seemed to be steaming towards the convoy. Malaya's patrolling Swordfish also spotted them and they relayed the information back to us. We suddenly had action stations and lay on full steam. So Malaya and Faulknor could haul out of the convoy at full flank speed. We joined Forester in a wide pattern putting all our big guns between the convoy and the enemy.

At 1630 Hrs we spotted the Scharnhorst on Malaya but it didn't take too long for her to spot us and turn tail. After a brief pursuit to scare her off we returned to the convoy. We were followed by Faulknor and Forester re joining the convoy at 1900 Hrs. Two days later on the 10th at 1500 Hrs battle cruiser Repulse, aircraft carrier furious and destroyers Duncan and Foxhound took over the escort of the convoy and the old lady Malaya and her Destroyers Faulknor and Forester detached and headed for Gibraltar.

11th March
President Roosevelt signed the Lend –Lease Act in support of British war effort.

12th March
We arrived back at Gibraltar. Yet again the grand old lady HMS Malaya showed her true colours on this convoy tasking. We had survived the U-Boats with great flare, because of great seamanship from her officers and crew. I was very proud to be a member of her crew. To top it all scaring off two of Germany's newer mighty battle cruisers without firing a single shot at them. We were going to have a good bash at Gibraltar but yet again it was called off, after only 24 hours in port we were off again.

13th March 1941
We sailed from Gibralter escorted by Destroyer Wishart. We were to cruise down to Freetown Sierra Leone to pick up SL68. A fifty eight-vessel convoy one of the largest convoys that ever came out of Freetown.

We all knew there was a U-Boat pack operating around this area, on Operation Berlin. Helping the battle cruiser Scharnhorst and Gneisenau but there had been no reports of their latest positions. At this time the submarine blockade was in full swing. The constant fear of the seaman was the knowledge they might get an unwelcome acquaintance of a torpedo from that underwater death-dealer.

I have not been able to find a complete list of all the ships of convoy SL68.

Aldington Court, Alexandra, Andalusion, Benwyvis, Cap De Palmas, Clan Macnab, Clan Macwhirter, Clan Ogilvy, Corbis, Cressdene, Djambi, Eemland, Empire Bronze, Glenshiel, Hoegh Scout, Jhelum, Jaarstroom, Mahana, Mary Kingsley, Mandalika, Medjerda, Meerkerk, New Columbia, Nicolau, Zografia, Riley, Saint Merriel, Strix, Solarium, Tapanoeli, Port Sydney, Port Auckland, Brittany, Saint Gobain.

15th March
We joined AMC Canton and corvettes Calendula, Crocus and Marguerite escorting the convoy.

16th March
We picked up an SOS message that a ship called the Almerk. Was crossing our convoy route behind us unescorted and a U-Boat attacked them.

So we knew the U-Boats were active in our area. We found out later it was the U.106 and it had attacked the ship Almerk from 500mtrs. One torpedo hit on the starboard side and a few minutes later after the U-boat had repositioned got a second hit on the portside. The crew abandoned ship in lifeboats and watched as she sank fifteen minutes later.

17th March

The first indication we had, that a U-Boat was hunting our convoy. Was suddenly out of nowhere the Andalusian got hit by a torpedo (tin fish). At 2107 Hrs followed only after a minute or two by the Tapanoeli. Both ships sank in quick succession. But all the crew from both of them survived and were rescued. We later found out it was the same U-Boat U.106. The corvettes with us carried out anti submarine sweeps and dropped a few depth charges. Believing they had either sunk the U-Boat or chased it off the convoy carried on steaming.

18th March

 Fifteen quite hours later at 0225 Hrs there was a huge explosion from behind the convoy. We didn't know it but one of the merchants the Medjerda was struggling to keep up with the convoy. She had slipped back and she was taken out by another U-Boat the U.105. Again she was hit by one torpedo on the port side near the engine room followed shortly after by another on the starboard side. This broke her back she then broke in two and sank within 30-40 seconds. With 54 officers and crew all hands on board a total loss.

Some of the merchant ships panicked and left their place in the convoy. It was a total shambles with ships scattering. We tried to get control of the convoy and get some resemblance of a convoy back. One of them the Alexandra collided with Cap De Palmas. Luckily both ships came off with minor damage and were able to carry on. Yet again we had a quite day all the crew on board our ship was restless it was a game of wait for it to happen. We all knew the subs would be back and probably during the night but you just never knew when. The Germans could be sneaky buggers and try it during daylight so it was an uneasy time for the crew and me. The only sort of comfort you had was everybody was in the same boat "so to speak". We all knew every crew on every ship of the convoy was going through the same thing.

Predictably nothing happened until after dark on the 19th. When at 0024 Hrs the Mandalika got hit by a tin fish. U.105 had fired off a whole spread but only got one hit. But it was a good one right in the portside by the engine room. The crew abandoned ship in several lifeboats as the ship slowly sank. Three of the crew were lost to Davy Jones locker. The rest of the crew all 65 were picked up by HMS Marguerite. The Corvettes did a sweep of the area. During the night in poor visibility and running dark due to the U-Boat threat.

Clan Macnab was in a collision with Strix. Strix was a tanker full of aviation fuel. She suffered minor damage and was able to carry on with the convoy. But Clan Macnab full of sugar and iron was badly damaged and sank.

It was turning out to be a real nightmare, a war of nerves during the day. Little to no sleep, on and off action stations, no body knew when and where to turn. It seemed like there were quite a few U-Boats around the area. The escorts seemed to have contained the situation again for a brief period.

20th March
The convoy was 200 miles due west of Cape Verde Islands. 2323 Hrs, "BANG WALLOP" every thing was in darkness the ship had been hit by two torpedoes from a U-Boat. It came out later that we had been hit by U.106. She was running just under the surface at periscope depth. She had fired a spread of two torpedoes with her stern tubes at a shadow in bad light. She thought we were one of the merchant ships and they tried their luck. At first it was thought one torpedo had hit us but it was two. They hit us next to each other at the same time in the port side causing considerable damage.

It was frightening to see all the mess a torpedo could make of the ships compartments and boiler room. What with burst steam pipes, twisted walkways and warped ladders everywhere was a mess. It was a good job everyone was alert enough and skilled at damage control. After assessing the damage done to the ship it was lucky not one of the ships company got hurt. It was amazing really we had lost two boiler rooms. Twenty other compartments were flooding: bathrooms, locker rooms, storerooms and the double bottom and air spaces. Eventually the ship was heeled and trimmed with only a 7- degree list to port.

We started to make a speed of 10 knots due east with a corvette escort from HMS Crocus. She stayed with us until out of range of the threat on the 23rd and she detached and returned to Freetown.

A few hours after we got hit we were trying to get everything under control. Whilst we tried to dodge any further encounter with U-Boats. U-105 resumed her attack on the convoy. Sinking British steamers Clan Oglivy killing 61 seamen only 24 survived. She also hit Benwyvis killing 34 seamen and only 21 survived that one. One man lasted 28 days in an open boat until rescue.

Whilst we were limping east the next day at 2200 Hrs she struck the convoy again. Sinking another British steam ship the Jhelum 8 sailors were killed 49 survived. They floated 650 miles and landed in Senegal where they were taken prisoner by the Vichy French.

U.S. Patrol boats came out to meet Malaya and escorted her on the rest of the route to Port of Spain Trinidad, West Indies. We got to Trinidad on the 29th and divers were sent down to find out the damage. It was found that extensive damage was done to the ship under water. All the crew rushed about finding supplies so we could get the emergency repairs carried out. It was a case of beg borrow and steal anything that could help everyone was helping on the scrounge. While temporary repairs were made the British Government were negotiating with the American's to fully repair the ship in one of their dockyards with a dry dock. We sailed up the U.S. coast at 3 knots to Brooklyn Navy Yard, New York. Where we was the first British ship to be repaired under the new Lend-Lease Agreement.

6th April
We arrived in the vicinity of New York. The ship became
an open target to the photographers and press on Staton
Island and Long Island. * Reference pictures 19, 20

The New York river police had their work cut out for
them controlling the boats that carried the news hacks.
Mind you anyone who used the Staton Island and Long
Island ferries had a very close view of the ship. But didn't
see any damage though as it was mainly below the
waterline. Before the ship could go into the Brooklyn
Dockyard, the main mast had to be struck i.e." lowered. So
she could pass under Brooklyn Bridge. After entering the
harbour, it took four hours to complete the docking of the
ship. As there was so much damage done they had to be so
careful in all respects. It was estimated that one could put a
fleet of buses in the cavity. So the Yankee dockyard
workers had a mighty job on their hands.

All the New Yorkers were shocked rigid that the war
was so close to their country. What surprised them was a
British warship in their fair city. We had Lord Louis
Mountbatten come and open the new Union Jack Club on
Lexington Avenue. Where we could go and relax and
where organised trips were being offered. There were
musical shows to see and visits to sporting events i.e.
boxing, ice hockey and baseball. Everywhere we went was
free entry as we had freedom of the city.
We had visits to the pressrooms of the New York
Herald, Tribune and the New York Times, having photo
calls, interviews etc.

I stayed with The Grand Old Lady Malaya only for 2 months in New York. I was especially grateful for my time there it was grand time of my life. Whilst we were in Brooklyn Navy Yard, we had the film star Robert Montgomery for our Naval Liaison Officer. His office was right opposite Times Square Building. We used to stand there looking up to see the latest news on the "Ticker Tape" display Good or Bad.

24th May. We saw the news coming in about the Sinking of HMS Hood by the German Battleship Bismarck.

27th May. Sinking of Bismarck by our North Atlantic Fleet it was a shame we could not take part in that battle.

I was sad to say goodbye to the old Battlewagon when I received my orders to be leave. I was attached with a few members of the crew to steam over the pond in the ex U.S. Coast Guard Cutters Sennen, Walney and Totland. They had been commissioned for Royal Navy service and re-flagged. Only by chance the German Battleship Sharnhorst was not about during our crossing from Newark New Jersey to the Clyde. We were sitting ducks to be taken at any time not even a flare gun for distress signals on board. At least they had Ice Cream Parlours and Banqueting Rooms but even they were not stocked so that was useless. The only good thing was we all had plenty of room to try and relax, when not on duty.

8th June. Allies invade Syria and Lebanon
14th July. British occupy Syria.

1

2

5.

6.

79.

7.

8.

9.

10.

80.

11.

12.

13.

14.

81.

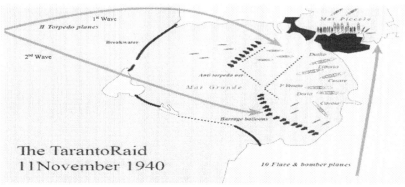

The Taranto Raid
11 November 1940

15.

16.

17.

18.

82.

19.

20.

83.

CHAPTER SEVEN

HMS DELHI

 As soon as we were back across our side of the pond I was told I was drafted to HMS Delhi. Which was then close to be nearly completed in Brooklyn Dockyard, New York. So it was back over the pond to join my new ships company. I thought that was a bit of a waste of journey, time and effort. But at least I got some shore leave at home to see the family before the trip back. I could look forward to getting some more time in the Big Apple (New York).
When I got back to New York I was helping out on the Delhi every now and then in the dockyard. But most of the time we had off as free time to let the dockworkers get on with re-fitting her.

4th May 1941
I got introduced to some very nice people who took me around New York to see the sights and a few Broadway shows.
*Reference Pictures 21, 22, 23.
Don Selkinker and "Pepe" Saddie Jackson I was very grateful to the both of them. I got to know them well I am afraid to say during the rest of the war years I lost their addresses somewhere along the way and could not get in touch with them. I always wonder what happened to them. (Note from his Grandson if any information is out there I would gladly receive it through my publisher).

They even took me to Jack Dempsey's restaurant on Eighth Avenue. He was the world heavy weight champion from 1919 to 1926. He opened the restaurant after his boxing career ended. We had a good meal and a few beers it was time to relax and chat it all seemed serial away from the war.

HMS Delhi was a Danae class Light Cruiser.
She was laid down in 1917 (launched 23 August 1918) and scrapped in 1948 after war service in the Atlantic and Mediterranean.
Builder: Armstrong Whitworth,
 Displacement: 4,927 tons standard (4,850 tonnes), Length: 445 ft (136 m)
Beam: 46 ft 6 in (14.17 m), Draught: 14.4 ft (4.4 m)
Propulsion: 2 × Brown Curtis geared steam turbines
Speed: 29 Knots (54 km/h; 33 mph)
Range: 6,700 nautical miles (12,400 km or 7,700 miles)
Complement: 450-469
Armament: (when built)
6 × 6"/45 (15.2 cm) BL Mark XII guns
2 × 3"/45 (76.2 cm) 20 CWT QF HA, 2 × 2-pdr AA
(Armament as refitted in 1941)
5 × 5"/38 (12.7 cm), 8 × 40 mm Bofors AA (2x quadruple mounts), 12 × 20 mm Bofors AA (2x twin mounts)

26th July
Roosevelt freezes Japanese assets and suspends relations.

14th August
Roosevelt and Churchill announce the Atlantic Charter.

13th November
A U-Boat sinks Aircraft Carrier Ark Royal off Gibraltar.

December 1941
Post refits sea trials.
A sea trial is the testing phase of a refit it is also called a shakedown cruise. Sea trials are conducted to measure a vessel's performance and general seaworthiness. Testing of a vessel's speed, crash stop capability, manoeuvrability, endurance, sea keeping, equipment and safety features are conducted. On board are technical boffins from the dockyard, governing and certification officials from both US Navy and Royal Navy and most of the crew and officers who are going to serve on her. Successful sea trials subsequently lead to a vessel's confirmation of the impact of any modifications and certification for commissioning. Sea trials can last many days it is a lot of work in the engine and boiler rooms. Finding maximum settings and measuring all average speeds at all levels this can be done several times in various sea states.

7th December
Japanese bomb Pearl Harbour to the shock and horror of every one. What a surprise they used our raid on Tarranto as a planning aid and virtually copied it. Right down to the torpedo adaptation for running torpedoes in shallow water.

8th December
United States and Britain declare war on Japan. At least with us working together we should give them something to think about.

11th December
Hitler and Nazi Germany declare war on the United States. Finally the Americans are in the fight.

12th January
On part commissioning HMS Delhi was sent for a second set of sea trials. It was for military readiness and gunnery trials at Fort Munro, Chesapeake Bay, Virginia.
We were finally declared a fighting ship. All the latest hi tech anti-aircraft equipment with R.D.F. (Range and Direction Finding) and Radar was fitted to her. Also we had automatic time fuse loading projectile system on all the guns. This cut down the reloading time of the guns so they could fire faster and engage more targets. It also prevented fewer mechanical problems and stopped human error on setting the fuses.

13th January 1942
Even over here on the other side of the pond. The Germans begin a U-Boat offensive along the east coast of USA.

21st January
We arrived back at Norfolk, Virginia prior to await return passage to the UK.

26th January
The first American forces arrive in Great Britain we all hope they can behave themselves with our women (like we wasn't with theirs).

4th February
Saying farewell to America, the ship was on route to Devonport, Plymouth. We got there on the 15th and waited for a couple of days for further refits to start. After the refits we had trials and shakedowns over the next two and a half months. For most of us that meant plenty of time off to visit family and friends a much welcome change to the last couple of years. By May the ships company was fully selected and she was retained in the Command for convoy defence in the channel and SW approaches.

June 17th
We were deployed to the Irish Sea Force. We were to provide AA defence for RMS (Royal Mail Ship) Queen Elizabeth. During her passage in the NW approaches on route to the Middle East. She was being used as a troop ship and being escorted by Destroyers: Bodicea, Leamington, Keppel, Salisbury and St Marys. This was designated convoy WS19Y. It was only a short stint lasting only 24 Hrs. Until we were relieved then we returned with the escorts to the Clyde on the 19th. To work up for operational service in the Med.

On completion of the build-up training we resumed deployment with the Irish Sea Force. For three and a half months we did AA defence of convoys in the western approaches. With little to no action at all with run of the mill jobs all routine.

27th October
Our ship was nominated for support of the planned allied landings in North Africa (Operation Torch). We took passage from the Clyde with a force of considerable strength. The fleet of ships we had with us consisted of the following. Battleship HMS Rodney, Aircraft Carrier Furious, Escort Carrier Biter and Dasher with Cruisers Jamaica, Hermione and Auxiliary AA ship Alynbank. We had been given the name Force X we was to join the Central Naval Force at Gibraltar. Arriving on the 5th November we stayed overnight.

6th November
We sailed with Rodney, Furious Biter, Dasher as escort for KMF (0)1. We first sailed towards Malta to make it seem, as we were a routine re-supply convoy.

7th November
The fast and slow convoys KMF (0)1 and KMF (0)2 met us 1600 Hrs. We all then divided into seven groups detailed for the three assault areas at Oran. All groups continued together towards Malta until at appropriate moments in the dark for stealth. They broke off individually and turned south towards their real objectives.

89.

We broke off with Battleship HMS Rodney, Cruiser Hermione, Aircraft Carrier Furious and Escort Carrier's Biter and Dasher. We acted as their close AA protection. We sailed to within twenty- five miles of Oran so the aircraft could provide air cover for the invasion. A surprise attack was planned to prevent the Vichy French and Germans scuttling their ships or escaping and destroying the port. Ex-American coastguard cutters, HMS Walney and Hartland would carry out a surprise frontal assault. They were to force their way in to the Harbours. "I thought it was a bit suicidal for my liking".

8th November
Just after 0300Hrs Operation Reservist took place. The Walney and Hartland both had 200 men on board from the American 6th Armoured Infantry Division. With two Fairmile 'B' Motor Launches providing a smoke screen headed directly for the port. They suddenly became aware that the defenders of Oran were not only aware of their presence they were full of fight.

Huge searchlights caught the Walney and Motor launches in glaring beams. All at once they came under heavy withering fire from all the ships in port and shore batteries. Undaunted by the heavy rain of shells the Walney drove head on crashing into the ports log boom. Once through this she found the harbour blocked by a Ville French Sloop La Surprise. The Walney narrowly avoided a collision but received a murderous crossfire of shells at point blank range. Rendering her a wreck and helpless with up to 75% casualties on board.

The captain of HMS Walney gave the order to abandon ship and they were taken prisoner. Shortly after she was abandoned she capsized and sank. The Hartland fared no better she too made it across the boom and into the harbour. Only to become a target, face to face with a Vichy French Destroyer, Typhoon. They immediately came under withering fire at extremely close range. With more than 50% casualties on board and the ship a mass of flames from stem to stern. Hartland was abandoned and the crew and troops were taken prisoner. They had to watch her get blown up later as she was not recoverable from the battle damage. The French Sloop La Surprise made it out to open waters and headed to intercept the troop transport ships. She was cut off by HMS Brilliant and sunk after a shot gun battle.

Shortly after daybreak four Vichy French Destroyers tried to break out. But they ran into HMS Aurora and her destroyer screen. After the smoke had cleared from the battle three were sunk. The forth one was forced back into the harbour to surrender.

By 0900 Hrs the tanks were landing on the Oran beaches. But not until noon was our land forces in full control and our prisoners were released. Our ship was released from duties at Oran with Battleship HMS Rodney and Aircraft Carrier Furious to join Central Navy Forces at Algiers. We were used for AA defence of the invasion force. At Algiers the same sort of sequence had happened under the name of Operation Terminal.

At Algiers two obsolete Destroyers; HMS Broke and Malcolm attempted to land a party of U.S. Rangers directly onto the docks. Again two Fairmile 'B' Motor Launches were used, as escort's to make a smoke screen. Light Cruiser Aurora was detailed for close support with her guns. Yet again it was foiled with heavy artillery hitting HMS Malcom she was badly hit and prevented from landing. Although Destroyer HMS Broke, on the fourth attempt charged the boom and broke through. Which enable her to dock and debark 250 Rangers. Hms Broke was forced to abandon the dock and driven back to sea under a blistering fusillade of gunfire. She suffered much damage and sank the next day.

We arrived to bolster the ack-ack defence and make a smoke screen. To cover the large troop ships containing the invading troops. Aircraft Carrier Furious used her fighter aircraft to provide air defence. All throughout this time we were under heavy air attack.

20th November

Around 0200 Hrs there was a lull in the attacks. I was going off shift in the boiler room and I had just passed through two bulkhead doors. When there was a tremendous explosion we had been hit by a bomb. I was very lucky I was thrown the entire length of the companionway to the next bulkhead door. I only received minor cuts and bruises I was a bit black and blue the next day .The entire stern section of the ship was blown away killing 59.

We lost the aft gun turrets and gun crews, which were manned by Royal Marines. The damage was extreme, to the extent that the whole of the stern of the ship. Down to the water's edge was blown apart exposing the whole stern.
*Reference picture 26.

The crew managed to control the ships stability by pumping more water into the front bilge and antiroll tanks. We Then managed to enter Algiers Harbour carefully at a dead slow. We were secured at the quayside for a further three days providing AA defence. For 3 days and nights we constantly pumped shells into the waves of German torpedo planes and dive-bombers. The ships log recorded "The guns became so red hot that rings of fire like "St Elmo's fire" hung round the barrels. Officers on the bridge had their eyebrows singed off, by the flaming cordite flashes from the forward guns. In one of the nights alone nine thousand rounds of ammunition were expended".

Army officers confirmed later that it was due to Delhi's persistent gunnery protection, that some 30,000 troops of the 1st Army were enabled to land. After those three days we could get started on the repairs. Having eventually assed the damage the shipwrights and damage control personnel were detailed to work around the clock. At least emergency repairs enough to make the ship seaworthy enough for the journey to Gibraltar.

Having succeeded to make it to Gibraltar we were dry docked. This was to assess the worthiness of the ship and make further repairs to make it back to the U.K. It took a couple of weeks there with a bit of shore leave added. We constructed a turtleback of steel plates covering the stern of the ship. It was not pretty but it was sufficient for the journey home. Leaving Gibraltar we made good progress with an escort to the U.K. Going up the west coast of England and Scotland around the north coast and then down the east coast. We went to Hebburn on Tyne to Palmer and Leslies Yard. They had to completely reconstruction of the whole of the stern of the ship. It was a three-month stint by both the ships company and the work force of the yard. In between working on the ship each watch had a considerable length of home leave. On completion of the work the ship was seaworthy once again. The ships company were informed we had to complete readiness sea trials at Plymouth. That took the whole month of April to pass muster.

May 1943
After sea trials we were retained at Plymouth Command for convoy defence. We also took part in interception patrols off the French coast.

14th May
We were sent on a deployment to escort a convoy. We were tasked with Destroyer HMS Tuscan and a Polish Destroyer ORP Orkan.

We assisted in saving the Tuscan after she struck a mine in the Bristol Channel. We escorted the Orkan that took the damaged Destroyer in tow. As soon as we were back at Plymouth we received orders. To take on provision we were released from Plymouth Command. We were to join a Squadron at Gibraltar

June
We were deployed with the squadron at Gibraltar but not for long. We were nominated for service in support of Force East. For the upcoming planned assault on Sicily (Operation Husky). But before that we had preliminary build up operations.

11th June
We deployed on Operation Corkscrew, The allied invasion of the Italian island of Panterlleria (between Sicily and Tunisia). A Royal Navy task force was sent consisting of; five Cruisers, eight Destroyers and three Torpedo Boats.

We took part in a combined naval bombardment of the main port. It was hoped that the island was being blasted into complete surrender. It was an attempt to stem the onslaught of the assaulting troops. The Luftwaffe called on aircraft from all over Sicily and Italy to repel us. But our skilled gunners on board the ships and supporting aircraft did a grand job. Spitfires from the a free French squadron shot down a Junkers Ju 88 bomber and a Focke Wulf Fw 190 fighter bomber on the way to the island.

95.

In all it was recorded that 23 enemy planes were shot down by AA fire by either our guns or the other ships that were there. Around 6,600 tons of bombs and shells saturated every possible target across the island. Hopefully this would bludgeon the defenders into submission. When the first of the Commandos landed the white flag was already flying it was a success.

After we had a brief stop at a pre-planned rendezvous location with re-supply ships to refuel and re-arm. The attention of our force switched to the smaller islands of Lampedusa and Linosa. It is during the subsequent bombardment of lampedusa on the 14th that an unlikely story unfolded. A Swordfish pilot on a rescue mission had engine trouble and was forced to land. The only place he could go was on the enemy held runway. Upon landing he was told the island wished to surrender to him. Sadly this story is unknown to be true.

When our taskforce arrived the enemy was still manning their positions. Our approaching ships were fired upon to no avail as the rounds fell well short of any ship. Our ships sailed up and down the coast bombarding any visible enemy positions and gun emplacements. A white flag was eventually seen on the quayside. A motor launch was sent ashore from one of the destroyers to investigate. The owner of this flag turned out to be lampedusa's second in command. His commander was away from the island on the mainland. He definitely wished to surrender the island to stop the bombardment. But he did not talk to the islands Governor due to language difficulties about the surrender.

The launch had landed a single company from 2nd Battalion Coldstream Guards to secure a landing site. It was discovered that the Governor of the island had not authorised the previous surrender. He was not willing to give up without a fight. He threatened to resist any landings with force. He soon changed his mind under the threat of levelling the entire island by shelling and bombing. The actual surrender was given and signed by the Governor and the military second in commander on the 15th. Thus 95 men from the Coldstream Guards were left in charge of 4,000 prisoners of war and an entire island and its population for three days. Until the main body of the battalion arrived to secure and defend the island.

After that it was seen that an islands could be taken with less effort than had been envisaged. A small force was despatched to deal with Linosa. This happened at 0530 Hrs on the next morning. HMS Nubian cautiously approached the steep, rocky island. All seemed quiet nothing was happening on the island. The landing party made ready to board the ships whaler (as their motor boat was under repair). Still it was too quiet until Nubian sounded her siren and then suddenly white sheets and towels began waving furiously from all the windows and vantage points ashore. The garrison almost to a man deserted their posts and rowed out to the destroyer to surrender. Nubian sailed around the small island picking up the members of the garrison.

Meanwhile the landing party went ashore at first initially the Garrison Commandant could not be found. He was not in his Garrison for he was sleeping elsewhere with a woman. When he was eventually located he refused to surrender. Until the CO of the landing party told him it was a futile gesture. As all 168 troops from the garrison had surrendered and were already in captivity on the Nubian. This quashed the Italian Commandant's pride and at 0615 Hrs he signed the surrender document. On the pier there was something of a farewell party for him before he was interred in the brig. The Nubian sailed away having first destroying the Italian gun emplacements and communications equipment with explosives.

1st July 1943
We joined with cruisers Newfoundland, Mauritius, Orion, Carlise and Colombo as the cruiser force in Force East to cover British landings at Syracuse for the invasion of Sicily.

CHAPTER EIGHT

HUSKY

9th July 1943
Operation Husky the invasion of Sicily we were assigned to an area called Acid Beach, not far from a village called Avola.

The plan for Husky called for the amphibious assault of the island by two armies. One of the landings was on the south-eastern coast which we were involved in and the other landing on the central southern coast. The amphibious landings were being supported by naval gunfire, tactical interdiction bombing with close air support and an airborne operation. Defenders had assumed that no one would attempt a landing in such poor weather conditions and strong wind.

Operation Husky constituted the largest amphibious operation of World War II. In terms of size of landing zones and number of divisions put ashore on the first day. The armada of 3,200 ships had 160,000 personnel, 14,000 vehicles, 600 tanks and 1,800 guns. Also 400 transport aircraft 144 gliders 3,700 fighter and bomber aircraft were used.

There were 610 merchant ships used in the operation all crewed by civilians. They were being tasked with getting the troops closer to the operations area. They then transferred on to the Landing ships and other vessels before going in to hazardous areas.

Allied Naval Command Military Vessels

Naval Task Forces: Commanders:	Western Rear-Adm H K Hewitt USN	Eastern Adm Sir B Ramsey
Naval Forces	**U.S.A.**	**British & Allied**
Battleships	-	6
Carriers	-	2
Cruisers	5	10
Destroyers	48	80
Submarines	-	26
Other warship	98	250
Troopships, supply ships, LSIs etc	94	237
Landing Ships and Craft (major)	190	319
Totals	**435 USN**	**930 RN**
Plus Landing Craft (minor)	510 USN	715 RN

In the afternoon of the 9th a force 7 north- westerly gale blew up. With these weather conditions it was very rough on the troops on the transport ships. They were suffering the double discomfort of seasickness and a drenching through to the skin. However these unfavourable conditions had a beneficial side effect. The enemy relaxed their guard in the mistaken belief that a landing in weather conditions such as this was most unlikely.

The air defence on Sicily was comparatively strong for the size of the island. Stukas and ME-110's strafed the invasion fleet whenever the opportunity presented itself. Not causing serious damage but spurred up enough panic to seriously endanger the success of the operation. Four British and American attacks by airborne parachute forces were carried out just after midnight.

When some of the C-47 transport aircraft carrying American Para troops passed over the American invasion fleet. Some of their inexperienced naval gunners nervously fired their anti-aircraft guns at the friendly planes. No damage was done to the planes but in the panic and confusion some pilots hit the green light. Entire sticks of paratroopers jumped early this sent the heavily laden men down in the ocean to disappear. Hundreds of men were lost to a bad mistake. The high winds of up to 45 miles per hour caused problems in the air too. The American troop carrying aircraft got blown off course and the Para troops were scattered widely over the whole of the south east of Sicily.

The British air landing troop's fared little better.The unlucky contributing factors were poor flying by inadequately trained pilots and the navigational conditions they faced. About a dozen of the gliders were released early from their transport aircraft and they crashed into the sea causing many casualties. Out of the 135 gliders that were released at the right point 57 of them received the same fate they got blown off course and crashed also in to the sea. The wind scattered the rest of the gliders so badly that only 12 of the gliders with their elite troops reached their targets. Nevertheless the scattered airborne troops maximized their opportunities, attacking patrols and creating confusion wherever possible. In spite of their losses the airborne troops had a positive effect as small isolated units. Acting with their initiative they attacked vital points and created widespread panic.

The strong wind also made matters difficult for the amphibious landings, but also ensured the element of surprise. The ships were rocking about like mad and the smaller craft were tossed about like corks. The Royal Navy was allocated their own landing sector in the east and also they provided a covering force against interference by the Italian Fleet. The main group included Battleships: Nelson, Rodney, Warspite and Valiant. With Aircraft Carriers Formidable and Inodomitable their aircraft would provide close air support and protection to the landings. Seven Royal Navy submarines acted as navigation markers off the invasion beaches.

There were advance reconnaissance beach landings of Royal Marine Commandos. Of the 13 officers and ratings put ashore 9 went missing it was presumed the weather had caused their disappearance. As the enemy did not seem alerted by them and 4 of them returned with vital information about conditions on the beaches.

Every boat and ship has a different dance in the water. A large freighter or warship for example, rolls from side to side very slowly and up and down very slowly and sometimes even nose to stern a bit. They all have their own rhythm and depending upon the size and weight of the ships and boats and how big their keels are each one is different. Landing craft of various sizes have a different dance because they are flat bottomed in most instances. So they can get into shore, and even the ones that don't have a flat bottom have their own dance. So now in the middle of the night you have all these ships in close vicinity with their own slow tango dance on the sea.

102.

You now have swarms of smaller landing craft and boats all between the ships with their fast foxtrot of a dance. Now if any make a mistake it's not toes that get stood on its lives lost or trucks, guns, tanks straight through the bottom of boats to the bottom of the sea.

10th July
02.25Hrs. All's well everything is set, all of a sudden flashes of AA fire could be seen from the beach as enemy guns fire at aircraft noises in the dark. Our Cruiser and others start turning starboard beam on to the beaches ready to bring guns to bear. Further out the Destroyers follow suit with their big guns.

0230Hrs. RAF bombers start to fly over and drop their bombs on the coast this is the start of the softening up phase.

03.00 Hrs. No shelling from the ships as yet the intensified bombing still in progress as all the landing craft and ships jockey for position.

0330 Hrs. Motor launches lay a smoke screen close to shore the odd enemy machine gun post exchanges fire with them.

0400Hrs. Machine gun posts on the shore now firing tracers into the smoke screens and they are really pouring it on.

04.15Hrs. We start to light up the beach with star shells and use our AA guns to strafe the coastal defences. The big guns on the destroyers start to take out the bigger fortifications that started to return fire towards us. The Italians defence plan was for the coastal formations to form a covering screen to take the initial impact of the invasion. This would allow time for the more centrally located field divisions to intervene and counter attack the invasion beachhead repelling us back to the sea. But this was not going to happen.

04.30Hrs. A heavy smoke screen is covering the island the rocket ships open fire with an almighty barrage. This was to try and clear the machine gun posts and any barbwire entanglements.

04.40Hrs. The first waves of Royal Marines start to go in to try and secure landing corridors. One of the Destroyers fires two complete salvos at targets just of the beach. By now shells from shore batteries fell uncomfortably close, as did bombs from a few Stuka aircraft.

04.45Hrs. Dawn has broken an enemy battery on shore opens up at our ship shots straddle the ship and make it shake. The enemy then suddenly switched fire on to the Landing Crafty Gun's (LCGs). It took all of five minutes for our guns to relay on to the new targets and return fire.

04.55Hrs. A couple of the destroyers must have noticed what was happening. They joined in the barrage of the enemy positions with their heavy guns. The enemy's guns were silenced in seconds and the bridge reported that one of us must have hit the enemy's ammunition dump as there was a large explosion close to the gun position.

05.30Hrs. We are not getting much reply from the enemy out at the anchorage off the beachhead. That can only mean the ground troops must be engaging the enemy positions taking their attention away from our ships. We are on full alert for enemy aircraft as we have heard the American sector is getting hit hard by aircraft.

Action becomes very heavy in the American sector losing quite a few ships. German aircraft sank the landing ship LST-313 and minesweeper USS Sentinel. Italian Stukas sank destroyer USS Maddox and the Indian hospital ship SS Talamba. In the following days aircraft damaged or sank Liberty ships SS Timothy Pickering, SS Sullivan and several more warships, transport vessels and landing craft. *Reference picture 27.

Italian Stukas named Picchiatello and Savoia-Marchetti SM.79 torpedo bombers coordinated their attacks with German Junkers JU88's and Ju87's coming in between the Italian strikes. However being close to shore the ships settled on even keels so a lot of the cargo on board them was salvaged or got off before they went down. Later on divers recovered some more of the valuable cargo that was needed ashore.

The British land forces did not meet strong resistance from the Italian coastal troops and swiftly moved inland leaving a very secure beachhead.

16.24Hrs. Four miles south of our position a small ammunition supply ship gets hit by enemy bombs. She can be seen in the distance as she blazes.

11th July
11.35Hrs. Our ship was directed to indirect fire at enemy positions near to Spaccaforno. We had to move position by several miles to within range and turned broadside on. To be able to open fire with all our 6 inch guns. After three salvos we received the message to cease fire target neutralized.

12.00Hrs. We were transferred from Bark West anchorage to Acid anchorage to act as AA defence. Acid anchorage had so far borne the greater part of the enemy's air attacks.

During the night we moved a small force to attempt to capture Augusta. On route we dropped of several of our Cruisers to carry out mission's .HMS Uganda stopped off to engage a hostile battery at the southern end of Augusta Bay. We also dropped off HMS Uganda and Mauritius who bombarded the enemy's line of retreat in the vicinity of Augusta.

106.

The rest of us were going to try and land some troops at Augusta to form another beachhead and split the attention of the enemy. We had Destroyers: HMS Blencathra, Nelson and Rodney with us. Our four ships went slightly ahead of the landing ships we were to bombard any enemy positions that gave their position away engaging us. On our approach we were being bombarded by numerous guns in hidden positions that we could not locate. The Captains of the Battleships relayed the information to HQ who in turn ordered the landings cancelled. This was fortunate as the land forces were advancing so fast they would be capturing Augusta within a day or so.

12 July

Our Cruisers were yet again bombarding Targets around the Augusta area. While this was happening the 14th minesweeping Flotilla were engaged in screening sweeps protecting us. HMS Seaham sighted a periscope shortly before 1300 Hrs. She closed in at the enemy at full speed with the intention of ramming the U-boat started to crash dive and avoided the collision just and Seaham scraped along her side. As the U-boat's conning tower started to slip under the water in a mass of bubbles. HMS Boston's 3" inch gun got a quick shot off and hit the periscope. The U-boat surfaced and the crew rushed to man her weapons. Seaham opened fire at her with all weapons available. The U-boat returned fire with her 4" inch deck gun and her 2 x 20mm machine guns.

The fire fight lasted less than half an hour. Seaham's 3"
inch guns reported direct hits on the U-boats conning tower
silencing her guns. HMS Seaham went alongside the U-
boat and some of her crew boarded her with tommy guns.
They climbed down the gruesome wreck of the conning
tower through the bits of bodies of the men that died to
capture the submarine. They found it was an Italian U-boat
and the remainder of the subs crew surrendered. Only
twenty of the U-boats crew survived out the commander
and 20 others died in the fire fight or drowned trying to
abandon ship. Later the submarine was repaired at Malta
and she was commissioned into the Royal Navy as HMS P
714. On 29 January 1944 she was transferred to the Free
French. She served as the Narval until 1949.

16th July
The weather turned nasty again we had a leak in the fore
store on Delhi. This required bailing out it was caused by
separation in the hull plates due to so many near misses.
HMS Indomitable was damaged by Italian torpedo aircraft
which had been wrongly identified during air attacks as a
naval Swordfish was returning to carrier. She left on the
20th as her repair was arranged in USA.

A little further around the coast was Syracuse and Augusta.
Where there was a heavy bombardment from the Capitol
Ships. Fighting between forces was also heavy on the coast
road to Catania. Eventually all of Sicily was captured
though in the meantime the assault and landings had begun
around Bari and the south of Italy.

About 170 enemy aircraft had been lost in the first week of the invasion. 57 of which were lost to our fighter aircraft and anti-aircraft fire in the first three days. The Royal Navy lost 314 killed or missing and 411 wounded. Four sailors were captured but later released by our forces.

17th July
We started to patrol the coast anti clockwise of the island. Stopping in some places when the captain thought it was safe for the crew to try and relax. Some crewmembers would swim ashore to get citrus fruits and grapes. But we would be back on patrol again in the evenings.

18th July
There was a clear night and the full moon made us an easy target to see. We fought off two air attacks with anti-aircraft fire. As we patrolled around the coast we would keep an eye out for enemy activity on shore. But most of the eyes were watching the sky for any threat.

Eventually we got to Palermo just after ground forces on the 22nd had captured it. So we put in to harbour for fresh water and a chance to go ashore for a few hours to see the sights. As normal that did not happen only a few of the officers got to go ashore for a few hours. We then received orders to return to Malta for the 30th July for ammunition and victuals (food and provisions) etc. So the officers got called back and we put to sea again.

Desmond Tighe war correspondent was on the island of Malta for the Royal Navy. He wrote for the Newspaper "Times of Malta". One of his articles was about the invasion of Sicily

Extract from the article in the "Times of Malta".

"HMS Delhi stooged around always off the most dangerous beach areas protecting the landing craft, Her men stripped down to the waist sweat pouring from their bodies in the oppressive heat manning the guns night and day".

That's when we got called "The Stooge Ship of the Mediterranean Fleet". That followed us around for a long time after that with sailors on other ships shouting. "Hey look here comes the stooge ship" every time we passed them in port. The sense of humour of the British military is one of the things that kept us going through out the war.

We were then nominated for service in the Northern Attack Force (TF85) for the planned invasion of Salerno, Italy.

August
The allies used this month mainly to build up the number and strength of troops ready to invade Italy. It was a race to deliver vital troop reinforcements from North Africa to Sicily and other places. For the future coming operations. So it was back and forth with troopships

CHAPTER NINE

AVALANCHE

Operation Baytown 3rd September 1943.
The preliminary step of the assault by British forces under Monty would depart from Messina on Sicily. They crossed the Straits of Messina in landing craft, as it was a short distance across. They would land near the tip of Calabria, Italy.

Operation Avalanche was the invasion of Salerno.
The Royal Navy in supporting the beachhead would send Force five. It would consist of a unique assortment of warships. Five Aircraft Carriers: Fleet Light Carrier Unicorn with Escort Light Carriers: Attacker, Battler, Hunter and Stalker. Ten hunter class Destroyers and four Anti-Aircraft Cruisers: Charybdis, Delhi, Euryalus and Sylla. The five Aircraft Carriers would have to work in a tiny area off the coast of Salerno. They would have very little room to turn into the wind for flying aircraft off and recovering them. The Aircraft Carriers lack of speed and restricted operational area would be a major flaw. The problem would be to have the carriers back at windward in time for each successive flying operation. This would eventually cost our forces quite a number of aircraft losses due to accidents.

Force five sailed from Malta on the morning of the 8th steering for the Straits of Messina rolling over heavy seas. Ahead were our Cruisers leading the five Aircraft Carriers, which were circled by their Destroyers. The summit of Mount Etna was hidden in cloud as the force passed it to port. As we approached the Straits darkness began to close in, Sicily was lit up like bonfire night. They were using Floodlights, great big bonfires and fireworks. They were celebrating the Italian surrender, which was announced that afternoon. But on the Italian mainland the war went on. The British Eighth Army crept up the toe of Italy dispelling the occupation of German forces. The bright flashes of distant gunfire and the red glow of verey lights and illume flares lit up the Italian sky.

As our force sailed north past the Lipari Islands and the volcano island of Stromboli we appeared to be the only ships at sea. Yet we all knew across the Tyrrhenian Sea from bases in Sicily and North Africa. The long lines of landing ships and transports plus more warships from the American Navy were slowly converging to meet us in the Gulf of Salerno.

Operation Slapstick 9th September.
British 1st Airborne Division would seize the port of Taranto using British warships. They were informed of this with such short notice the operation got the nickname "Operation Bedlam".

9th September 1943.

We were off the coast of Salerno.

About 0320 Hrs in pitch darkness, the rocket LCT(R) let go their barrage. The rockets were fired in bunches with a loud whoosh that was terrifying, enveloping their craft in brilliant sheets of flame. The rockets soaring high up, over and down toward the beach. Where thunderous explosions took place this was the pre landing bombardment.

At 0330 Hrs the first waves of assault troops landed in their small crafts. This was followed by waves of: LCVPs (Landing Craft Vehicle Personnel), LCIs (Landing Craft Infantry) and LCTs (Landing Craft Tank). Sometime around 0430 Hrs four German artillery shells fell into the water near a LST (Landing Ship Tank). They had a causeway attached running ashore. The explosion's enveloped everyone on board with water. The Savannah was the first American ship to open fire against the German shore defences in Salerno bay. She silenced a railroad artillery battery with 57 rounds and completed eight more fire support missions that day.

When the small craft began hitting the beach the German panzers opened up with everything they had. They soon were to be joined by all the big guns, 88s, and machine guns. Our cruisers joined the USS Savannah, Boise and Philadelphia (Galloping Ghost) in returning fire. Galloping Ghost was Philadelphia's nickname. Because the Germans pronounced prematurely they had sunk her three times by mistake before this operation.

We returned fire and were blasting with everything we had. German bombers started coming over, so even the guns on the LSTs started firing. Good god it was hot and the sky was bright with tracer.

A division of German Panzer Grenadiers was opposing the Allies landing force. They were supported by a myriad of well-sighted 88mm gun positions in the surrounding hills. Far inshore their gunfire sent brown clouds of dust rolling over the countryside. Now and again a tower of water sprouted up on the water's edge showing they were ranging in on the beachhead the action was fierce.

The Monitor Lord Roberts was brought into action. She was a floating gun emplacement. She had a twin, 15 inch gun turret and two 12 pounder (76mm) secondary guns. Also she had a single 47mm anti-aircraft pom-pom gun. Being of shallow draft with a flat bottom she got in very close to the coast and pumped 15" shells up into the high terrain. She was trying to put the Jerries and Italians gun batteries out of action. Or at least keep their heads down so they were afraid to mount their guns. She was also trying to shoot observation posts their spotters were using to bring down fire on us.

Off to the left of the beachhead we could see one of the LSTs approaching the causeway running to shore. She was about a mile off the beach when she suddenly must have ridden up on to a loose mine. As there was one hell of an explosion and most of the twenty-four or so men that were on the causeway were blown off in to the water.

114.

As it was getting light the carriers moved into wind to begin their work. From the massed aircraft on their decks the first Seafires (naval versions of the Spitfire) roared off. Plane after plane formed up in the sky before heading to the beachhead to cover our advancing troops. The first day at Salerno was a maelstrom of air attacks, bombardments, sea attacks, landings and counter attacks.

One of my mates who was on deck at the time said he saw a YM minesweeper about two miles off shore. She must have seen a large Italian mine which had been swept to the surface loom in front of her. She tried to franticly avoid it but not being quick enough she rode over the mine. Just seconds before it went off against the side of the ship. There was a blinding flash with flame and water towering up. It hurled objects off her deck aloft. Then a deluge of water and oil fell on to her decks. The explosion ripped into the ship's crew quarters killing and seriously injuring a few of them aboard her. It was a hard sight to witness.

We were in constant action on Delhi throughout the day. USS Buck (DD-420) sunk after being torpedoed by the German submarine U-616 off the coast. That night we had a particularly heavy air attack. A few enemy bombers made it through at 2152 Hrs dropping 31 sticks of bombs in the crowded anchorage. One attacked our ship whilst we tried manoeuvring to avoid them two near misses landed close to us. When the spray and smoke cleared we were on a collision course, at HMS Uganda another of our light cruisers.

115.

We could not avoid her and clashed a glancing blow to her, slightly damaging our hull. When the flak that went up it was so thick you could not put a finger up in the air in between the shell bursts. Nine enemy planes were brought down during the night. When you have been through something like that who could be afraid of fireworks and bangs now? Ocean Tug (AT) USS Nauset (AT-89) was also sunk this night in the gulf of Salerno by enemy aircraft.

On the second day the 10th the air attacks in the anchorage continued. Our ship born forces came under attack from torpedo bombers. They were met by a furious flak barrage from our ship and others. The barrage seemed to put a wall up in front of the enemy planes. This forced some of them to turn tail. Our land forces fought to expand the beachhead.

On board our ship we were again in frequent action. Our guns shot down at least two enemy aircraft over the southern anchorage while a third plane seemed to explode in mid-air. Captain Peachey reported that the ships company had applied to remain continuously at actions stations. The ships routine was modified according to this. As there was nothing wrong with a bit of competition between gun crews. Within seconds again our guns opened fire as another of the attacks started. We suddenly were aware of the whistling of the bombs coming towards us.

Luckily they were near misses. We were shaken three times as they exploded drenching men on our stern fantail. The concussion burst a few pipes down below with the pressure wave. As soon as they went off an enemy plane swooped over us. He raked the decks with machine gun fire. Drilling holes in the deck until suddenly one of our gun crews got a bead on him and blew him out of the air.

On the third day the 11th, the USS Savannah was lying in her support area. Waiting calls for gunfire support. She was not far away from us on the Delhi. At 0930 Hrs 12x Focke Wulfe 190's were reported approaching from the north. All the ships started their avoidance manoeuvres. A heavy bomb exploded close to Savannah's hull to the stern of the ship.

You could see the whole stern of the ship lift in the water. A few sailors on deck lost their balance and fell over. Ten minutes later a Dornier Do 217 K-2 bomber approached from out of the sun. The USAF's P-38 Lightning's and the Savannah's anti-aircraft gunners were tracking it at 18,700 feet high but could not stop it. Savannah received a direct hit on No.3 turret from a heavy radio controlled bomb (at a guess a Fritz-X glide bomb). The bomb had penetrated through three decks. It detonated in the lower ammunition handling room of the turret. The blast wiped out the crew of the stricken turret and the No.1 damage control crew in the central station. It blew a gaping large hole in the ships keel and opened a seam in her port side.

For at least 30 minutes secondary explosions wreaked havoc in the turret and its ammunition supply rooms hampering any fire fighting efforts. Working quickly, the officers and sailors of the Savannah's crew sealed off flooded and burning compartments. They then tried to correct her list by pumping out the water. With some assistance from the USS Hopi and the USS Moreno rescue tugs putting out the fires. The Savannah got underway on her own steam by 1757 Hrs, and steamed for the seaport at Malta. The Savannah lost 197 crewmen with 15 other sailors seriously wounded. Four crewmen were trapped in a watertight compartment for about 60 hours. These were not rescued until the Savannah had arrived at Grand Harbour Valletta, Malta on the 12th. She left Malta after emergency repairs on the 7th Dec and headed stateside for more permanent repairs.

Force five was withdrawn later on in the day all the Aircraft Carriers and Destroyers headed to Palermo, Sicily. To re-store essentials, ammunition, refuel and to embark replacements for planes lost, before returning to the beachhead on the 13th. All the cruisers headed for Bizerta, Tunisia for the re-store of essentials, ammunition and refuel before returning to the beachhead on the 13th. Apart from us we moved off the beachhead. To rendezvous with an American re-supply vessel who re-fuelled, re-armed and repaired our hull damage. We then returned 24 Hrs later to our duties at the beachhead.

USS Rowan the Benham class Destroyer was another casualty on this day she was torpedoed and sunk off the coast 10 miles or so from Salerno. A Kriegsmarine E-boat did this with the loss of 202 of her 273-member crew. That was another shock but you just had to thank your luck that it was not your ship.

The James W Marshall a US Liberty ship arrived at Salerno and was immediately hit and set on fire by a 250-pound bomb. The brave crew extinguished the fire and the ship continued unloading its essential supplies to the beachhead.

12t h September 1943
On the fourth day we were under repair away from the danger area. We was all a bit disappointed that we was not in the action but we were kept fully informed of events happening and as soon as we were ready we would get back to it.

The Luftwaffe furnished their brand of entertainment throughout the day to the ships at sea of Salerno. They delivered this entertainment with Junkers JU-88s and Dornier DO-217s these delivered bombs and torpedoes. The Dornier's also launched a new version of guided bombs or radio-controlled bomb, also known as a glide bomb or standoff bomb.

This type of bomb allows it to be released at a distance from the target so the aircraft is not in danger from the flak. LCT (5)-215 was sunk with one of these and an Hs-293 rocket propelled glide bomb damaged LST-312. One of the crewmembers John Herbert showed rare courage and presence of mind for one so young. By cutting loose a burning landing craft full of ammunition and flooding the aft magazine to stop it from exploding. The William Bradford was also lucky she had two bombs explode 25-30 feet off her port bow and another close enough to splash water on deck. She was also strafed and had her life boats riddled by machinegun fire but she gave some back. Shooting down two aircraft, no one was injured aboard her.

The Fifth day 13th
We returned to the beachhead amidst all the havoc. The Germans were now making a terrific counter attack on our precarious landing area. Some of the Tiger (Mark VI) tanks were moving south along the beach to threatening beachhead. The Delhi and USS Edison (American Destroyer) were tasked with counter battery fire. On to the tanks and other Wehrmacht gun emplacements. One of the enemy 88's fired upon the Edison. It had a unique piercing sound as it passed us. It went over the Edison between their fire directors armoured observation position and their No.1 smock stack.

120.

We had been used to the fluttery sound of large artillery projectiles in arched trajectories. Like our guns and other ships guns that were subsonic. But the enemy 88 had a round that went 4,000 feet per second. When you heard that petrifying sound the projectile was long gone. They had to hit you directly to set off their impact fuses. They were designed to be an anti-tank, armour piercing round.

Edison and our ship were carrying out evasive manoeuvres. Accelerating or slowing down, making course reversals, dodging bombs and shells. All the lookouts kept an eye out for any "floaters" sea mines that were set adrift in our area. All available guns were being used even personal weapons were being used to shoot at the floaters. Since we both were firing constantly the water around the ships was full of spent cartridge cases (brass).

The Wehrmacht's surviving tanks and infantry finally turned around. Leaving tank wrecks piled up in a twisted mess among the rubble. We all thought that the German forces had been blunted this time. While our forces fought to expand their beachhead the Germans defended stubbornly. The Germans tried to mask the build-up of their reinforcements for a counter offensive. This was noticed by the Allies intelligence units and reported up the chain of command.

United States merchant ships were under attack for most of the day the James Woodrow recorded eight dive-bombing attacks.

The armed guards on board the James Woodrow claimed to have destroyed three enemy planes. she was finally hit by an anti-personnel bomb in the late afternoon wounding four of her armed guards.

One very sad loss of life was to take place on one of the Hospital ships anchored off the coast. The Hospital ship was thought to be at a safe distance out to sea. The ship was brightly illuminated and carried standard Red Cross markings to identify the hospital ships. Supposedly under the protection of the Geneva Convention! They were purposely attacked twice during the day so were moved further off the coast for the dark hours. At 5am the hospital ship was deliberately hit on the boat deck by a large bomb. Unfortunately all the fire fighting equipment was destroyed and the fire took a strong hold of her. The fire eventually set the oil tanks on fire. Her crew and passengers were evacuated and she was towed out to see to be sunk as the damage was beyond repair. Sadly six of the nurses and all the doctors on board lost their lives.

That night the 504th Parachute Infantry Regiment of the 82nd Airborne Division did a night drop. To support the 5th Army that was in danger of being pushed back into the sea! They landed south of the river Sele. Their LZ (Landing Zone) came under attack virtually straight away and was shrinking. In order to guide the C-47 pilots to the shrinking drop zone. Oil drums were filled with gasoline soaked sand and ignited every 50 yards when signalled. 1,300 troopers landed that night infusing a new sense of confidence to the beleaguered soldiers of the 5th Army.

Sixth day 14th September 1943

Yet another casualty was HMS Uganda she was hit by a FX1400 glider bomb when she was providing naval gunfire support she sustained major damage with serious flooding she survived but was put out of action for the majority of the war.

The first United States Liberty ship to be sunk at Salerno was the Bushrod Washington. She carried 7,000 drums of aviation gasoline, 75 tons of bombs and some 105mm shells. After continuous air attack she was eventually hit with a 500lb bomb that ignited the aviation fuel in number four hold. The fire heated up her cargo, until it resulted in a tremendous explosion. Throwing 50-gallon drums in the air like rockets. These exploded raining burning fuel down on what was left of the ship. The explosion had destroyed the entire forward section of the vessel. But by chance it had only killed four of the crew she sank shortly afterwards. At least her armed guards claimed they got one of the planes.

The Lewis Morris suffered minor damage from shell fragments by several near misses three armed guards were wounded and one died later from his wounds.

On the afternoon the Battleship Valiant and Warspite with Aircraft Carrier Illustrious left Malta for Britain. They didn't get too far when they were ordered to Salerno at 2000 Hrs, with their six Destroyer escorts. To support the landings, Destroyers Nelson and Rodney were ordered from Malta to converge on the beachhead as well.

That night the 505th Parachute Infantry Regiment of the 82nd Airborne Division was dropped in. This was to reinforce the 504th near to the same landing zone as the night before.

The James W Marshall US Liberty ship was hit for a second, time this time by a guided bomb. It plunged right through the ship in to the engine room and exploded. This split her hull plates flooding the engine room and No.3 hold. It started fires amidships and ignited the fuel oil that had leaked in to the sea. Watching from nearby was a nightmare, wild panic seized the crew as they struggled and fought to get over the side. Some of them jumped when it would have been easier to go down a ladder to the safety of a raft. They jumped from the bridge and the stern of the ship, right into the melee of a cauldron of burning fuel oil on the surface of the sea. Some of the crew attempted to launch a lifeboat but they swamped it in panic. The flames were dancing and leaping at them as they blindly jumped into the sea. Also US Liberty ship SS Boyd Washington was hit but she managed to control the fire eventually extinguishing it with the aid of a rescue tug.

Seventh day 15th September
In the morning hours it was the turn of the Liberty ship SS James W Marshal who was anchored 1.5 miles off shore. Ten Stukas cut loose from formations and dropped their sticks of bombs on her whilst she was unloading her cargo. Her armed guards knocked down one plane and damaged another.

One bomb went right through the bridge but it was a dud and didn't explode. It was dealt with later as all hands were busy. Another bomb dropped dead centre of a barge tied up alongside loading. The barge went up in a puff of black smoke ablaze. A Destroyer close by pulled it away to a safe distance and sank it with depth charges set with time fuses.

Air raids continued throughout the day. The German planes were back again and again and we had to fight them off like swatting off one or two wasps from a swarm. Valiant and Warspite arrived a magnificent sight in their war paint with battle ensigns flying. They took up positions a few miles off the coast steaming up and down. It took most of the day briefing the gunnery officers and landing their spotter's on shore. Eventually they were ready to start shelling. During this time the ships at anchor still suffered from the air attacks even with the extra AA defence they brought to the party.

The Derwent dale one of our English tankers was about seven hundred yards off our starboard quarter. She was hit and blew up with a deafening roar around midday. During another of the air attacks in the afternoon the James W Marshal came under attack again at 1440 Hrs. A 250lb bomb struck a 20mm gun shield on the starboard side of the bridge. The shell glanced off and pierced the deck exploding in the master's quarters and office. The explosion caused a small fire but the crew quickly extinguished it, she was to survive.

Two days later planes attacked the James W Marshal again and a glide bomb penetrated the boat deck. It exploded near the crew's mess room and the engine room. A fire broke out and the engine room and No.3 hold flooded. Two LCTs loaded with gas lay on the port side of the ship caught fire adding to the inferno. Eventually the fire was extinguished and she was towed to Bizerte by the British steamship Empire Perdita. The loss of life during this attack on board was tragic one officer 12 crewmen and fifty of the Army stevedores who were unloading the ship.

LCT (5)-19 and LCT (5)-241 were both sunk from bomb hits. This lost a large number of infantry and equipment and all the tanks on board them. The 325th Glider Infantry Regiment was landed at the beachhead amphibiously (without their gliders) successfully. They were tasked to support the other airborne units fighting on the ground.

The USS Mayo was tasked with targets by the river Sele it was engaging the enemy at 1,000 yards. Her gunners and fire control could not see direct to the targets as they were over a hill. Its targets were German Tiger Tanks, which were advancing down the banks of the Sele River. They fired more than 1,200 rounds of five-inch projectiles. The Destroyer was getting numerous requests for fire support in that area, as the tigers just kept on coming. They came close to burning up their guns from over use. Afterwards when the Germans fell back the spotters on the battlefield reported.

"There was a layer of dense smoke over the devastation. The air was filled with flying steel and the stench of explosions choked the throats and nostrils of the men ashore in that area".

At 1752 Hrs Warspite and Valiant opened fire with a thunderous report. The fire was extremely accurate and an excited radio operator signalled back. That of the thirty rounds of 15-inch shells fired into the Altaville area in the first salvo nineteen had fallen on target. This was naval gunnery at its best. The Battleships were firing at ranges between 19,000 and 24,000 yards. The effect of those heavy shells upon the enemy was reportedly a horrific sight it was like dropping a freight train from an equal height.

The evening of the fifteenth was calm and clear, with a bright moon that put us all on edge. Soon after dark the first German Torpedo bombers arrived. All the ships of war were steaming about firing an onslaught of ant-aircraft fire into the sky. Even Warspite and Valliant were in action as they steamed up and down outside the bay. This action against air attack occurred on and off for the whole knight in the bay.

The Eighth day 16th September
Early on Warspite and Valiant returned to their bombardment positions, half a mile or so off shore. It's a unique experience being under the over flying bombardment. Just after the initial thunderous out clap of the salvo comes the sounds of the rounds like large whistling, steaming kettle's flying over.

127.

Fifteen inch shells from our big ships ranged all around the German positions far inland. Then at 1300 Hrs the fire was switched to enemy traffic concentrations and ammunition dumps. Thirty-two rounds were fired, again with great accuracy. But the Navy was not going to be allowed to have it their own way. The punishment caused by the accurate and effective shelling of the US Cruisers and our two Battleships. This motivated Marshall Kesselring to order a maximum concentration of effort against us. He also increased intensified bombing attacks of our fleet at Salerno. Just after 1400 Hrs, Warspite was under way after completing a bombardment changing position for a further bombardment. She also intended to keep the enemy guessing where she was. Twelve fighter-bombers (FW190s) attacked straight out of the sun. Warspite's anti-aircraft guns and ours engaged the aircraft with an outpouring of lead and steel. Our pom-pom guns shot down one of the fighter-bombers. This put the rest off their mission, causing them to fail in their attack.

Unknown to us their purpose was to divert attention from a more dangerous attack then approaching. At 1427 only a few minutes after the fighter-bombers had disappeared we got an alarm. The Warspite's lookouts and our spotters sighted a group of high-level bombers approaching. From which were launched three of the dreaded feared FX1400 glider bombs. Our captain was first to spot them at 15,000 feet they turned together in synchronism in a vertical dive. From the time of sighting to the impact was only seven to ten seconds.

No time for a warning and evasive action of the ships. They were controlled from aircraft far out of the range of our guns. Tracer shells and anti-aircraft bursts raced out from the assembled ships to no avail. Off the three bombs launched from the enemy planes, two found their target. Warspite was making 10 knots and in the congested anchorage it was impossible to take avoiding action due to her size. One of the bombs hit Warspite amidships. The bomb penetrated straight through six decks to hit her double bottom near to No.4 boiler-room where it detonated. A second bomb about two thirds of its flight down curved toward the ship and was a near miss. Hitting the water amidships abreast of the ship where it detonated underwater creating a gigantic waterspout. The third bomb was a near miss on the starboard side aft of the ship causing another massive eruption of water.

The near miss had made a long gash in her starboard side amidships running through several compartments. Astonishing with all her damage only nine men were killed with another fourteen injured. One boiler room had been completely demolished, and four of the other five were flooded. All steam was lost and she was dead in the water the ship could not steer so drifted uncontrolled. All communications and radar were temporarily out of action due to the loss of power. About 5,000 tons of water had flooded her lowering her in the water by five feet.

At 1615 Hrs Warspite prepared to be taken in to tow by U.S. tug Hopi. The Delhi was tasked with being her close protection anti-aircraft cover. Two more U.S. salvage tugs, Moreno and Narragansett, soon turned up to help and a course was set for the Straits of Messina at 4 knots.

2000 Hrs

HMS Warspite was still dangerously near to the action at Salerno. She was still at tow from the three U.S. tugs slowly making headway. HMS Euryalus and Scylla both Dido class cruisers were assigned with us to protect her. At 2300 Hrs despite the best efforts of the tugs Warspite started drifting sideways. Euryalus was given permission to help the tugs pulling abreast of the battleship's bulky bows to pick up another towing hawser. As soon as this tow was secured Euryalus went to dead slow ahead taking up the slack. Unfortunately due to a communications failure the salvage tugs cast off their own tows. As soon as Warspite's waterlogged dead weight was on Euryalus's single tow. The hawser snapped up taut out of the water momentarily it was held bar taut and quivering, before falling back to the sea. For all the effort it was worth nothing. Warspite might have well been secured to land for all the effect the tow had on her. A second attempt was made and Euryalus's engines were put slow ahead but the same thing happened, not a single budge on the battleship. On the third attempt as the hawser became taut Euryalus notched up her engines. Suddenly the hawser parted with a gunshot of a snap.

130.

The cable whipped viciously back into the Euryalus quarter deck. The cable vanished through the fairlead, mooring pulley blocks and pedestals at a hundred miles an hour. It struck the quarterdecks officer's legs breaking both of them. He was lucky to keep them as it could have sliced them off like a cheese wire. All that had been achieved was an injured man and a two and a half hour delay. Until the three U.S. tugs had picked up tow again and had her underway once more. A speed of 4 knots was maintained all that night. Sometime during the night Valliant and her escorts passed us on route via Augusta, Sicily to Malta then eventually to Gibraltar. They passed a few miles to the westward.

Valliant and her escorts were firing up a blaze of anti-aircraft fire to distract the enemy planes from our group of ships. But the enemy aircraft were searching too far to the south to find our group and Valliant's. By the next morning Warspite's list had increased to 4.5 degrees and we had only covered 45 miles from Salerno very slow progress. At least the damage repair parties aboard her had got diesel dynamos going providing electric power. This enables her pumps to get on top of the flooding and prevent it from spreading.

By mid-morning two more tugs, the British Nimble and Oriana, joined up with us. It took numerous attempts to secure towlines many with parted cables. They had secured their extra towlines by midday and speed was gradually worked up to 6 knots.

In the Straits of Messina the salvage ship Salveda joined our cortège. But the southward current was so strong that all the towing hawsers except one broke and parted. The waterlogged ship went through the Straits broadside on. Warspite drifted on the rapid current through the night between Sylla and Charybdis sometimes stern first but mostly beam on to the current. Eventually she emerged at the southern exit of the Straits. Where the tow was picked up and resumed with three tugs towing ahead. Warspite could only be pointed in the correct direction by the tugs lashed to her sides. For extra steerage the salvage ship pulled to either direction from astern. Our group finally made it to Malta on the 19th, where she was patched up.

We was released and after taking on stores, ammunition and fuel headed back to Salerno. We resumed duty with the northern attack force when we got back in the fray late the next night. We found out on our return that Force Fives role had ceased on the nineteenth. The enemy had withdrawn from the beachhead and it was confirmed by recce troops. The rest of Force Five had been reassigned elsewhere but we were asked to stay with the landings to provide AA defence. As the command group were well impressed with our service.

21st September 1943
In the morning the next large group of merchant ships entered Salerno Bay. There were some 13 United States ships in this convoy. Disaster struck before they had even anchored off the beachheads.

Shortly after 0900 Hrs an explosion took place alongside the Oliver Hazard Perry. This was the commodore's ship in charge of the convoy that had just arrived. A few minutes later a torpedo hit the William W. Gearhard the crew-abandoned ship. William W. Gearhard's Armed Guards officer went back aboard. He had learned that wounded armed guards had been left aboard by mistake. He got them off to safety by himself bravely. 24 hour later when she was being towed clear of the beachhead. The forward part of the ship split off and sank the rest of the ship had to be sunk by gunfire as a preventative. So it would not drift off and be a danger to other shipping.

I saw a particular violent explosion, made by an ammo ship exploding after being hit by a bomb. She also had a quantity of petrol on board. Smoke and flames went up to about five hundred feet in a fireball. Burning debris spit off the explosion like flying Catharine wheals in all directions. That night we had a rather heavy air attack. A couple of large British merchant ships were hit and set on fire. The whole anchorage was lit up by the mass of fire. Apparently one of the merchant ships had petrol on board in tins. All the empty cans and debris were floating around the rest of our ships in the morning.

Every night without fail we could see fires and gun duels in the front lines. They were getting further away from the beachhead every night. Also the air attacks were getting less and longer periods of quite between them.

133.

LCA675 sunk on the 24th,
LCT (5)-196 sunk 27th,
LCP(R) sunk on the 28th,
LCT (5)-342 sunk 29th.
These were the only incidents that happened on the
following days.

I believe all of them hit mines that were floating free
(Floaters). Enemy aircraft were getting sparse on the
beachhead as they could not get to it.
    Our captain asked those that be (The higher
Command element) for the release of our ship from the
attack force at Salerno. Which was given, and we made
way back to Malta for some well-deserved shore leave.
Whilst at Malta we finally got some repairs done to the
ship. This Included repairing the damage of the collision in
the first day at Salerno to a higher degree of excellence.
Repairs were complete and all was rested and recouped by
the Twentieth of October and we were awaiting orders.

Captain Peachy gave an interview to Desmond Tighe from
"Times of Malta" and said.

"I have a grand ships company. The men have done
magnificently. They never complain although for weeks we
have been without home mail and provisions of food and
water ran very low .The time came when there was not
even a cigarette to smoke. The gun crews became so
enthusiastic, blazing a mass of wreckage into the sea.

There was so much individual competition. To which they asked permission to remain at permanent day action stations in case they missed shooting down any German planes.

But as well as the gunners and the men on the bridge, it's the men of Delhi's engine room who deserve very high praise.

When the ship is in action, and there are very few moments when the guns are silent, these men down below have no preoccupation. They stand faithfully doing their jobs as shells roar away into the heavens and bombs hurtle down with fearsome crashes. They don't know what's going on and patiently hope for the best. The ship shudders and lurches with each near miss.

Indeed Delhi has an astounding record of good service in the Mediterranean she's only been damaged once off Algiers although she has had over a hundred near misses at Salerno alone we have fought off fourteen day attacks and eight night attacks with her guns blazing away five confirmed German planes fell and scores of others must have limped home feeling much the worse for wear".

I was really proud to have been one of the crew of the ship after reading this especially as I was a stoker in the engine room.

2nd November 1943
We took passage to Gibraltar to be deployed for convoy defence. In the western Mediterranean and Atlantic or so we thought.

At that stage in the war, there were so many ships anchored in the harbour you literally could not park a rowing boat between them. We had a good idea they were preparing for the upcoming campaigns and operations. But three days later we woke up in the morning and looked out to see we were virtually the only ship left in Gibraltar. We were docked at Gibraltar for a further 12 days. We then were confined to the ship for an upcoming tasking the next day.

We were told Winston Churchill was on route to Gibraltar on HMS Renown he would then fly to Cairo. But the flight had to be cancelled. So it was reorganised to proceed on Renown to Malta for the 17th. With Destroyer's: HMS Inglefield, Ulster, HMCS Athabaskan and fast Cruiser HMS London as escorts. We would join the escort as their AA cover all the way to Alexandria for the 21st.

As we passed Crete two German aircraft buzzed our flotilla but they didn't attack. The senior Flotilla officers thought they were reconnaissance planes. This might represent a worrisome visit from more of the Luftwaffe later on. So we all slipped in to top gear and were making 32 Knots. From Alexandria Winston Churchill would then go on to Cairo for a conference "Codename Sextant". It would be held on November 22nd to the 26th. Between Churchill and Roosevelt who was aboard the USS Iowa and the Generalissimo Chiang Kai-shek of the Republic of China.

The Sextant conference was to make decisions about post-war Asia. Winston Churchill would then fly with Roosevelt to the Tehran Conference "Codenamed Eureka". That one was on November 28th to December 1st. That was with the big three: Churchill, Roosevelt and Joseph Stalin to plan the war against Nazi Germany and Operation Overlord. While there Churchill presented the Sword of Stalingrad to Stalin by command of George VI. As a token of homage from the British people to the Soviet defenders of Stalingrad.

Then it was a return flight to Cairo for the second Sextant conference. Witch was December 4th to the 6th with Roosevelt and this time the President of Turkey Ismet Inonu. This was to address Turkey's possible contribution to the Allies. Then it was a mirror image of the Escort duties and chaperone trip alongside Battleship USS Iowa. We would return through the Mediterranean to Gibraltar then back to England. But that was to change due to circumstances out of anyone's control.

Winston Churchill had been feeling far from well as he left Britain, with the effects of a heavy cold. Luckily he had his doctor travelling with him in his entourage with his bodyguard. The cold had been exasperated by a reaction to the inoculations against cholera and typhoid that he was given. I cannot confirm or verify it but to my recognition some time on this operation. Two Vichy French Destroyers attacked us. We fought them off and chased them away from Renown. Renown fired at them over the top of our ship. With her heavy guns until they were out of range and running.

137.

The out ward trip and half the return journey went well apart from the previous statement I alluded to.

The exhausting programme of conferences and the travelling had taken their toll on the Prime minister health. He was deteriorating rapidly and his doctor and the captain of the Renown were beginning to get worried.

12th December 1943

On the route back off the coast by Carthage, Tunisia it was found out he had contracted pneumonia. Churchill was difficult to persuade by his doctor not to go home to the cold British weather. So our flotilla was ordered to put in to the port of Carthage. There the Prime minister would be flown to the safer location of Morocco. We heard later he had suffered a heart attack two days later. Whilst staying at the Villa Mirador in Casablanca. There the US President Roosevelt visited him after catching up on the USS Iowa. He recovered from that and both Winston and Franklin wanted to visit Marrakesh. So they travelled together and stayed a further ten days convalescing at the Villa Taylor. General Charles de Gaulle visited them both to see how Churchill was recovering and to go over events that had been happening and upcoming operations.

14th January 1944 Churchill flew to Gibraltar to embark on the HMS King George V to return to England.

HMS Delhi was back at Gibraltar by the 15th of December looking forward to celebrating Christmas in a fairly secure port.

CHAPTER TEN

ANZIO

January 1944

HMS Delhi was nominated to provide AA defence at Anzio during the landings. So we set sail and headed for Naples. Where we were given a briefing and all the ships began forming up. Task Force 81 was made up of two parts British and one part American.

Winston Churchill originally conceived operation Shingle in December 1943. A month ago while he was bed ridden in Marakesh when he was recovering from pneumonia. Because the operation came from the heads of state it was rushed through as a matter of importance. The operation was to be commanded by American Major General John P Lucas. The operation was intended to outflank German forces on the winter line across Italy and enable an attack on Rome.

Task force 81 consisted of:

Task Force Peter (British)
1x HQ Ship, 4x Cruisers, 8x Fleet Destroyers and 6 Hunt Destroyers, 2x Anti-aircraft ships, 2x Dutch gunboats, 11 Fleet Mine Sweepers and 6x Small Mine Sweepers, 3x Landing Ship Infantry, 4x Landing Craft, Gun, 4x Landing Craft, Flak, 3x Landing Craft Tank, Rocket, 30x Landing Ship Tank and 30x Landing Craft Tank, 40x Landing Craft Infantry, 200x DUKW.

Task Force X-Ray (American)
1x HQ Ship, 1x Cruiser, 8x Destroyers and 2x Destroyer escorts, 6x Mine Sweepers, 12x Submarine chasers, 20x Submarine chasers, 18x Motor Mine Sweepers, 6x Repair ships, 5x Landing Ship Infantry, 1x Landing Craft rocket, 50x Landing Ship Tank, 56x Landing Craft Tank, 56x Landing Craft Infantry, 250x DUKW

Landing Ship Infantry could carry 2,000 infantry.
Landing Ship Tank could carry 12 tanks or 33 loaded trucks or 200 troops.
Landing Craft Infantry could carry 200 men to the beach.
Landing Craft Tank could land five Tanks or nine trucks.
DUKW could carry 12 troops or 2 tons of equipment and a 50cal machine gun.
Landing Craft Gun had two British 25 Pounder Howitzers and could carry a number of troops.
Landing Craft Flak had eight 20mm Orlikons and four QF 2 Pounder pom-poms.
Landing Craft Rocket had in excess of 700 launch tubes with 5,000 reloads capability.

As well as what the German had in resistance and coastal defences that awaited us. There were two natural obstacles, bad weather and poor beaches. All told this made the landing at Anzio in January extremely hazardous. Winter was the worst time of year to launch an amphibious assault even in the Mediterranean. Rain, low clouds and high seas would complicate the landings. It would make the re-supply over the beaches hazardous and hamper the air support.

21ST January 1944

In a pre-Anzio deception plan: three Motor Gun Boats; MGB-657, 658, 663 and three Motor Torpedo Boats; MTB-640, 655 and 659. They departed Bastia, Corsica on Operation Lurcher at 1700 Hrs. They met up with US Navy PT Boats 203, 209, 211, and 217. Where they formed two columns and headed for the Civitavecchia coast. At 0147 Hrs PT 209 reported radar contacts off her port bow at 2800 yards range. The US PT's continued with the diversion operation. The British MTB's and MGB's investigated the radar contact.

Destroyer leader HMS Inglefield, Destroyer HMS Kempenfelt and Cruiser Dido carried out a bombardment of Civitavecchia over the top of the US PT boats.

At 0207 Hrs the MTB's and MGB's identified the contacts as a Marinefãhrprahm. They were large German landing Craft which we knew as a Flak Lighter. They were being escorted by two E-Boats. There convoy were heading on a south-easterly course at 7-knots. The MTB's and MGB's run past the convoy on a parallel course at their top speed at 0211 Hrs.

The MTB's and MGB's engaged and repeatedly hit them with gunfire from all six boats. The British boats turned in unison on to a reverse opposite return course for a second run at the enemy. The Flak Lighter is hit again and one E-Boat is set on fire. The E-Boat stopped dead in the water with engine failure returning fire with all her guns through the smoke.

The other E-Boat makes off and flees the engagement. The British boats turn again to make a third run. The Flak lighter is set on fire but the defensive fire from both Flak Lighter and the remaining E-Boat damages MTB 655. Who disengages and heads west to safety.

At 0220 Shore batteries open up on the boats but they manage to evade any damage and break off contact. They all retired to assist MTB 655 as they left the area. They witnessed in the distance the Flak Lighter exploding and sinking.

22nd January 1944

We sailed through the evening; it was a restless quite calm evening for most. What might come? What might the next few hours hold in store? Did the Germans Know we were coming?

A beacon submarine, HMS Ultor, had been lying off shore since the day before. Taking compass bearing fixings on the beach and checking for mine fields. They were mapping the beaches to help the minesweepers in their task clearing the approach channels. Part of our naval task force passed Anzio as part of a decoy operation. It was to deliver a bombardment to Civitavecchia, north of Rome at H-Hour and carry out dummy landings. Hopefully to distract the Germans and attract there forces to that area instead of ours with luck. The minesweepers went ahead of the assault ships. To start clearing the approach channels at 2030 Hrs.

The minesweeper sweep was only just a success due to not enough rehearsals or even a proper briefing. There was a lot of fouled gear, near collisions and narrow escapes from floating mines. All this was done in pitch darkness with a strict no lights policy. The Germans must have known or suspected something was going on off shore but they lay low.

At five minutes past midnight Task Force Peter arrived in the murky blackness off Cape Anzio. The assault convoy dropped anchor and rode easily on a calm Mediterranean Sea. It relaxed our duties in the engine room and I was able to go on deck for a bit of fresh air. Unknown to most of us as soon as it was dark enough Royal Navy Commandos had landed. The Commandos went ahead of the convoy to neutralise minefields prior to the arrival of the landing craft. They would approach the beaches in dinghy's and swim the last few tentative 20 mtrs or so ashore under the noses of the Germans. They used metal detectors to find the metal mines switching their use, for their trusted F-S daggers (Fairbairn-Sykes) to find the rest. To probe the sand for wood encased mines, which the detectors could not find. A secondary task was to locate Sand bars that could prove to be a hazard to the landing craft.

Aboard all the assault ships there was a murmur of subdued activity, as officers gave last minute instructions. Men clambered into stubby assault crafts. Then their davits were swung out which lowered them in to the sea.

Patrol boats wove in and out of the milling craft herding them into formations. It looked like an old cowboy film with the cowboys herding up a lot of stray cattle. Then they were off leading the first wave into the moonless night.

To gain surprise the guns of the escorting warships kept silent in the dark of the night. It was only light enough to see the dark silhouettes of all the ships lined up. They were facing broadside on to the smudge of land 3 miles distant. The sea was still all you could hear was the muffled rumble of silenced landing craft manoeuvring about getting ready in the distance. Then just ten minutes to go before H-Hour the silence was suddenly broken.

With a frightening roar as three of the Landing Craft Rocket opened up. With a deafening roar as their deadly flights of rockets tore through the night. They flew in the direction of shore each trailing a line of fire. The rockets were lighting the night sky around the ships with a bright intensity. Within seconds another flight roared away and then another and another and another five devastating volleys. We then could only see the fiery tails from the last set of rockets thundering off into the distance. The darkness closed in and all was silent once more. It was a spectacle beyond my imagination more than anything I witnessed before. After a few seconds the rockets were hitting the beaches with devastation. It must have caused terror in the hearts of the defenders and played havoc with any mine fields and beach defences. There was one thing for sure now and it was certain they must know we were there and where we were!!

144.

Off went the light assault landing craft of the first wave. In the dark like horses out of the bleaches engines galloping away spewing smoke from their exhausts. Reaching out and racing to the beach in double quick time just in case the Germans opened up. Resistance had been expected in hand full's but the first waves got ashore relatively unopposed. In fact, surprise was so total that some of the German troops were captured asleep at their posts. That was a surprise despite all the rocket firing and the whining of the five-inch shells. Thrown in for extra impact after H-Hour by the off shore destroyers. Some reports came in that the beaches were still heavily mined. Including sea mines just offshore some of the beaches reported shallow draft. Others were shelving but the first flights of assault landing craft had disgorged their troops. They were already trying to thread their way back to give room for others.

The work of the engineers in the first wave of the landing troops was to remove land mines. This caused heavy congestion at the water's edge. No amount of persuasion from the officers would induce the troops to advance through a minefield. The mines were eventually cleared at 0400 Hrs and the DUKW's began to roll in. But there were serious delays due to not enough exit lanes planned. The first of the LCT's beached at 0645 Hrs. The first 18 of the LST's and 24 LCI's arrived even later at 1045 Hrs. Due to the serious delay in rigging pontoon causeways to help unload them. The LST's had arrived at 0715 Hrs from Napels and had been impatiently milling about waiting.

145.

CHAPTER ELEVEN

ANZIO AIR RAIDS

We were anticipating the Luftwaffe almost from the start. It wasn't long about noon that they turned up doing strafing runs along the beaches and at the unloading landing craft. Before attacking the shipping there also was some long range shelling of the port area.

The DUKW (colloquially known as Duck) were boats that rode on land or a 4-tonn truck that floated on water. Or better to say a large motorboat with wheels. The name DUKW comes from the model naming terminology used by GMC:

"D", designed in 1942, "U", "utility",
"K", all-wheel drive, "W", Wheels dual rear axles.

They were used to bring troops ashore from assault ships and then to re-supply them. They were on the go 24 Hrs a day. The DUKW's got off pretty easy during the Anzio landings. Two were destroyed by land mines and one was unlucky to be hit by a bomb completely destroying it. A forth one sank under dubious circumstances into the sea never to come up. Probably due to bad handling being swamped by a wave broadside on could sink them. Without the DUKW the beachhead was at risk. They carried the lifeblood of re-supply transporting ammo and rations ashore. Enemy shells and bombs followed them about through the day. They had a casualty list of nine men killed and 30 injured.

146.

One of the LST'S was attacked by a number of Stuka dive-bombers. The ·30" and ·50" calibre guns mounted on her returned fire to deter the enemy. But one Stuka dived down low and dropped its payload of bombs. As we watched they fell towards the deck of the LST we were waiting for the explosion to hit them. But by chance they missed falling very close to the side and hit the water exploding but caused no damage.

USS Portent commenced her minesweeping duties as soon as it was daylight. She could only just navigate between the landing craft waves going ashore. She found out there was much work to be done in the mine-infested waters. She was working in tandem with the other minesweepers. The captain of Portent "CPT Plummer" reported at 0930 Hrs that there were no mines left in the area. He then proceeded to do a second pass along the beachhead to make sure. She had just passed USS Mayo and was in her rolling wake when suddenly a massive underwater explosion rocked her. A mine had detonated near her starboard screw at 1000 Hrs. Sending a 150-foot spout of water in the air. This lifted her fantail clear out of the water by three feet. The Portents keel cracked and the seams in her hull opened up. The cracks and seam splits allowed massive amounts of seawater to enter the ship. The mine explosion had blown the mine gear stowage hatch completely off and it went flying into the sea. Immediately she began to settle by the stern. Her engine room filled with oil and water.

147.

`USS Portent rolled 45˚ to her port side at 1010 Hrs. CPT Plummer realized that the ship was lost and ordered abandon ship. Portents crew aided the injured men from her engine room into life rafts. The crew stepped over the side themselves leaving 18 men dead. Within minutes she had rolled over and sank in shallow water. This left fifteen feet of her bows sticking up visible for months.

Shortly after noon during one of the air attacks. Focke Wulf fighter-bombers swooped down over the beachhead. Dropping bombs among the LST's and LCI's clustered around the two pontoon causeways at beach red. A 500lb bomb smashed through LCI-20 and exploded below her bottom, destroying her. Our ship HMS Delhi was off Peter Beach. Her guns were firing a dense field of ack-ack. Causing hundreds of black puffs of exploding shrapnel in the air. Our gunners aimed at the swarms of enemy's hornet like dive-bombers.

Aided by the calm sea and the virtual absence of opposition our invaders quickly established themselves on shore. It was so uneventful the second in command of the Irish Guards called it "very gentlemanly, calm and dignified". In all January 22nd had been a highly satisfactory day. By midnight some 36,000 men, over 3,000 vehicles were already on shore. Approximately ninety per cent of all the personnel and equipment had been brought onshore from the ships.

Casualties had been amazingly light in VI Corps; 13 killed, 97 wounded and 44 missing with 227 prisoners captured. The Casualties of the Navy, from the sinking of Portent and LCI-20, were somewhat higher.

Peter Beach was not ideal. The beach shelved gently and sand bars had formed preventing a close approach inshore for the ships. To overcome this, the invasion force had formed a number of pontoon floating-roadway's stretching from the shore to deeper water. These were narrow with a minimal distance either side of a vehicles wheels to the edge. The danger was slipping off the side of the pontoons into the water, losing vehicles. That might even damage the pontoons themselves thus holding up the unloading of the ships. This thought filled everyone with alarm. So it was go steady but try and be quick and safe like walking on a tight rope.

A Royal Navy Destroyer was lying broadside on ready to fire in support of those ashore not far from us. A deadly game of cat-and-mouse was being played, between the ship's commander and enemy artillery piece's ashore. A shell exploded to the stern of the ship the next being beyond the bow thus bracketing the target. The next was sure to land between the two and hit the vessel. In the short interval whilst the gun was being reloaded. I observed the ship move forward very slowly. The next shell came and surely enough it landed between the first two. Where seconds before the ship had moved she had been. And so it went on with the ship imperceptibly changing its position.

The artillery shells coming in just missed their intended target. All praise to the RN Commander. The game ceased suddenly and I presume the German gunners saw the wisdom of removing themselves whilst the going was good. Before they were taken out by a retaliatory barrage from the ship hit them.

In support of the landings on day one allied fighter and bomber squadrons flew more than 1,200 sorties. Heavy bombers blasted key bridges and road junctions. This was to attempt to block all the enemy's avenues of approach to the Anzio area. Fighter-bombers and fighters flew along the main highways day and night. Enemy traffic that was surging toward the beachhead was being bombing and strafed. Other fighters gave continuous air cover to the landing force. Together with the anti-aircraft fire from the ships they repelled 140 enemy air attacks on the first day.

When night closed it was with heavy black clouds. You could see flashes of artillery fire reflected in the cloud far inland, and patterns of red tracers in the sky. The Luftwaffe was equipped with very good machines and brave pilots. The nearby airfields around Rome soon woke up to the fact that unwelcome invaders were on their doorstep. The beehive had been thoroughly disturbed by us as we arrived. As we were approaching a new position for the dark hours, over they came. The sky became alive with tracer. The guns of every ship around us let fly. Thousands of rounds of ammunition yet no plane took a plunge into the sea. It is not surprising that it is remarkably difficult to bring down a plane. They are so small and are diving at 350 MPH, dodging our small calibre weapons.

150.

Our attackers were intent on sinking ships by dive-bombing. I was on deck having a break in a good position to view the scene. I could see that one plane had singled out our ship with unfriendly intentions. In it came at a steep dive dropping its deadly cargo. All I can say is that its bomb must have skimmed over the deck to burst alongside us.

Another ship to fall foul of the mine menace on the first night after D-Day was HMS Palomares. She was an auxiliary anti-aircraft ship converted from a "Banana Boat". She was more used to bringing fruit from the Caribbean, than fighting and patrolling. The crew manned quadruple 2lb pom-pom anti-aircraft guns. She was a tripod masted ship fitted with all the latest radio direction finding equipment. Her job was to detect the approach of planes and pass information to the other ships. To do this the closer to shore HMS Palomares could get herself, the better. But the whole of the area she wanted to go into was mined. She carefully got in to the location she needed to be in and was hemmed in on all sides. The crew were exploding mines around her with gunshots from rifles. That night seemed to go on forever. There was hardly a lull in the air attack red; all hands were on deck at action stations. As the night wore on, up and down, up and down, alert after alert. It began to take effect of the crew. With hardly a moment to spare, not even to have a sip of "ki" (coffee with a shot of rum) in between action stations. Some crewmembers began to feel they wanted to ignore the alerts.

Suddenly the most horrific explosion rocked HMS Palomares. Bits and pieces were flying everywhere a mine had hit astern of the ship. The deck rolled up like an opened sardine can. The Palomares survived this incident and she had to be towed to Naples for repairs. In the rest of the war she saw more action than most and served on the ill-fated PQ-17 Russian convoy.

23rd January 1944.
It was the second day of the initial landings; the Germans staged their first all-out attack on the ships. As well as moving every available force that could be mustered to the Anzio area. The Luftwaffe was instructed to make available two groups of Heinkel He111's and all the Junkers Ju88 torpedo bombers in southern France and move them to Italy. The Germans had reacted with characteristic vigour and efficiency. There was a dispute raging with the Allies high command, weather to push forward or not. The unfortunate decision of consolidating its positions at the beachhead and only slightly increasing the size of the beachhead was made. The Germans took advantage of this and rapidly encircled the beachhead.

There was soon to be no safe area at Anzio from attack either on the front line or in the rear with the gear. If you were at Anzio in any area you were in the thick of it. No bunker, no foxhole, no ship was safe it was a vision of hell. The bombers were merciless and the sky was ablaze with shellfire. The big problem of an invasion beachhead is re-supplying the forces landed.

The Captains of the liberty ships were civilian merchant officers, therefore not under direct military control. When cargo arrived at the beachhead they would often refuse to unload it. After their work hours had finished, as they were not paid over time. The Navy would have to sit and wait until they were ready. Also because of the German shelling they refused to go in close enough, to be unloaded by the Army DUKW's as they did not want their ships sunk or damaged. Admiral Lowry finally had enough of their castigation. He was obliged to personally assume liability for any damage to the Liberty ships that might result from enemy attack.

One of the real heroic units at Anzio was unquestionably the African American Army soldiers who manned the DUKW's. They braved attacks from German shore batteries and sporadic strafing by enemy fighter planes. Whilst trying to survive in their un-armoured, ugly platypus, amphibians. They did so with good-natured courage, style and vigour. In spite of submarines, mines, air raids and artillery fire, there was a steady inflow of supplies.

The Germans brought forward their latest weapons, and unveiled them at Salerno. The dreaded feared FX1400 glider bombs and the Fritz X guided missile. This had an armour-piercing warhead with 320 kilograms of amatol. The Allies had prepared for this they had equipped three of the Destroyer escorts. With the latest: jamming devices, radar and early warning systems. They were so efficient that it could detect the German bombers in the air outside Rome.

Then it was a desperate game of cat and mouse, with the bomber pilot and crew trying to keep his glider bomb on target. While the destroyer men fought to stay on the beam of the radio frequency to miss direct the bomb. The destroyers HMS Janus and HMS Jervis had been giving fire support for two days supporting the beachhead. They had both laid down nearly 500 salvos of 4.7-inch shells. HMS Jervis had a reputation as a lucky ship. She had completed a long and active career and 5 ½ years of war and 13 major actions. Not one of her crew was lost to enemy action, a unique record on its own and she was to prove that luck again. There was another air attack with 30 to 40 Luftwaffe aircraft. They came over the area and circled at a very high altitude releasing their bombs. While two American Destroyers; USS Davis and USS Jones tried to jam their controlling frequencies used to guide the bombs. Unfortunately some got through.

HMS Janus was hit on the bridge and forecastle her forward magazine also exploded. She broke in two and capsized with the loss of 100 or more officers and men. It took the Janus a mere 20 minutes to sink. PC-621 rescued seven survivors and recovered one body from HMS Janus.
HMS Jervis had the forward part of her bow demolished. Astonishingly, not one of her crew was hurt. She was taken undertow by HM tug Weasel who rescued survivors of Janus along with HMS Laforey. HMS Jervis was then towed to Naples stern first for repairs. The loss of HMS Janus and the damage to Jervis was a sad blow to us.

"Red Anzio"
Are the words that were shouted and they were stamped on the minds of all the Anzio survivors in nightmares. These are the code words signifying a call for all gunners, fire control men and ammunition handlers to man their battle stations. Load and make ready their guns because here come "the Boche" "the square heads" "the krauts".
"Red Anzio" immediate danger",
"Yellow Anzio" cautionary
"White Anzio" all clear.

They were alternately piped dozens of times each day aboard the scores of ships anchored and patrolling. We were kept busy on the Delhi with bombardments of the coast road at Formia. The most amount of "Red Anzio" was piped was I think five times in a two-hour period. It is difficult these years later to imagine the strain and terror of the call to battle stations. All the alerts could be called in quick succession night and day. This provided little to no time for sleep or even to get some food down our throats. It was shattering the nerves of everyone on board the ship's and demoralising the troops on the beleaguered beachhead.

The high level enemy bombers were like circling vulture's high up around 15,000 feet or more. Circling around lazily safely out of range of our guns, until spotting their targets to strike. Enemy: Fighter's, Stuka's and Torpedo bombers came in low in swarms like hornets or wasps. Deadly swooping throngs of stinging insects. We would try and swat with all our ack-ack and pom-pom fire.

155.

Flares were dropped from the enemy planes at 1756 Hrs and bomb explosions were observed. Anti-aircraft fire opened up from the ships in the vicinity. But none of the aircraft came close enough, within the range for our ship's guns. USS Plunket was reported bombed and on fire at 1800 Hrs, but even though it looked serious she reported the fire was under control. USS Mayo was sending a continuous barrage of gunfire wherever it was needed. By this time the Germans had moved up some troops and artillery pieces to threaten the American sector. The enemy were fighting their way across the bridge at the Mussolini Canal. The American landings were being slowly pushed in to the sea by this new counter attack. Mayo seeing the imminent danger shifted position. To get her 5inch guns in to action towards the bridge and halted the German advancing troop movements across the canal.

24th January 1944

As the Allies strengthened the landings, the Luftwaffe increasingly launched attacks, with intensity and ferocity against the beachheads and anchorages. Small flights of fighter-bombers strafed and bombed the beach and port areas every few hours. The most serious threat however. Were the raids of medium bomber squadrons that were brought from Greece and the torpedo and glider bombers brought down from France by the enemy. They skimmed in low at dusk and throughout the night. They weaved through all the smoke and blizzard of ack-ack fire toward the crowded anchorage.

There were numerous "red Anzio's" called at 1735Hrs by numerous ships. There was a concentrated torpedo and glide-bomb attack by fourteen aircraft that lasted 17minutes. USS Plunket was the next victim the JU-88's picked her out of the ships assembled at 1738 Hrs. Two JU-88's attacked on her port beam and two approached from in front of her bow. They did it to give them more of a chance of hitting her and split her anti-aircraft fire up. The Plunket's speed was increased and she manoeuvred radically to try and avoid the attack. She sent up a hail of fire sending two of the hostile aircraft crashing into the sea. The glide-bombs were finally dropped at 200 yards distance. Plunket had little hope of avoiding both glide bombs that was sent towards her.

At 1757 Hrs USS Plunket took the hit. A 550lb glide bomb exploded into the side of a 1.1inch gun platform. Killing 51 officers and men wounding many others it started a raging fire. Exploding ammunition and depth charges fuelled the fire. This caused extensive damage rupturing the main fire fighting water pipes to the aft magazine. Her heroic crew that were left alive fought the fire and jettisoned the burning depth charges and ammunition. They secured the steam-filled fire room and extinguished the flames by 1821 Hrs. This was done without stopping her remaining other guns defending her. Although under manned and damaged with all fires out she successfully cleared the hazardous area. Got up steam and proceeded to Palermo on one engine for temporary repairs.

The next casualty for this day of never ending air attacks of deadly buzz flies. Was the USS Prevail she was mine sweeping new corridors and extending the old ones. She was subjected to an intensive air attack. It was like a pack of wolves singling out the lone weak dear from a herd. Prevail was attacked by horizontal approaching bombers. Armed with glide bombs luckily the bombs missed but one exploded close by her hull damaging her. Her crew worked hard to stop her from taking on too much water. Plugging the damage with blocks of wood and hammering patching in the cracks. This forced her to retire from Anzio she preceded to Palermo for emergency repairs.

During the same air raid US Freighter SS F.A.C Muhlenberg was hit amidships and set on fire. It could have been disastrous if it had reached the cargo of ammunition and gasoline. But fortunately the ship's crew and the crew of the rescue ship extinguished the fires just in time. There was much damage done, but her cargo was unloaded safely. Tragically six of her crew and one of the armed guards had been killed. The ship was finally repaired in New York.

One of the most shocking events of Anzio was to happen to HMHS St David. As always anything to do with hospitals or medical treatment i.e. all First aid points, vehicles and personnel are protected under the Geneva Convention. Having their hulls and superstructure painted white easily identified the hospital ships at Anzio. Large red crosses painted on all sides and on top of the roofs with Red Cross flags flying. They were highly lighted of a night looking like Blackpool illuminations.

This however did not stop the ships being attacked by the enemy. Firing on a hospital ship was considered a serious war crime. All day HMHS St David, HMHS St Andrew and HMHS Leinster were anchored five miles off the beachhead-receiving casualties. At 1715 Hrs, the three hospital ships were ordered back to sea for the night.

They had an outer screen of destroyers with them in close proximity for protection. At 1810 Hrs they were subject to a heavy aerial attack by enemy bombers and torpedo-carrying aircraft. At 1825 Hrs a distress signal from Leinster stated that she had been hit by a bomb and was on fire. ST David turned towards the stricken ship, offering assistance. Seven minutes later St David received another signal from Leinster "no assistance required, fire extinguished, am proceeding". The group of ships resumed their former course and headed toward the open sea.

St Andrew reported being bombed at 1840 Hrs but the fire was under control and she didn't require assistance. The three hospital ships were well clear of all merchant shipping and the outer Destroyer screen by 1900 Hrs. Twenty five miles south-west of the beachhead. They were steaming at 14 knots in a south-westerly force 3 wind. There was a heavy south-westerly swell on the sea. Shortly after 1930 Hrs, an enemy aircraft flew over the ships from starboard to port, releasing four flares. The flares illuminated the whole area like daylight so there was no mistaking they were hospital ships. The aircraft were about 5,000 feet above sea level with plenty of visibility.

The enemy aircraft suddenly dived like swallows on an ant's nest. Their dive brought them to mast high before releasing two bombs on unlucky St David. She was struck in No.3 hold, near the aft end of the promenade deck by one of the bombs. The other exploded hitting the water next to her hull, the ship shuddered violently. The aircraft turned and began another run towards the St David. Two more bombs exploded alongside No.2 hold ripping open her hull water poured in her hull fast. Another bomb explosion had blown away the radio aerials thwarting any attempt to send distress signals. All the lights went out and the engines stopped the water had got to her generators and engines. St David settled rapidly by the stern, listing 20 degrees to port. Without hesitation Captain Owens gave the order to abandon ship and the crew attempted to evacuate all the patients.

However, the water ambulances situated along the starboard side were fouled in wreckage. This made them impossible to lower, despite the second officers repeated efforts. The port side presented a very different picture. No 2-water ambulance, weighing nearly two tons. Was lowered into the sea she had a large number of patients aboard her. This Included six stretcher cases and some of the ship's crew to help handle the craft. Unfortunately, loose ropes fouled the ambulance's rudder and propeller. Because of the heavy swells, it proved very difficult to release the water ambulance from the davit falls.

Owing to the weight on the hooks and spring clips they would not undo and retained the water ambulance hanging. Time was not on their side, and they only just managed to free the ambulance. It hit the water just before the St David sank, stern first, all this happened in just ten minutes after the initial hit.

No's 4 and 6 water ambulances, also situated on the port side, were not so lucky. The heavy hooks could not be released in time and both were dragged down with the sinking ship to their doom. They went down taking an unknown number of unfortunate people kicking and screaming with them. No 8-lifeboat, stowed on the third class deck, was successfully launched sinking almost instantly. Four Carley rafts also floated clear of the condemned ship before anyone could get on to them. Officer B. Howell-Mendus and 19 others were in No. 2 water ambulance. Taking command, he circled the area dragging aboard another 19 other survivors seriously overloading it. While lifeboat No. 8 had 10 people on board at first then picked up a further ten other survivors.

At first the captains of the St Andrew and Leinster thought that the captain of St David had extinguished his Geneva lights to avoid being attacked. It was not until the chief officer signalled, "St David sunk, SOS", by torch. They suddenly realised their misunderstanding. Thirty minutes later after they got close enough, they lowered lifeboats and began the rescue.

By 2115 Hrs all the survivors were on board the other two ships about 100 in the Leinster and over fifty in the St Andrew. Captain Owens had been last seen swimming in the water. He was not seen again losing his life with 12 of his crew, 22 patients and 22 Royal Army Medical Corps. St Andrew and Leinster saved 165 injured people form the water and the water ambulances in total.

This was an atrocious blow to the moral of all the troops on the beachhead, knowing that they were not safe anywhere. Even when they had been evacuated to a so called safe zone or ship! Patrol boat PC-621 was credited with downing one of the attacking Heinkel-111's.

USS Mayo had now virtually been continuously shelling Nazi targets for nearly 48Hrs. Then a sudden explosion at 20.01 Hrs believed to be a mine exploded on her starboard amidships. The explosion created a huge gaping hole in her side measuring 12 by 20 feet. Wrecking and flooding the: aft engine room, fire control room and rupturing the bulkheads between the two compartments. The concussive blast caused the main deck to bulge and knocked out both propeller shafts from their bearings. This was unfortunate as she was drifting out of the swept area into mined waters. The night sky was still full of flares so that no lights could be used aboard ship to spot the mines. The ships main deck aft had sunk to the water's edge as a result of the flooding. The crew was wading around in a foot and a half of fuel oil and saltwater below decks.

The flood water was flooding the first living compartment aft. The crew worked like banshees and succeeded in plugging the leaky seems thus preventing further flooding. So the pumps could get ahead of the deluge. With the loss of 6 men killed, one missing presumed dead and 25 wounded the crew desperately battled to save the ship. The explosion broke her keel almost breaking her in two.

The Mayo was kept above the water and under orders from the skipper the Chief Bosons Mate had to let go the anchor. He fully expected it to be blown right back up in his face as it hit a mine as he dropped it. But it didn't and the anchor held the ship for the time being. They were safe from mines they just had to hope they escaped detection by enemy planes. At 2300Hrs they was taken undertow by the British tug Prosperous and slowly crept out of the area. At dawn they were a good twenty miles away from the action and were not molested by the enemy in any manner. The stricken ship survived the tow to Naples for emergency repairs, where a temporary patch was placed over the hole in her side. Due to the outstanding damage control efforts and the courage of her crew it saved the Merry Mayo to fight another day. A lesser destroyer would have sank the USS Mayo went stateside for permanent repairs.

In total on the raids since dusk the Germans sent in ninety-five aircraft. In total eleven of the raiders were shot down by the anti-aircraft fire.

The next setback that night was the weather. As a storm blew in the wind picked up and the waves pounded the beaches destroying the pontoon roadway. So no further shipping could be received for the British sector except through the small port of Anzio itself. This further increased congestion of the ships and made them easy pickings for the attacking planes. The attacking aircraft had to avoid the many barrage balloons that had been put up for air defence and the anti-aircraft fire.

25th January 1944

Air raids were relatively light due to the bad weather. After two full days of harrowing mine clearing, the motor minesweeper YMS-30 was on over watch providing close air cover for fellow minesweepers. She was operating in a previously swept and cleared area close to shore while trying to maintain her station in the foul weather. The YMS-30 was suddenly lifted up and rocked in her forward bow by a tremendous explosion. Caused by a drifting mine that had cut loose from its anchor by the large swells of the sea. The force of the explosion blasted a massive hole in the wooden hull of the ship, and within seconds the ship was going down by the bow. The crewmembers that had survived the holocaust of the initial blast were all a bit shell shocked and dazed. They abandoned the ship before she sank bow first bellow the waves. Fourteen crewmembers survived, although some of them were badly wounded. The other half of the crew fourteen in total was either killed in the blast or missing in action later it was decided to declare them dead. Some of the sailor's remains were never to be found.

164.

During the same raid submarine chaser USS SC-676 was damaged by a near miss.

The final units were landed on Peter beach and it was decided to close the beach for any further landings. All other landings would have to use Anzio port and Yellow beach. This was to compound the ships at anchorage into a tighter space. This Provided the Germans with a more concentrated target area to hit with anything they could throw together. The weather had its downfalls as well. Rough seas off the coast tossed the landing crafts like discarded matchsticks. It had its good points too putting off any German air attack.

26th January

LST 422 had arrived off the coast about 1am and set anchor. To delays caused by the backlog of ships unloading at the Anzio docks she had to wait. In the next couple of hours an intense storm whipped up with gale force winds and waves 20 to 30 feet high. The wind blew LST 422 into a known mine field, about 12 miles off shore. At 0520 Hrs there was a blinding flash followed by a terrific explosion they had hit a mine. It had blown a huge hole in the bottom and starboard side and the ships fuel oil supply had immediately ignited. From afar you could see twenty-foot flames coming from all the ventilators on the tank deck. The flames illuminated the deck like daylight in the pitch black night. The vehicles on the tank deck started to cook and had begun to explode.

This in turn had set fire to the ship's diesel fuel oil that had sprayed out of its tanks the moment it hit the mine. The explosion had ripped a massive fifty-foot hole on the starboard side in the area between the main and auxiliary engine rooms.

Most of the men of the 83rd Chemical Mortar Battalion aboard LST 422 were asleep on the tank deck. Which was first to flood it sealed the fate of over four hundred men. They had no chance of escape, so they either drowned or burned up in the fiery inferno. You only hoped that they never woke up to feel it. The men on the main deck had a grim ultimatum. Either abandon ship or be consumed by the raging firestorm approaching them. The aft hatch collapsed open like the doors of a car ferry opening. Allowing ammunition and rockets to escape like meteors trailing smoke tails. Then some of them in flight fell onto the vehicles on the upper deck causing havoc. Shrapnel had fractured tanks of gasoline on the upper deck. Within two minutes the entire upper deck was a sheet of flame. Soon the bridge was on fire and all the landing craft was ablaze and fell into the sea from their davits. The crew made an attempt to start the auxiliary fire foam motor. But shrapnel and flying metal from the exploding ordinance had damaged this. All the Army personnel were ordered to abandon ship but only four Carly floats (life rafts) were left undamaged. All the floatable materials that could be found were thrown overboard to assist the men in the water. Many of those who took to the water perished in the frigid sea before anyone could come to their rescue.

166.

Luckily LST 301 who stood nearby came to assist the trapped men they pulled up alongside 422. Sadly one of the men escaping the fire fell to his death between 301 and 422. The disaster this night was not to end soon enough. As LCI-32 came to assist in the rescue she hit a mine and sunk herself killing 30 of her crew and wounding 11. Two minesweepers USS Pilot and Strive came to the aid of 422 along with vessels LST-16, YMS-34 and 43. Heavy seas and high winds made it very difficult to find the unfortunate men in the sea. Most of them were either too cold or too nearly drowned to help themselves. It was only a matter of time until they were overcome and gave themselves up to the sea. At 0845Hrs no more floating bodies were visible in the water due to an extremely heavy hail storm, 150 survivors of LST-422 and LCI-32 were rescued from the stormy water conditions.

The gale during the night blew ashore all the pontoon causeways and beached twelve LCT's, one LST and one LCI. The weather eventually calmed down at daybreak, it was a tremendous break for the recovery crews and rescue ships. But it had its downfalls as it gave the green light to the Germans to begin their air attacks again.

The liberty ship SS Hilary A. Herbert (7,176 tons) took more punishment, than most ships are made to take and yet survived to sail another day. She reported seventy-five air raids and twenty-seven actual bombing attacks since the first day. On the first day 22 shells landed as close as fifty to a hundred feet away, the second day eight shells landed about fifty feet from her stern. She got her first plane on January 24th and counted a probable the next day.

On the 25th three bombs landed about fifty feet from our ship. Again the big question on everyone's minds was when it was going to be your time to catch one? Odds on nearly every ship in the anchorage had been hit either partially or fatally. Again this day we were in the fray and the Germans let slip the dogs of war. The Luftwaffe again struck again at our ship with bombs and strafing runs. The bombs were landing close and the bullets even closer but no cigar for them they missed and we got another enemy plane to our scorecard.

In the early evening two bombs landed within five yards of SS Hilary A. Herbert and did considerable damage. A few minutes later her armed guards shot down another plane but unluckily the plane exploded. Scattering itself all over the deck of the ship with a vicious fireball. Causing severe damage its two bombs slipped off the deck exploding in near misses causing no damage. The ship was beached away from the beachhead to save her from blocking routes in and out. SS Hilary A. Herbert discharged her cargo of ammunition, gasoline and other vital supplies during a terrific aerial and shore bombardment. The crew and armed guards never left their posts. Whilst the armed guards protected the ship the crew put out all the fires. The armed guard got another enemy plane the next day during an air raid on the 28th. With bombs coming close to hitting her again and she was strafed over and over again. German artillery finally got the range and a shell hit the stern of the ship. Next on the 29th a glider bomb missed by only fifty feet and on January the thirtieth shells fell around her.

Still the crew and guards stayed at their posts, finally on the 1st Feb she left under tow for Naples. Admiral H.K. Hewitt said "The captain and crew showed extraordinary ability and courageous action under fire and outstanding devotion to duty."

The liberty ship SS John Banvard 7,191 tons was unloading her cargo, when she was bombed during the concentrated air attack this day 26th Jan. Two glider bombs that ignited fires within her cargo struck her. The explosions split and prised apart her hull plates. She was so extensively damaged that her captain gave the order "abandon ship". Notwithstanding the danger of spreading fires and further explosions the chief engineer remained on board the stricken ship. He promptly and fearlessly entered the engine room and amidst bursting steam and water lines. The chief engineer regulated valves and repaired leaking pipes in the darkness. This enabled him to quickly restore auxiliary power his skilful untiring efforts in effecting emergency repairs was a godsend. With the crew and armed guards returning the ship was able to get underway. SS John Banvard under her own power proceeded to the port of Naples. The John Banvard reported 72 alerts and lots of bombs were dropped 25 times near to them, whilst they were at Anzio. With numerous close calls with bombs falling fifty to three hundred yards away from her.

Bad weather intervened again and the German Luftwaffe had a fruitless raid for once they couldn't hit a thing in the foul weather.

The night passed mostly quite apart from the storm, which blew ashore all the pontoon causeways and beached twelve LCT's one LST and one LCI.

27th January 1944

As the weather cleared in daylight the sounds of high-pitched German airplane engines approaching started the nerves going in everyone. The sound of bombs exploding and anti-aircraft fire drowned out all human sounds except from your own hearts as the sound beat again and again in your ears as the anticipation grew. Air activity was on the increase and growing more intense each day, and continued at night with high level bombing.

The enemy airfields being only a few minutes flying time away made it easier for them to attack the beachhead. Compared to our own airfields that were way back somewhere behind Cassino. This caused fuel consumption problems and limiting time above the battlefield at Anzio for our planes. Low-level air attacks during the day happened so quickly and without warning. There always seemed to be aircraft somewhere in the sky but not that many of ours. Although I did see 2 X US P38 Lightning's doing their best for us, but they got shot down into the sea. The Luftwaffe's main action appeared to be directed against our ships crowded into the small bay at Anzio. But on this day they didn't manage to sink a single ship. They were not averse to amusing themselves with any target on the ground when they could get close enough.

170.

US liberty ship's SS Lawton .B. Evans had arrived on D-day she had an untrained gun crew. Sixteen of the twenty-eight members of her armed guard had never been to sea before with only one of which that had seen battle before and been under attack.

Before she left her guard would be veterans with five enemy planes to her credit. She had been shelled a number of times before today and a bomb had hit her port wing on the bridge damaging the life boats and No.2 hold with jagged pieces of hot shrapnel she got one of the planes as they retreated. On this day 27th she was shaken as bombs landed within fifty feet of her and her gunners blasted two of the planes out of the air.

This day turned out to be a day of near misses as a US submarine chaser SC-534 received damage by a near miss. But the score of the Allies anti-aircraft fire had considerably increased, with a confirmed nine Luftwaffe planes shot down in 24 hrs. SS Bret Harte reported once again close near misses with one of the bombs exploding within forty yards of her littering the ship with fragments.

28th January 1944

Everybody and every ship were at danger at Anzio from all kinds of hostility. From sea mines, aerial attack, the coastal defence guns, artillery fire and even U-boats. Losses were considerable with ships sunk, damaged and disabled. At the anchorage the ships suffered even though we were fighting of attack after attack.

171.

With a shield of anti-aircraft fire so intensive a fly would find trouble getting through. One of the minor casualties was submarine chaser SC-534 again for the second day running. She suffered damage by a near miss bomb. Sometimes the trip from Naples to Anzio was even more dangerous. Nobody was exempt from the danger, not even the commanding general himself. He was dissatisfied with the progress of the beachhead and the limited attacks from ground forces. So Lieutenant General Mark Clark Commander of the US Fifth Army was determined to go to Anzio. He wanted to confer with General John P. Lucas about tactics. He took his operations officer; his intelligence officer and his army engineer with him. They went down to the mouth of the Vloturno River to board PT boat 201.

Clarks trip to Anzio could well have resulted in being his last trip ever. The seas were rough and they found it difficult manoeuvring the small boat in the swells of the sea. The prospects of the trip became more uncomfortable as word reached them, that enemy air raids and shelling were causing considerable damage at Anzio. The German E-boats on the prowl along the coast added to the dangers of the trip even more. Nevertheless he was determined to get through. PT-201 made it almost to Anzio without major difficulty. When Clarks party aboard PT-201 reached a point seven miles south of the beachhead it was still dark. They encountered an American minesweeper AM120 USS Sway. They felt no cause for concern when they were immediately challenged by them. The commander of the PT boat sent up the routine signal in answer.

He fired green and yellow recognition flares and backed it up with flashing the designated Morse code signal on the boats signal light to identify himself. The minesweeper, however, misread the signals from the PT boat and let loose with 40mm and 5-inch shells. The captain of the PT boat was wounded in both legs and fell to the deck. With chaos and confusion aboard General Clark picked the Very pistol up and fired the signal again, with still no results. With five officers and men wounded Clark took command and shouted "Let's run for it". The PT boat mustered all the speed she had and retreated to a safe distance.

Eventually reaching a British minesweeper HMS Acute the PT boat fired the same signal again and Acute fired the correct recognition signal answers. They unloaded the wounded and organised a rendezvous with a replacement PT boat. By a twisted turn of fate the new PT boat encountered the same American minesweeper once again. The skipper of the new PT boat fired the same signal again and it was answered so they pulled up alongside minesweeper AM120. Through a megaphone he delivered a corrective and profane telling off to the captain of the minesweeper for firing on the General. The captain of the minesweeper could not present an adequate excuse of course as much as he tried. He lost much faith within his crew and the navy. It was not the only delay for General Clark as when he eventually arrived at Anzio. The third air raid of the day was in progress and he had to wait until it was over and the all clear was given before they could land.

173.

29th January
By now at or near the beachhead, the Germans had
formations and units of six Divisions. They had another
two divisions assembling not too far distant in reserve.

How can I describe Anzio? How can a man describe
hell? Anzio was a terrible error in tactics. Thousands of
men and boys died on the beachhead and on the ships. The
beachhead and anchorage was many times in flames and
the sky was alight with fire and smoke. The Luftwaffe
during this period controlled the airspace. As their
formations of planes came in the sight would numb us.
With lads saying "god save us" and "for what we are about
to receive God please get us through this". I could still see
the goose bumps standing up, each with a hair at its centre
it will chill my dreams until the day I die.

The USS Edison fired 101 rounds to support the
troops on the beachhead. One of her targets she hit was a
parade of Nazi trucks and armoured vehicles. She turned
them into a roadside junk pile. A mass of signals came
from exuberant shore fire control parties to her radio
operator. She received one congratulatory message after
another.
"Fire effective, very good, it brassed off a bunch of
Krauts." "Many enemy troops killed by your fire good
work." "Your fire was very effective you were hitting right
on the artillery pieces you were firing at." "Effect of fire,
machine-gun emplacement in building totally destroyed."
"Your last target was a tower being used as an observation
post you demolished it completely."

The USS Edison returned home the start of February after firing: 1854 rounds of 5-inch ammunition at 21 separate targets.

The iron determination of the Germans was demonstrated once again, when sixty aircraft in all varying types appeared at once. Junkers 88's, Dornier 217's and Heinkel 177's came down to smash the shipping in Anzio harbour. The fire of our guns and our sister ships caught the formation far out to sea. This forced the aircraft to strike in one single harassing attack to put them at an advantage. The Allies ship borne anti-aircraft guns succeeded in destroying 5 planes. By disrupting the mass plan of coordinated attacks, vital ships were saved but of course there were casualties.

The anchorage and beachhead were constantly in danger during the day from the hazard of the German 88's in the nearby hills. The ships were constantly on the move to put off the shelling from the feared 88's. Time after time the ship would move to gain a few hours respite. Before the German gunners got the range again and fired. Many a time we would move just in time to see shells hit the precise spot we were just in. But the German shells would eventually follow us like a game of tag.

The SS Lawton B had a successful day making lucky hits with her pom-poms on the enemy aircraft. She knocked down a couple of fighter planes in to the sea. Also by chance her guns knocked a glide bomb out of the air and also got the bomber that dropped it.

The bomber blew up and left nothing but a carburettor which landed on the deck of the Lawton. The armed guards made it a prize souvenir in their mess for their marksmanship. As dusk fell we all expected the increase of the air raids, and we was not wrong. The Liberty ship SS Alexander Martin serving as a troopship was heavily damaged by strafing. But there were no fatalities among the ships compliment.

HMS Spartan a brand new Dido Class Light Cruiser with all up to date equipment was being used for anti-aircraft protection duties off Anzio. Like the duties our ship Delhi was doing and she was positioned not far from us. For some reason or other not known to us she was anchored. The rest of our ships were under way making it harder for the Germans to hit any of us. I can understand a cargo or troopship being dead in the water for unloading. But this was just making her a sitting duck, giving her no chance to avoid the threat.

At sunset the enemy began to attack smoke had been ordered in the anchorage. But was not fully effective owing to the short time it was in operation and the strong breeze off shore. The Spartan was making smoke from funnel to stern and behind. But she was not covered as the wind was in the wrong direction blowing it away from the ship. Eighteen enemy aircraft approached from the north. They circled over the land ready to deliver a beam attack against the ships. The ships were silhouetted against the afterglow of a brilliant sunset.

176.

The timing of the attack 1800 Hrs prohibited the aircraft from being sighted and radar was ineffective owing to land echoes. By the time all the ships received warnings and had opened fire it was too late. The bombers had already released their deadly cargo. Six-glider/rocket bombs were already approaching the anchorage. Most of the bombs fell into the water harmlessly. But one of the radio-controlled bombs hit the Spartan amidships just astern of the aft funnel. It detonated high up in the compartments abreast of the port side above one of the aft boiler rooms. It blew a large hole in the upper deck. The main mast collapsed and the boiler rooms were flooded. Due to the hull plates being separated and prised apart by the explosion. Steam and electrical power failed due to flooding and a serious fire developed. Within a few minutes the ship was ablaze from stem to stern. She started to heel over to port taking on a list.

We were one of the first ships on the scene taking on survivors. We aided them fighting the fire with attaching our hoses so they could get some water. But we were a fighting ship and not a rescue tug or ship. We never had enough water pressure in our hoses to fight a fire aboard another ship sufficient enough. About an hour after being hit she had to be abandoned it was getting too dangerous. Ten minutes later, she settled on her beam end in five or six fathoms of water. The sea was too rough to be able to tie up alongside but we were of some assistance. Until a couple of fire fighting tugs came along to take our place.

177.

We then circled around the seaward side picking survivors up out of the sea. I think Delhi rescued about a hundred of her 530 ships company of men. In all five officers, 41 ratings lost their lives and 42 ratings were wounded. At that time we didn't know whether we were going to get hit next or not. Ammunition was cooking off flying in different directions aboard her. Some of it dangerously toward us, and enemy planes were still overhead like vultures. She burned for two days, and then turned over she was a red glow all over until she sank I will never forget those scenes.

Another of the anti-shipping guided missiles (rocket glider bombs) slammed into the US Liberty ship SS Samuel Huntington 7,181 tons. At the same time as Spartan. The bomb penetrated the hull and went through most of her decks. The bomb exploded in her boiler room killing four men. The force of the explosion blew out two of her cargo hatches and launched a jeep off her deck into the bridge. With no power hence no way of fighting the fire. Samuel Huntington's master ordered the ship abandoned. A number of the crewmembers escaped aboard LCT-217 and 277. The rest of the crew lowered her lifeboats and headed away from the ship. But some of the armed guard gunners remained on board to man her guns. During their brave protection duties they claimed to have shot down five planes. Fifteen minutes after the bomb's blast, part of her cargo of fuel and ammunition exploded rocking the ship.

178.

The explosion aboard Samuel Huntington threw a cloud of debris over 300 meters in the air. Raining shrapnel landed on the ships as far as 1.5 miles away. The explosion lit up the night sky. After the second explosion, Samuel Huntington settled to the bottom. Because the seabed had only been 3 feet below her keel, most of the ship remained above the water. There was not enough water flooding her to stop the fires. The rest of the armed guard was taken off by ATR-1 rescue tug that was fighting the fire. They stayed alongside her until the tug suffered minor damage from near miss bombs.

USS Weight a rescue and salvage ship was commencing a rescue operation to pull LCT-223 who had stranded herself on the beach. When she was shook from the explosion of Samuel Huntington. After dragging the LCT off the beach she got underway to fight the blaze on the wrecked Liberty ship. The salvage vessel trained both its monitors (large deck mounted water cannons) and a 2-inch fire hose on the wreck. They began fighting the inferno of a fire that ravaged the freighter. When the task seemed accomplished at 18.35Hrs, Weight pulled away with the wreck still smocking. The fires flared up again four hours later at 22.07Hrs. Weight returned to fight the conflagration and renew her efforts to contain the flames. However USS Weights work on the Huntington was not yet done she was needed elsewhere. In the company with British salvage vessel HMS Weazel and aided by bulldozers ashore. She attempted to salvage the grounded British landing craft tank, LCT-542.

179.

After re floating 542 Weights divers cleared the fouled screws of submarine chaser SC-497 close by and the ship's crew repaired LCT-288. It was a busy night for the Weight tending to other ships damaged during the raid. Weight returned a third time to the Huntington but by the early morning of the 30th January. Any hope of salvaging Huntington or her cargo ended. The fires reached her load of canned gasoline heating it up rapidly. Weight was lucky to have pulled away from her when the resulting ferocious explosion completely destroyed the ship. Again there was another pyrotechnic display, which rained shrapnel on nearby ships. When the smoke cleared only a burning hulk remained.

30th January
HMS Delhi was kept busy with her sister ships. We carried out further bombardments of the Formia areas on enemy positions and build-ups.

February 1944
German forces numbered some 100,000 troops around Anzio's beleaguered beachhead. The Allied forces by this time totalled 76,400. The Luftwaffe showed no signs of stopping their attacks. But off the coast at the anchorage it seemed they had eased off on us. They were concentrating on the harbour and beachhead. The planes made run after run over the harbour, staging areas and hospital tents. Dropping their bombs turning to repeat their attacks until their bombs and ammunition had been spent.

Their main targets seemed to be the airstrip, the anti-aircraft batteries, the ammunition dumps, the fuel dumps and the motor pool. All of them were located on the edges of some part of the tented hospital area. But that didn't stop the Luftwaffe from dropping bombs on the hospital tents or in the hospital area. Incoming artillery shells also fell often among the hospital tents. The hospital tents were hit so frequently that the American troops (GI's) nicknamed it "Hells Half Acre". The wounded regularly proclaimed their reluctance to be sent there for medical care.

February 3rd
The Germans forces launched a full counter attack at 23.00Hrs. They targeted all the ground forces at Anzio in order to "iron out the front line". After the attack the Allies coherence of the frontline had been shattered. With the evening and gradual darkness, German planes began unrelenting attacks. The night was filled with sounds of exploding bombs and anti-aircraft guns. Tracers threaded the night skies with snakes of fire. Flares from German planes lit up the beachhead with an eerie green glow. That lit up our faces like an apparition of ones nightmares. The night was a cacophony of noise of exploding bombs, flying shrapnel and projectiles.

4th of February
In the early hours several regiments had been cut off and were surrounded in a pocket. They held their line all day taking heavy casualties.

Our cut off regiments were eventually ordered to pull back, making a fighting retreat to the main force at the beachhead. That night again there was no rest for the wicked exploding ammunition dumps sent long fingers of flames upward into the night sky. As if a giant was trying to capture the enemy aircraft and fling them back to earth.

HMS Delhi was rocked this day by the only near miss that came close to us. I was in the engine room on duty and didn't know what was happening above. It was a little scary because when the bomb went off right by the ship. It lifted our ship right out of the water and I was thrown to the deck. So of course it kind of shakes you up a bit. You get up and think, now what happened? Did they get us? I was told later that the plane was so close you could see the outline of the pilot. Now that's a little too close for comfort.

CHAPTER TWELVE

THE ANZIO EXPRESS

February 5th 1944

It was a clear day nothing in the sky not even flying Krauts. Suddenly out of nowhere the first few gargantuan rounds started hitting the beach. The American and British commanders soon realized that a new threat to the beachhead and anchorage had arrived. Railway guns were not obsolete, as they had thought. The huge shells passing overhead sounded like an express train. The rounds quickly got the nickname "the Anzio Express" coming from the gun "Anzio Annie". The Allies did not realize that there were actually two guns involved.

The Germans had always loved big guns and had moved two of them in to the area. They were "Leopold" and "Robert" they both had 280mm (11 inch) gun barrels with a length of 70 feet and could fire 20 miles. Mounted on a railcar and designated K5-E's. They were sent by rail to a town named Ciampino in the Albano hills about 19 miles from the beachhead.

With the troops and supplies penned into a relatively small area, targets were plentiful for the big guns. They took out ammunition dumps, gasoline dumps and various harbour installations. Also under threat were the ships that had to come close to shore to unload.

Because of the threat by these big guns all ships had to be anchored at least three miles out to sea. This greatly slowed down re-supply efforts and evacuation of casualties. Commanders at the beach demanded that Annie was to be found and destroyed. The American's came up with a planned reply and it was twofold. The first part of it was to use their artillery in counter battery fire. The second was to use air power to hunt down any guns firing at the beachhead and bomb them into oblivion. Search planes were scheduled to over fly the area every hour if weather permitted.

This wasn't going to be effective the range of the enemy's guns was too far, beyond anything the Allies had. Hunting them down and bombing them from the air wasn't going to be easy. The Germans had cleverly located their firing position just outside of a railway tunnel. Any time they were not actually firing they would roll them back into the tunnel. Well out of sight of any allied aircraft patrolling. To further confuse things, the Germans also built several dummy railway guns. Out of wood using telephone poles mounted on flatbed railcars, painted and covered with camouflage netting. These were positioned to distract Allied bombers from the true targets. The Germans also set up flash simulator pyrotechnics across the countryside. At night it would look like muzzle flashes of big guns to confuse the Allied spotters.

The Germans had an array of artillery guns moved into the area already like the German 88's. But they also had captured Czechoslovakian 210mm gun battery and a captured French 240mm gun battery. This would make things more difficult for the Allies to be positive they got the right guns. They could easily be mistaken for the big ones though they neither had the range or the payload of the K5-E's. The Germans firing the K5-E's would use Deuneberger salts to reduce the muzzle flash and make it less visible of a night. It took between four to seven minutes to reload them and fire again. So in half an hour they could fire six to eight rounds. Then the gun would disappear back into the safety of the tunnel as its rounds rained down devastating the target.

From February 5th to February 7th
Both sides employed heavy artillery concentrations and bombers to try and disrupt the other side. The bombing and the shelling went on day and night, day after day on shore it was clobbering time. The explosions followed by the sharp sounds of shrapnel tearing its way through canvas hospital tents or anything that got in its way. This noise added to the dark of night had its own special terror to the soldiers on the ground. A night filled with the overpowering odours of burnt flesh, diesel fuel and cordite. Everyone on shore and out on the ships in the anchorage became expert at distinguishing incoming and outgoing rounds. Each type of gun had very subtle differences of sound when fired and the sound would reach different ranges.

185.

Each calibre of round had a different flight noise as well as the obvious difference in the end result explosion: Whether it was the crying sound of 88mm shells, or the low soaring sound of the 110mm she: To the frightening metal on metal brakes sound of the anti-aircraft shells, especially when the Germans fired them at troops on the ground. But everyone knew the express freight train sounds of Anzio Annie soaring in to spoil someone's day.

It was decided from now on the Cruisers, HMS Dido, Phoebe, Penelope, Mauritius and our ship was to operate out of Naples. We would operate in pairs with one of the US Cruisers, USS Brooklyn or USS Philadelphia. So we would be on the beachhead for a few days than back to Naples for a break out of the fray. Then off again to whatever tasking they gave us, to and fro the beachhead. So we could be used for escorting merchant ships to and from the beachhead and AA defence while we were at the anchorage.

February 7th
The Anzio port area was bombed and strafed by Focke Wulf 190's and Messer Schmitt 109's at 0810Hrs, 1135Hrs and at 1525Hrs. High explosive and anti-personnel (butterfly) bombs were dropped from the occasional enemy bomber. In the harbour area one LCI and one LCT were damaged with thirty men killed and forty wounded.
In an effort to gain altitude when attacked by a Spitfire one German plane jettisoned its load of anti-personnel bombs. They fell into the area of the 95th Evacuation Hospital.

186.

Twenty-eight hospital staff and patients were killed and sixty-four were wounded, including the Commanding officer. Anti-aircraft gunners shot down seven aircraft and damaged nine others, while Allied fighters destroyed seventeen with twelve probable hits.

Life on the beachhead and anchorage was regularly noisy the Germans were very methodical "set in their ways". Every day when everyone was having their meals on shore, they would shell the rear lines. At every stand to time (dawn and dusk) they would mortar bomb the front lines. Intermittently and quite randomly throughout the day when there was no spotter planes flying to spot them. They would bring up the huge railway gun with 12-inch shells. As they passed over the noise was deafening like a train in a tunnel.

The Liberty ship SS Tabitha Brown departed on this day after being at Anzio for eight days waiting to unload and unloading. She reported 78 air raid alerts the closest near misses fell within 300 yards on February 6. She accounted for one plane probably destroyed and assisted in shooting down another. Arriving with her at the same time and also leaving with her the SS William Mulholland. At the same air raid on February 6th bombs fell within 50 yards of her hull. Showering the ship with bomb fragments and causing deck plates to crack and seams to open in the skin of the ship.

Shells landed in SS William Mulholland vicinity right up to the time she departed. She claimed one plane destroyed and probably another damaged form her guns in over 62 air raid alerts.

8th February 1944

USS Ludlow (DD-438) had arrived at Anzio on D-day with the rest of us. In less than a week, Ludlow had splashed two bombers, one fighter and three rocket glider bombs. The Ludlow was working its way close to shore, to deliver close range fire support. A large German artillery shell, of a calibre likely more than five inches, hit her. The projectile must have come from extreme range. For it went vertically through the torpedo director deck and the pilothouse. It went through several decks and ended up in the galley scullery. Fortunately it did not explode it was a dud causing the Ludlow to retire for emergency repairs. On its destructive way through the Ludlow's pilothouse smashing everything fragile with its concussive air flow. A fragment of the shell's rotating band flew off slashing Commander Creighton the skipper of the Ludlow's leg. (Rounds rotating bands are made of softer metal they form a gas seal around the round. It is scored by the gun barrel's grooves to make the shell rotate and be stabilized in flight. This made the rounds more stable in flight, accurate and travel further.) The round left him with a severe wound twelve inches long and down to the bone it was bleeding profusely.

188.

Chief Gunners Mate James D. Johnson located the remains of the hot projectile. This was already spilling a portion of its high explosive charge on the deck from its cracked casing. He carefully picked it up wrapped it with his shirt and he carried it all the way topside. Cautiously he gently threw it over the side to safely dispose of it before it could go off. With Lt. Cutler of the US Navy Reserve now acting CO, the Ludlow retired to Naples for emergency repairs and re-arming. USS Plunket that was already at Naples having a rest volunteered its crew to re-arm the Ludlow of ammunition. So Ludlow's crew could get on with the repairs and try to get a nights rest before returning to Anzio. Ludlow arrived the next day in time for the morning air raid.

The number of planes destroyed in an attack is not the measure of the fully effectiveness of the anti-aircraft fire. A large percentage of the planes making the attacks on Anzio, jettisoned their bombs in the water. Many times the enemy aircraft dropped their bombs on their own troops or the wrong targets by mistake in their haste to abandon their attacks. The devastating fire from all the ships and shore batteries must have been the reason why they were put off. On every occasion where the enemy employed eight or more planes, he lost at least one plane got completely destroyed, and in some attacks 30 to 40 percentage of his raiding forces were damaged. The Nazi's were forced to abandon their large-scale daylight attacks from fear of losing all its aircraft.

189.

The Luftwaffe noted in all the night attacks that no fire was received from light anti-aircraft units in the forward areas of the beachhead. Knowing that our heavy guns on board ships could not engage low flying aircraft in that area without endangering our own troops (blue on blue). The Nazi's started to take advantage of this and their aircraft began to come in at low altitudes, with high explosive and anti-personnel bombs. The anti-aircraft commander promptly countered these tactics. By organizing fire control orders and permitting controlled barrages in any of the three sectors or all at once. Fears were raised that it would outline troop positions and bring on concentrated artillery fire. But this was quickly dismissed when the on mass firing of hundreds of guns quickly drove the enemy aircraft from the area. The enemy tried a few further half-hearted attempts at bombing attacks a couple of more times. They also tried some ineffective shelling of a few of our light gun batteries but they could move position quickly so the enemy could not effectively hit them sufficient enough. The forward areas of the beachhead were added to the territory forbidden to the Luftwaffe because of the danger.

10th February
B-17 Flying Fortresses were flying over our anchorage and the beachhead they were a magnificent sight with their comforting groaning engines. Their operation was to give a massive walloping to the German positions surrounding the Allies during daylight.

The enemy ack-ack was very thick protecting their troops, but the Fortresses ploughed right on through it. They were eager to get at the enemy boxing in the beachhead and try for Anzio Annie. Enemy ack-ack got a direct hit on a fortress, which was flying in the second wave. It was seen to catch fire start smoking and rapidly swung out of the formation. It tried to turn back for safer skies but it did not get very far when it exploded. None of the crew was seen to bail out as no chutes were reportedly sighted the fire must have set off its fuel tanks and payload in the large explosion.

The Liberty ship SS F. Marion Crawford during her nine days at Anzio logged more than 200 near misses from German 88's. She shifted anchorage every few hours to disrupt the German range finders. On this day fires were started by a shell that hit the top of a hatch just above a cargo hold filled with 75-millimeter ammunition. The merchant's fire control drills were swiftly put in to action. The fires were extinguished within fifteen minutes, saving the crew, ship and cargo if the cargo had cooked off they would have stood no chance.

So the days rolled into one another as the saying goes "ground hog day" at ground zero. The only break in the normal sequences of the day was when Anzio Annie raised her ugly head. She attempted to unleash hell at our ships with her deadly shells. If a ship got hit by one of her massive shells it would stand no chance of surviving.

191.

Anzio Annie would often send a round towards a ship singled out from the rest. If you were lucky and it was a miss your ship would shudder from bow to stern. A great spout of water would erupt from the sea reaching at least 100 feet in the air as it exploded. Of course the spotters would be then relaying the information so the gunners could lay corrections. As they reloaded the gun and then they would send another screaming train engine block of steel and explosives of death our way. They would try to bracket the ships to get the correct range and aim off for wind. As soon as the first round exploded the ship would get up steam to move locations, to throw the spotters off with their aim. Everybody aboard would be very tense and ready to snap at the first momentary lapse in concentration.

The crew would be hoping the ship would move fast enough, willing her across the waves. This game of tiger and mouse would be played out many a time with all the ships in range of her. She would come out and pummel the troops with its high calibre gun each round would be devastating in its impact. This gargantuan sized gun could wipe out artillery or armoured vehicles with one gigantic shell. If it had hit our ship I don't think there would have been much left of her except a smouldering wreck. Some of the destroyers would be tasked to fire at likely positions periodically during the day. They would try and keep her at bay with indiscriminating shelling or put the spotters off their job with smoke and fragmentation rounds.

192.

13th February 1944

Another weather front was in with gale force winds and slashing rain. It was whipping up stormy seas with mountainous waves cresting thirty to forty feet high. Rain was coming in at right angles to the ship splattering the sides like little bullets. We lost landing craft tank LCT-220 in the heavy weather, as she was forced beam on to the waves by the wind. She was swamped by a humongous onslaught of water sending her down to the sea floor. Luckily no souls were lost as all the rescue ships were on full alert to save any ship in distress. For just this type of incident and all her crew and troops aboard were wearing lifejackets already just in case they went into the water.

15th February

At around midday an extremely strong sirocco wind blew up. It was just one of those unfortunate times LCI (L)-2's engine decided to pack up. She drifted into a mined area and triggered a mine off. Luckily she got away with only slight damage.

Major air attacks came in once again at dusk. It was one of the most concentrated attacks the Germans would throw at the ships at the anchorage.

Destroyer USS Herbert C. Jones was on duty with all the latest electronic wizardry. To jam the remote control frequencies, of the German guided rocket glider bombs. She was lying off the beachhead by 3 miles at the edge of the anchorage. Towards the direction we expected the enemy aircraft to approach from.

Destroyer USS Herbert C. Jones spotters sighted the build-up of bombers far out past the range of her guns. Coming in low and informed the bridge who ordered the sparkies to start their music. (She started to jam radio frequencies). As expected the bombers released their deadly cargo out of range of our guns, so the guns could not get the mother aircraft. As they're screaming infants flew off towards us (Hs-293 Rocket propelled glide bombs). The Herbert was unlucky this day it threw off some of the bombs from their controlling frequency. But one got through and impacted within 50 feet of her. The tremendous explosion close to her hull caused minor damage and sprung a few hull plates. The explosion had knocked out her electronics with the blast wave. So she moved out of the anchorage ten miles or so to reset all her electrics as fast as she could

To reduce the number of ships offered as targets to the enemy at the anchorage with important and essential resupplies. The Allies had set up a regular shuttle service from Naples in convoys which we were protecting but it had its backlogs. Since arriving at the anchorage on the 13th the Liberty ship SS Elihu Yale, had been a too attractive target to the enemy. She had to keep moving around into different positions constantly. As she waited to get her cargo of ammunition unloaded and off to the troops. Eventually she moved to within a mile and a half of the beach to unload as fast as she could. The craft doing the donkey work could go faster back and forth from her with there cargos.

LCT-35 was tied up alongside her loading shells when the air attack started. It was an unlucky glider bomb that struck SS Elihu Yale in No4 hold which was full of ammunition. She exploded with a tremendous thunderclap of a bang. The explosion caused an enormous cloud of smoke, which drifted over the beachhead. The LCT alongside was caught in the explosion of the ammunition ship and was destroyed.

Almost miraculously only twelve men were killed. Two of the forty Armed Guards, three of the 45 man merchant crew and seven stevedores of the 182 who were working the cargo. Just four other Armed Guards were injured seriously. Fire fighting efforts by fleet tug Hopi (ATF-71) ultimately proved successful in extinguishing the flames. But Elihu Yale was later written off as a total loss due to the extensive damage done to her, she was literally a wreck. LCT-152 came to the rescue of the survivors picking them up out of the melee.

16th February 1944

The Germans launched a new offensive (Operation Fischfang) against the Allies troops on the beachhead. They had the strongest attacking force yet they could get together. As well as this the German Luftwaffe struck again and again at the ships in the anchorage, harbour and beachhead. They used every known trick in there tool bag with everything from fighters to heavy bombers. During the day, German aircraft flew 172 sorties. But the results of which, hardly justified the effort expended.

Only one landing craft was sunk with one English Destroyer receiving minor damaged and one landing ship was damaged. Near miss bombs in the anchorage damage destroyer USS Hilary P. Jones (DD-427) but after emergency repairs she was up and running quite fast.

Here is the story of the landing ship that was damaged. HMS landing ship tank, a 6,000-ton ship, was a specially designed landing ship built by Harland and Wolff, Belfast in 1941. It could carry 20 tanks in a hanger on the lower deck. She had a lift, which took light vehicles and guns to be stored on the upper decks. She was designed for running the ship ashore to unload. As you can imagine it can get tricky, when you put a 6,000-ton ship on the beach. The Captain has to be very experienced and a good seaman with skills knowing: weight of his ship and cargo, specifics of the design and workings of his ship, tides and actions of the sea. When you do hit the beach with a 6,000-ton ship at two to three knots you have to be cautious.

You don't want to hit too hard, because you have to get off the beach after unloading. When approaching the beach you let out your stern anchor, which is a kedge anchor. Then when you unloaded all the tanks, vehicles and troops off the ship onto the beach, you still had to get the ship off the beach to safety. So you would winch in the stern anchor pulling the ship right off the beach, well sometimes! This time the ship was stuck hard on the bottom so they put the ship into full astern and pulled on the anchor. But at this time it didn't work either they were stuck fast. They had a problem there was something wrapped around its propellers and shafts.

196.

The crew wanted to send down divers, but because of the air raid they could not risk it. Any bombs or shells falling in the water up to around 300 feet away would seriously injure any diver with the concussive blast underwater.

As the ship was stuck there a German shore battery opened up and a shell landed alongside the ship. Shrapnel showered the deck of the landing ship and killed the Petty Officer and a number of others were wounded. The landing ship eventually got off the beach getting a pull off by an ocean going rescue tug. They hoped that the propellers wouldn't get mangled after she had released the towing line. She tested her engines and propellers and found they had cleared. So she made headway further off the beach. This was when a German aircraft sent two 500lb bombs at her. Luckily the bombs skimmed the side of the deck and exploded in the water. The explosion in the water caused minor damage to the ship's hull. Having completed her tasking she returned to Naples to await a convoy to Malta.

Once clear of the threat the landing ship tank, crew would do one of the saddest things I have ever seen, and have witnessed. In the Royal Navy during war, when you have a crewmember who has died you bury him at sea with full military honours. You would sew him into his hammock. With the last stitch through his nose to make sure he was dead because if he were just stunned he would flinch at that. Then slide his body off a board covered in the white ensign. Blowing the boson's whistle then the armed honour guard would fire a salute. It is one of the saddest moments aboard a ship I have ever witnessed.

197.

In the afternoon LST 418 sailed from Anzio for Naples. It took the risk of being unescorted to her bad luck! She was carrying 53 empty vehicles and about seventy-five Army personnel. At 14.30 Hrs she was spotted by U-230 a U-boat that was patrolling the area looking for targets going to and from Anzio. The U-boat obtained a firing position within forty minutes. She fired a GNAT (German Navy Acoustic Torpedo) at 1511 Hrs. The torpedo struck the ship after running for 60 sec in the LST's port side aft. The engines stopped and all power failed and the LST began settling by the stern. At 15.37 Hrs a second torpedo struck her in about the same place performing a coup de grace. The LST ordered abandon ship and she sank shortly after by the stern with 21 dead. The survivors were rescued by an American landing craft USS LCI (l)-194 that was passing.

17th February
The Liberty ship SS Richard Bassett had arrived at Anzio on the 13th. She was in the thick of it from the start with bombs landing in her close proximity. Another stick of bombs landed close by her on the 15th. Followed on the 16th by artillery shells landing next to her but luck was still with her. But this day was not her most glorious moment in history. An American plane was shot down by mistake by her Armed Guards. She left in a convoy on the 21st and had close calls from a U-boat that sank two other ships in that convoy. She made it in one piece and the crew was thankful for it.

198.

German bombers attacked the anchorage straight out of the dawn sun. They singled out SS James W. Nesmith who was by chance at the edge of the anchorage sitting by herself as the closest ships were 500 feet away. Her Armed Guards had managed to knock down one of the German bombers that attacked and put the others off their aim. She survived the attack later in the day as she moved closer to the shore to unload. Artillery shells landed so close to her some of the crew said you could have reached over the side to catch them. She was forced to shift her anchorage many times with the rounds following her like a bad luck omen. Luckily every time she moved it was just in time as shells immediately hit the spot she had just vacated.

18th February
Heavy German air attacks, as well as artillery fire continued on the beachhead and anchorage at Anzio. Harbour tug YT-198 is sunk by a mine off the beachhead.

HMS Laforey carries out a bombardment of Formica with good results. USS Pilot (AM-104) minesweeper was at Naples she received orders to rendezvous with the US merchant ship SS Samuel Ashe. She was to escort her to Anzio in company with YMS-55. Unfortunately SS Samuel Ashe collided with Pilot and one man was killed. Pilot was towed back to Naples by YMS-55 for repairs as SS Samuel Ashe bravely went on alone to Anzio.

HMS Penelope (Light Cruiser) nicknamed Pepper pot. (From a previous battle because of the number of holes in her hull and superstructure that had to be repaired) She was anchored in the bay of Naples at 22.00 Hrs on the 17th. Captain Belben received a signal ordering him to prepare for sea immediately, "Return to Anzio to take the place of HMS Dido". Dido had been in a collision with a landing craft and needed repairs so she was making her way back to Naples. The position at Anzio was so critical not one cruiser could be spared so replacing the ships damaged was essential. Every ack-ack gun was needed to repel air attacks and every other gun that could support the troops to drive back the enemy. The enemy was driving our land forces dangerously towards the sea it was life or death teetering on the edge. The crew toiled late into the night to re-supply the ship of oil, ammunition and provisions. She was finally ready to be underway and slipped anchor at 0600 Hrs on the 18th. They left Napels bay and increased speed to 26 knots and steered a NW course to make for Anzio. On the regular run route between Ponza and Cape Circe. Zigzagging as she went to avoid possible submarine attacks.

The Germans still owned this bit of shoreline and their lookouts could help their submarines. Early that morning unknown to the Allies U-410 had moved into the area. Commanded by lieutenant Arno Fensky aged 25 they were running on the surface in the shadow of the coast. He had already destroyed a 7,000-ton supply ship on the 15th.

Suddenly at 0653 his look out on the conning tower cried "enemy ship". The captain ordered diving stations to periscope depth and they dived quickly closing in fast on Penelope. The captain matched bearings and ordered fire trying to get a quick lucky shot in on the fast moving ship. A GNAT (German Navy Acoustic Torpedo) leapt from its tube with a whoosh. It ran at a depth of 6 meters towards an unsuspecting Penelope. It took just 35 to 40 seconds to reach her. Then there was a thunderous explosion on the port side. The detonation sent chaos around the ship, as the stern lifted out of the water. The hit was well below the water line and she was taking on water fast abaft the engine room. It fractured oil tanks and flooded the aft engine room stopping the engines and generator. Other compartments quickly filled with water. An emergency signal was immediately got started, but before the full message was sent the power failed. That put an end to any radio signals being sent there was no backup power left in her batteries. Penelope listed to starboard as the sea rushed in through the gaping hole in her side. As her steering gear was damaged she began circling to starboard because of the rate of knots she had been travelling.

In effect she had no lights, her aft engine room out of action, no steering, no radio and a nine-degree list to starboard. Communications around the ship was knocked out apart from mouth to ear. She was a sitting disabled duck. The captain ordered counter flooding to stabilise her. Then ordered a signalman to us the spot light to try and signal nearby ships.

LST 165 and 430 a few miles distant returning to Naples empty to pick up more troops received the signal. "Close with me assistance needed". By then Penelope had come to a complete stop dead in the water. She had huge clouds of smoke and steam belching from her aft funnel.

It was then lieutenant Arno Fensky ordered, "Fire tube's 2 and 3". With mark V torpedo's to give the coup de grace. Then 30 seconds later the second earth-shattering explosion to hit Penelope happened. It had hit the starboard side abreast of the boiler room. That was closely followed by the third torpedo making a third thunderous explosion that caused the aft magazine to blow up. Penelope capsized and as water rushed into her funnels it released a horrendous cloud of vapour and smoke belching from her. The boiler room exploded sending a column of water into the air. The steam escaping made a horrendous hissing noise like something from the depths was dying. Penelope had broken her back the ship was in two pieces. With the two ends bow and stern pointed upwards towards the sky. The stern was at an angle of fifty degrees showing her rudders, screws and red leaded bottom. The crew immediately abandoned ship.

Diving over the side into the icy, rough, oil covered sea. Most just wearing their work wear: overalls, roll neck sweaters, jackets and sea boots. Swimming as fast as they humanly could in their condition after that sort of experience. Attempting put as much distance between them and the ship. In case of further explosions from the depth charges and other munitions and being sucked down.

202.

Other men still in duffel coats sank straight to the bottom, because of the weight of the water soaked into them. The ship then sank it had vanished in less than two minutes too fast for the crew below decks. A large number of men were trapped inside sealed to their fate. No lifeboats or rafts were released from the ship, as there was not enough time and they went with her. Many men died in the water from lack of strength and oil ingestion from the oil slick that was left from the ship. As the stinking oil would sting the eyes, clog the nostrils and if swallowed poison the seamen or coat their lungs so bad they suffocated, basically drowning from the inside.

The first of the landing craft from the LST's reached the scene in an hour and three quarters. But they didn't have any scramble nets to throw over the side. So could not help the men in the water to board the landing craft over the high sides. The Army lads aboard the landing craft from the Queens Own Regiment threw ropes over the side. The seamen in the water with the strength left in them grabbed the ropes. They were pulled over the side onto the deck like oily fish, this was difficult being soaked in oil and tired. Many men slipped back into the sea and were never seen again.

Out of a compliment of 618 officers and men only 203 survived. The U-boat commander Lieutenant Arno Fensky certainly knew his business. He carried out his attack in almost copy the book style. He still holds the record for hitting the fastest travelling ship with a torpedo. A very sad day for all the Cruiser crew's in the Royal Navy especially us on her sister ships at Anzio.

203.

PT boat Lieutenant Commander Barnes and his colleagues had been completely frustrated with their Mark 8 torpedoes. They refused to run shallow enough to engage the enemies Marinefãhrprahm large German landing craft barges (Flak Lighter). They had flat bottoms which meant they had a shallow draft and the torpedoes would go under them without exploding. They had their three US PT boats PT-211, 202, 203 adapted with ad hock beach rockets on a launch tube system. The rockets could deliver the force of a 5-inch shell explosive content without the use of a big gun. They had 8 tubes loaded with rockets so that's an instant 8 rocket barrage into a small target area in seconds devastating whatever you fired at.

One of the strangest enemy encounters I have ever heard of happened, just after midnight on the 18th February. PT-211, 202, 203 on patrol between Giglio Island and the Argentario Peninsula PT boat Lieutenant Commander Barnes was in command with his colleagues. Suddenly they saw a target come out from the peninsula on the radar. The enemy were heading toward one of the smaller islands south of Giglio. They ordered the rocket racks loaded and made ready, then preceded to advance on the enemy to see what they were taking on. Before they had got to within striking distance the enemy had ducked behind one of the islands. They knew it was going to be dangerous to try and re-pin the rockets and unload them. In pitching seas and in darkness so left the rockets ready in the racks. Just in case the same enemy reappeared or a spontaneous target made itself vulnerable.

204.

A little time went by and they picked up two more targets appearing on radar. They approached them to expend their dangerous rockets before an accident happened with them. They advanced toward the enemy and had just got to within a thousand yards. When they suddenly realized it was not just two targets appearing from behind the island. The convoy was a large concentration of enemy vessels numbering: two units of E-Boats and several Flak Lighter's. Suddenly they were outnumbered and virtually surrounded as they were so close. Barnes gave the order for all three boats to open fire with the rockets, but not to fire their guns. Hopefully the firing rockets would not give away their positions like the guns would and the rockets would cause confusion. During the firing of the rockets and 11-second flight nobody fired a single shot. Then the rockets landed and exploded everywhere all virtually at once all hell broke loose amongst the enemy.

A dozen enemy vessels opened up in all directions in panic spontaneously like there were a lot of nervous trigger fingers twitching. But not toward the PT boats, they went to move off but in a strange turn of events. PT-211's engine coughed and died and PT-203 lost all electrical power. So PT-202 circled the other two boats laying smoke. They were smack dab in the centre of the whole mess with enemy firing on all sides with a terrific volume of ammunition. PT-203 cleared its problem and both 203 and 202 eventually got out of the melee. By dodging in and out the enemy creating even more confusion.

The enemy E-Boats accidentally started shooting at each other thinking they were shooting at the PT boats. Eventually with a bit of luck on their side PT-211 drifted clear of the enemy. They could work on the engine without giving away their position and trying to be quite with hammer and wrench. They soon had the engine started and got their bearings as to where they were and which way to go to meet the other PT boats. She reached the designated rendezvous with no further engine faults and the other two boats were still there. They all inspected there boats expecting to find their boats pretty shot up, but they found none of the boats had been damaged. They were sure the Germans sank at least one of their own E-Boats and at least one of their Flak Lighter's. It had been a very lucky night for them.

19th February
Light Cruiser USS Philadelphia (CL-41) arrives of Anzio. She was to provide gunfire support to the defenders of the beachhead. Instantly she was put under fire from the enemy shore batteries. She came under fire on over three occasions throughout the first day. This caused her to move locations between engagements to avoid being pinpointed. Destroyer USS Madison (DD-425) conducts an unsuccessful hunt for an enemy submarine believed off the coast of Anzio. Liberty ship SS Charles Goodyear that had arrived the day before. Had a near miss with artillery shells that landed within fifty feet of her hull.

Another Liberty ship USS Samuel Ashe scored hit on an enemy plane that crashed into the sea near her scraping the tip of the wing along the ships side. She also fired at a glider bomb and luckily damaged it causing it to crash into the sea less than 50 feet from the ship but luckily it didn't go off.

20th February
USS LST-303 was made for the US Navy in December 1942 and was transferred to the Royal Navy as HMS LST-305 under the Lend-Lease Agreement and made its north transatlantic passage in convoy SC-122.
Landing Ship Tank 305 sailed at early evening unescorted from Naples to the beachhead anchorage. Her task was for radar picket duty, the 5th consecutive night she had done this duty. On reaching the position she anchored and stopped engines with the bow facing 050° at the request of the RAF controller aboard. At 1755 Hrs U-boat U230 spotted the LST in the failing light by chance as she did a irregular periscope sweep of the horizon to confirm her position so she moved in for the kill. At 1837 Hrs U230 fired one GNAT (German Navy Acoustic Torpedo) at maximum range and after a run of 3 minutes and 25 seconds the submarine's crew heard detonation at the end of its run. At 1851 Hrs, another torpedo was fired to deliver the coup d'état but the LST remained afloat. Her side was blown open in a gaping hole and she was taking on water fast because of the weight of the water she had a 15° list.

Merchant cargo ship XPC Sheppey arrived at 19.25 Hrs to assist. But it was clear any towing attempt would cause her to break in half as her structural integrity had been seriously compromised. By dawn she was sinking by the head and was starting to roll over, by 0710 Hrs she was on her side and then disappeared within five minutes. No casualties were reported and all crew and Armed Guard abandoned ship with the RAF controller.

USS LST-348 was steaming toward Anzio unescorted at 0157 Hrs. She was 22 miles southwest of Gaeta, when a FAT Torpedo hit her on the port side forward. (Federapparat Torpedoes run a wandering course with regular 180-degree turns. These were useful against convoys as they were more than likely with luck to hit a ship). The Torpedo came from U-boat U-410 who fired in a submerged position 600 meters from the LST. The torpedo struck the hull at frame 16, rupturing bulkheads in several compartments. The explosion pealed up 40 feet of deck directly aft of the elevator hatch. Damage control parties proceeded to close and dog all watertight doors. In all the troop compartments as far forward as the damage extended. Lookouts spotted an unidentified object off the port quarter. They thought it was the U-boats periscope. One shot was fired from the 3-inch gun with no secondary explosion or bubbles. They knew they had hit nothing. All most to the second of the shot being fired a second torpedo hit LST-348 at 0221 Hrs. The explosion broke the ship in two, just forward of the main cargo hatch.

The explosion of the torpedo against LST-348 split open the main fuel tank spraying out its contents. The fuel oil sprayed covering the two halves of the ship with a layer of greasy oil. Every single man that was on the deck was sprayed with oil coating skin and clothes. The oil almost instantly ignited in a violent fireball that swept down the entire stern section like a rolling sheet of flame. The fire lasted several minutes as it burnt off the oil residue and ignited anything flammable. Several men were thrown overboard by the explosion and others had no choice but to jump into the sea to escape the inferno. But most of the seamen where set instantly alight as they were all covered in the oil. Some of the crew died in the flames but all the survivors were burned in various degrees of severity. The order to abandon ship was given as there was little hope for the ship or its cargo.

All the remaining life rafts that had not been destroyed were launched. This was only five out of the ten they had on board. Out of the five (Landing Craft Vehicle Personnel) LCVP on board only one could be lowered. Three had blown up in the fire and explosions and another had jumped its davits. With the impact as the torpedo's hit and fell into the sea capsized and sank. The LCVP was loaded with the wounded and any essential first aid equipment that could be found. After thoroughly searching for any injured crewmen, the commanding officer was the last man to get aboard. The LCVP cast off about 30 minutes after the second torpedo hit.

The surviving LCVP would not move the propeller had become fouled with flotsam and they could not free it with the use of the motor. The crew knew they had to move away from what remained of the ship just in case of secondary explosions. So the crew use stretcher boards to paddle away from the wreck. No mean feat in itself with a craft that weighed in excess of two tons. With a crew that was exhausted trying to survive the incident.

USS LCI (L)-195 and 219 observed the first explosion. They were five miles away to the stern of LST-348. They increased their speed to catch up to her to help when they observed the second enormous explosion from two miles away. 195 and 219 reached the area shortly after 0300 Hrs. The wind and swell of the sea made securing a tow impossible so they both came alongside. They immediately transferred the men from the disabled LCVP on board their own vessels. Once they had evacuated the LCVP they began to traverse the area picking up other survivors. Most of the survivors were picked up before dawn. Only three more men were found later in daylight. 219 had saved the commander, six officers, 66 ratings and recovered bodies of two officers. 195 had picked up one officer, five ratings and recovered one body. The forward section of the ship had disappeared shortly after the Landing ship broke in two and the stern section eventually sank at 0630 Hrs. It was a sad loss of four officers and 20 ratings from the crew of LST-348.

At 0745 Hrs, submarine chaser USS SC-627 arrived on the scene. She was sent to escort both the Landing craft to Anzio. Where the 31 injured men were transferred to the British hospital ship HMHS Leinster. They were mostly suffering from second- degree burns, shock and exhaustion. All the remaining survivors were on board LCI (L)-219 after unloading the wounded at Anzio returned to Pozzuoli arriving on the 21st.

PC-621, was serving in multi roles at Anzio they were extremely busy little boats. They were multi tasked with: anti-submarine, anti E-boat, smoke screen layer duties and in between that they also had to do escorting duties between Anzio and Naples. While PC-621 did her tasks her crew were always on the lookout for downed aircrew to rescue. During her time she saved six downed USAAF airmen. The sad part of her duties was recovering a number of bodies. One of which was an airmen he was a downed pilot of a P-38 who landed in a minefield. PC-621 entered the minefield to try and rescue him but it was too late. Their flotilla CO was a stickler for the rules and reprimanded the skipper and crew for endangering their boat entering the minefield.

21st February
Was a quiet day but once it was dark there was attack after attack. In one hour we had been on the receiving end of six attacks. But the German Luftwaffe went away with a zero scoreboard. Nil Points to the Bosch.

During this night of air attacks PC-621 was on picket duty at the northern boundary of the anchorage fleet. She detected and engaged five German E-boats. Successfully sinking one of the E-boats and damaging two or three of the others. She managed to successfully divert their attack and turn them back. She avoided numerous dangers during this attack raging from shallow floating mines, enemy gunfire and acoustic torpedoes.

22nd February

Five German E-Boats approached the anchorage with great stealth. They used the coastline to great effect blocking our ships radar's. They were hiding in the reflective noise that the coast caused interfering with our radar. One of the E-Boats got into a position to be able to fire one of her torpedoes. Towards the Liberty Ship SS Samuel Ashe but failed to hit it. Another E-Boat attacked LCI (L) 33 also failing to hit their target. USS Gleaves and Submarine Chaser PC-621 managed to chase off the E-Boats. 621 claimed she sank one of the E-Boats and drove off another into the shallows by the shore. Where it ran aground ripping her keel apart and sank.

The German Schnellboot or S-Boot, meaning Fast boat, was the German designation for their fast attack boats. They were similar to our MTB Motor Torpedo Boats and our MGB Motor Gun Boats. We used the term E-Boat as in Enemy Boat.

25th February

HMS Inglefeild had come from Naples ten days ago escorting an ammunition ship. She had been doing various tasks: bombardments, AA defence and anchorage sentry and so on while she was at Anzio. This night she had taken up a defensive position to protect the anchorage 3 miles off Anzio lighthouse. During an air raid she sustained a direct hit by a rocket glider bomb, it created a massive explosion on her port side.

A US LCI (L)-12 was on salvage duty about a mile away. But she didn't realise at first that the British destroyer had been hit. After several minutes the LCI skipper suddenly realised that the smoke coming from her was a hit. He observed her listing over to port and headed to her to give assistance. As the LCI approached they could see at least fifty men were floating in the water. The entire midsection of the ship to the main deck was under water. The stern and bow were angled skyward the explosion had broken her back. It was now 18.25 and getting darker by the minute and they could hear frantic cries for help. But now could only identify the men in the water by the tiny red lights attached to their life jackets. So they quickly acted launching four rubber boats, both life rafts and several life rings in to the dark sea. Five members of the LCI's crew dove into the water to assist several struggling men. They towed the survivors to either side of the LCI on floats where they had nets slung over. The skipper threaded the LCI carefully through the survivors in the water picking them up as he went along.

LCI (L)-12 tried two attempts to nudge up to the destroyers bow, attempting to take off survivors from the stricken vessel. But the rough sea and high wind prevented them from holding their position long enough. On the third attempt two members of the LCI's crew rescued four of the destroyer's crew to safety. Before they lost position and had to pull away. The four survivors that had just got aboard then told the skipper there were three more casualties left alive aboard the remains of the Destroyer.

So he told USS Pennant YMS 64 a minesweeper close by their location to try and attempt a rescue. With their more powerful engines they might be able to hold position long enough to complete the rescue. She went in and successfully recovered the last surviving sailors. HMS Inglefeild sank at 18.50Hrs the whole incident had only taken just over an hour. LCI (L)-12 continued to patrol the area for survivors for more than four hours. In total she rescued twenty-four men including the Inglefeild's commanding officer. Minesweepers and other Destroyers came to the rescue of the rest of the remaining crew in the water. It was amazing work in extremely hazardous weather conditions. Out of the ships company of 192 they lost 35 crewmates.

HMS Delhi with HMS Laforey and HMS Faulknor was deployed to intercept possible E-Boats approaching the anchorage. We received a message that LST-349 was floundering in rough weather near Sabaudio. HMS Laforey was detached to see if she could assist the LST.

But before she got there the LST had run aground and sank in shallow water off the coast. They crew managed to swim to the safety of the shore. So HMS Laforey returned to our mission and continued patrolling with HMS Faulknor and our ship. Later that night Laforey and Faulknor split off from us to carry out a depth charge attack on a possible submarine contact. That they detected by chance we never did see the E-Boats we were sent to find.

The Germans would use acoustic torpedoes if they didn't have a good shot on our ships. Or if they were short of time to set up for a shot. The torpedo would zero in on the vibrations from the ship's engines through the screws (propellers). It was a bit like a blind man homing in on a whistling kettle. As long as they fired a torpedo in the right direction, close or even remotely close to a ship that was moving. The torpedo would be attracted to the ship's screws. It didn't have to hit the ship, it just got within a certain range and a proximity device to detect the ship would detonate the warhead. The explosion would either destroy your ship's screws or knock them out of alignment. This would damage them enough to cripple the ship making your ship a sitting duck for a final coup de grace and the submarine would finish the ship off. All our ships were issued with a noisemaker. The noisemaker consisted of two steel bars, loosely held in place with about a half-inch space between them. You would tow them behind the ship at a range of fifty yards. The water would rush between the bars and make them vibrate.

They would make a noise loud enough to divert the torpedoes off the ship. They would explode against them safely behind the ship. We all called the noisemakers CAT for short (Counter-Acoustic Torpedo) gear.

26th February
In another bout of foul weather LCT-36 sinks after running aground off Naples. HMS Laforey had a near miss on a patrol, a submarine attacked her firing an acoustic torpedo, and luckily it exploded in her wake against her CAT. The explosion destroyed the Cat totally causing no damage to the ship. Laforey with HMS Hambledon and HMS Lamerton dropped a series of depth charges in a pattern for several hours with no results but it must have scared off the submarine.

29th February
Landing Ship Tank LST-197 is damaged by enemy shore battery fire off the beachhead she reported No casualties and the damage was minor. The evening brought on another heavy air attack. Liberty Ship SS David S. Terry reported in sixty flaming minutes of the attack. That from 40 to 50 bombs were dropped and 15 to 20 landed in their vicinity. She scored a probable hit on one of the planes but it was not seen to go down. Luckily no ships were sunk when the aircraft had finally finished and the all clear was sounded. The rest of the night went by quite quiet there was the occasional artillery shell fired into the anchorage. We think it must have been a bored gun crew trying their luck firing blind in hope or was it just to keep us awake.

2nd March

Liberty ship SS David S. Terry left Anzio reporting five attacks in her eleven day stay. She had 54 red Anzio alerts and enemy planes were sighted 18 times. Some damage was done to her stern gun by shrapnel from a near miss and reported that enemy fire from ashore continued to be dangerous and annoying.

By March 3rd the guns nicknamed Anzio Annie had fired some 315 of their huge rounds into the Allied beachhead and anchorage.

4th March

The Allies believed they had gotten a lucky break in locating the guns. After heavy shells had hit the beachhead the Allies requested air support to try and find the guns. One of the planes spotted railroad guns firing from the Ciampino rail yards. Eight P-40 Lightnings carrying 500 lbs bombs were scrambled to destroy the guns.

They arrived over the target at 11.50 Hrs to find the guns still in position. This was the first strike of four missions that day to flatten the rail yards and anything in them. Dodging deadly anti-aircraft fire the pilots dove on the target over and over again. They Dropped bomb after bomb in to the target area causing chaos. That afternoon the top brass thought at last they had heard the last from Anzio Annie. The news made its way quickly around the troops on the beachhead and onto the ships "Anzio Annie would not bother us again".

Unfortunately it wasn't the case the guns Leopold and Robert had been safely parked in their tunnels. They were moved minutes after firing that morning back into their tunnels waiting for the reprise attacks. Long before the spotter and bomber planes had arrived. The planes had attacked wooden decoys with flash simulators. That had been positioned to distract the Allies. They did a good job even fooling ground reconnaissance by Special Forces.

The German Commander of artillery in that area phoned the commander of the guns. After hearing the Allied announcement that both guns had been destroyed. He told him laughingly "You're Dead".

It was getting too dark for aircrew in the spotter planes to spot anything on the ground so the planes returned to their bases. Captain Borchers the gun commander waited an hour after he had seen the last plane. Then he decided to give the Allies the good news that they were wrong he and his guns were alive. They wheeled out one of the gigantic guns and they fired four more of the 280mm rounds into the battered beachhead. To the shock of the troops on the ground the gigantic rounds struck out of nowhere. The Allied commanders wondered where they went wrong. They demanded the spotter planes to increase their sorties and make sure they were correct in their reports.

9th March 1944
High command ups the amount of bombing in Italy.
B-25's strike the docks of Porto Stefano, Port'oErcole and the bridge at Montalto di Castro.

218.

A-20's bomb Tank repair depot North of Tivoli,
P40's destroy gun positions West of Campoleone, west of
Pratica di Mare and south of Ciampino,
A-36's bomb Capranica railroad station and targets nearby
Fighters fly uneventful patrols over Anzio.

American Destroyers USS Edison DD-439 and USS
Madison with four British Destroyers: HMS Blankney,
Blencarthra, Brecon and Exmoor. Start a search for a
reported submarine that was sighted heading to the Anzio
area. A huge pattern of depth chargers was dropped. Until
Edison discovers a sonar contact further away. A short
game of cat and mouse ensues. Eventually Edison damages
U-450. The damage is enough to force her to the surface
where her crew abandons sub. The Edison destroys the sub
with gunfire 42 German submariners survive the whole of
the crew.

The Liberty ship John Murray Forbes left Anzio to
return home. During her stay of fourteen days she reported
artillery fire was kept up intermittently day and night. Shell
fragments hit the ship on numerous occasions. There was
air attacks throughout her stay, too numerous to count but
only once did the bombs fall even remotely close.

10th March
The US Liberty ship freighter SS William B. Woods was
on route to Anzio. Italian Destroyer Aretusa and two
British Motor launches were escorting the convoy. The
small convoy was steaming at 8 knots and was 47 miles
northeast of Palermo, Sicily.

U-952 was by chance patrolling the area hoping to catch Allied ships on the hop on route to re-supply the beachhead at Anzio. The weather was brisk with a strong wind with swells rising 10 to fifteen feet. The ships thought they were safe from U-boat attack. The waves would make it difficult for submarines to spot anything out of their periscopes. Submarines would have to be on the surface and the convoy would spot them from miles away.

U-952 spotted the ships by chance on a routine navigation check. They fired off a GNAT (German Navy Acoustic Torpedo) in their general direction. SS William B. Woods was hit on the port side in the No.5 hold. Opening a hole twelve feet wide, breaking the propeller shaft. The explosion blew off the hatch cover of the hold and broke beams. The blast ejected some of the cargo up through the hatch spreading it over the deck. The crew was lucky though as the explosion didn't ignite the bombs and ammunition stowed in the hold. If it had the ship and crew would have been incinerated instantly. The master (Edward Ames Clark) tried to save the ship. But the engines had to be secured as she settled by the stern. Most of the crew: officers, crewmen, armed guards and 407 US Army troops on board began to abandon the ship. Twenty-five minutes after the torpedo strike in four lifeboats, one raft and 14 Army rafts. Seventy men had to remain on board and construct makeshift rafts before they could jump overboard. As there was not enough rescue equipment still intact. The ship sank by the stern at 1940 Hrs with the loss of one-armed guard and 51 troops.

The survivors were picked up by two small British escort motor launches. Eventually the survivors were transferred to the Italian escort and taken back to Palermo. Complaints were made about the slow actions of the Captain of the Italian Destroyer escort. This was due to his lack of speed to respond to the incident and deplorable little rescue efforts they had made. It was hoped this would force the Italians to replace the Captain of Destroyer Aretusa.

12th
Light Cruisers USS Philadelphia and USS Brooklyn provided gunfire support.

13th March
The Cruisers: USS Philadelphia and USS Brooklyn come under fire from enemy shore battery fire. But swift actions on the ships switching positions on numerous occasions prevented any damage.

Submarine chaser PC-624 is damaged when she runs aground three miles east of Palermo Sicily she is repaired in a couple of days and back in action.

The long stalemate at the beachhead demoralized the Allied ground forces. They were forever put down by the German propaganda machine. Leading this was the radio show hosted by Axis Sally with her sidekick George. They would broadcast daily from 06.00 Hrs until after midnight.

The honey toned propagandist Axis Sally, called the Anzio beachhead "the largest self-supporting prisoner of war camp in the world". She would describe the Allies activity and movements of troops so accurately and up to date/on time. They knew what was happening before most of our commanders knew. Most thought they must have HQ (Head Quarters) bugged or was intercepting all official signals and messages. Or they might have an overlooking OP (Observation Post) in the Alban Hills watching the beachhead through powerful binoculars. Troops loved her inclusion of up to date music and her comic book descriptions of the Allied high command. Any military man knows the lower ranks love it when someone takes the mick out of their officers.

13th march
The Allies were stuck on the beachhead. They had rounds from Annie and other German guns landing on top of them day after day. The Allies High Command came up with another strategy against the guns called Anzio Annie. Instead of going after the guns, they would bomb all the rail lines and roads coming into the region. That carried the weapons re-supply of ammunition to them. "Let's bleed them dry of the ability to fire those bloody great shells at us" was the phrase used. The damage wasn't just in casualties and the destruction of supplies. It was the psychological toll of the shells roaring overhead. The new campaign was called "Operation Strangle" was to interdict supply movements of the enemy.

The new air offensive kicked off at a high pace:
B-26's bombed the railway bridges NW and WEST of
Sarzana and the rail tracks South of Viareggio.
South African Air Force (SAAF) light bombers bombed the
marshalling yard at Fabriano.
B-25's bombed Spoleto marshalling yards levelling them to
the ground. They also bombed the East and West
chokepoints and the line to Terni hitting them hard. They
gave the Perugia marshalling yard a going over but with
less successful results.
P-40's hit a supply dump near Valletri and gun positions
along a beachhead defensive line directly South of Rome.
While 24x A-36's bombed the railroad station between
Orte and Orvieto.
A-36's were making their way to a target when they were
jumped by 25 German BF 109's and a few FW 190's. The
Americans claimed three downed Germans but lost three of
their own. On the route back they were jumped again losing
yet another plane.

14th March
In part of Operation strangle huge bombing raids hit targets
leading in to Italy. This was to try and suffocate all the
enemy in Italy not only the ones affecting the beachhead.
234 US Fifteenth Air Force B-17's and B-24's, escorted by
a hundred plus fighters, bombed the air depot at Klagenfurt,
Austria. A hundred and fifty plus B-24's also hit the air
depot at Graz, Austria and the marshalling yards at Knin
and Metkovic, Yugoslavia.

The Luftwaffe fighters gave a fierce opposition and along with AA fire shot down 17 bombers and one US fighter. The US Air Force claimed to have shot down 30 enemy fighters in aerial combat but this was the usual American exaggeration.

Closer to the beachhead in Italy the US Twelfth Air Force sent all their B-26's to attack a road West of Arezzo and port installations at San Stefano al Mare.
B25's bombed a bridge approach into oblivion in South Orvieto. The marshalling yards at Avezzano and Orte was destroyed and a bridge at Orte.
The tank repair shops near Tivoli were bombed by A-20's. While P-47's and P40's concentrated their strikes at enemy troop concentrations, fuel dumps and guns in the Anzio battle area north of the beachhead.

We all were overjoyed to see the increase in air cover over the anchorage and beachhead. Every time we saw a formation of our bombers heading inland a cheer went up from all the ships. An even greater cheer went up whenever we saw our fighters swoop in to sweep the sky of the enemy around us. You could hear the cheering over the noise from the engines down below. We started to see a difference in the amount of German shells dropping, in the anchorage and on the beachhead. The Air raids started to ease as the amount of air cover increased for us. The Germans started to protect their assets more with what they had left. But occasionally they would strike at the anchorage at Anzio or at Naples.

During the air attacks at Naples bombs damage US freighter Liberty ship SS James Guthrie. There are no casualties among the ships company and the damage was light they were still up and operational. Landing Craft LCT-277 is lightly damaged in the same air raid with no casualties. Bomb fragments damage US freighter SS China Mail but this was just classed as a new paint job was needed. The duty rumour mill was put about Delhi that we were going to Naples, for a well-deserved rest some vital maintenance and the re-supply of the ships food and ammo. It turned out to be true we left Anzio that night, when it was dark enough to cover our transit. The prospect of a break from the rigorous demands of action for so long came happily to us all. Some of the crew looked at times like the walking dead they were just in automatic gear getting on with their jobs with no emotion.

21

22

23.

24.

226.

25.

26.

27

CHAPTER THERTEEN
VESUVIUS

15th March 1944

     Over the next few days we had time to rest do some letters and catch up on our own admin. All the stokers in the engine room worked diligently taking their time to do a complete boiler clean and general maintenance. The rest of the crew did vital overdue essential maintenance on the rest of the ship. Like greasing the working parts of the guns and swabbing out the barrels in other areas like the kitchen they did a deep clean. The ship was a beehive of activity all working and resting in shifts. We were all working to get the ship spick and span and operating at a high standard. We had to do it all without shore leave. But anything that granted us a relief in harbour. Away from the monotonous bombardment of unseen guns and being bombed and strafed, was a bonus. To be able to sling our hammocks up for a change and have a good night's sleep was indeed a luxury. Anyway in Naples they had a strict curfew and all the bars were closed and the local population were locking their daughters away from all the military.

     On the first day in Napels we were just looking forward to the normal work and respite. When we were just finishing supper, someone called down to us to come up on deck. We all saw what the commotion was about there was smoke and steam venting from Mount Vesuvius. The fierce furnace within the mountain was reflected in the night sky. An eerie iridescent spectacle of magnificent colours that could be seen as the mountain started to wake up.

228.

This night was interrupted the once when 20 to 30 enemy planes attacked the shipping off Naples. USS Narragansett (AT-88) an ocean going recovery/rescue tug was bombed and sunk. Also a liberty merchant ship was slightly damaged due to shrapnel from near miss bombs. The Hospital ship Aba with her red crosses and her doctors and nurses was of course a ship of neutrality. A stick of bombs was dropped right on top of her. One bomb went right through the matron's cabin when she was asleep on her bunk. It did not disturbing her until it blew one of the ship's hull plates out three decks below her. The bomb left a two foot wide hole through the ship to where it exploded even with this the ship survived, it's a miracle it was not sunk.

16th March

All through the day we were interrupted in our work with the mountain rumbling and groaning. The mountain was causing earth tremors, which inadvertently caused the sea to pick up increasing the swell. All through the Town of Naples in the Harbour and across the anchorage was the smell of sulphur and ash. It was like all the eggs on board the ship and throughout the local area had gone off. Whilst above us all, the giant woke up coughing, emitting gaseous clouds of suffocating chemicals.

On the second night again we had an evening of quakes with tremendous roars, similar to thunder. The vibrations could be felt on board ship as if the engines were running up. It's amazing to think the vibrations radiating from the monster within the mountain would travel through the earth and be transmitted to the sea and through its liquid to the ship.

229.

The sky was shot with bright colours of red, orange, green and turquoise. I was a truly remarkable sight a night time spectacular light show. We didn't know where we would be better off? Here or back at Anzio's anchorage with all its hazards. Is it better to know the devil that you are sat by waking up? Or another set of devils trying to kill you and your shipmates at any time!

17th March

Vesuvius was erupting! The great mountain was afire; huge red streams of melted lava streaked the mountainside. As we watched the streams like giant fingers flowing down the sides, it was a sight to behold. The streams were like its living veins transporting its lava like blood. Every so often huge gouts of brilliant red ash and magma belched from the bowels of the earth high into the sky. It was awe inspiring, nature in her most violent mood. Emitting a kind of fog, which in fact was a cloud of ash, majestic yet deadly. In comparison to the might of it, our endeavours were so feeble and insignificant. As we stood there on the deck we felt silly with our little guns on our ship compared with its monstrosity.

We had an air raid whilst this monstrous satanic event was happening. The German bombers must have snuck in whilst the majority of ships crews was watching the volcano. US Liberty ship freighter SS James Guthrie is damaged by a bomb no casualties were inflicted though and the ship was repaired quickly.

Off the coast of Anzio the Destroyer's: USS Madison (DD-425) and USS Eberle (DD-430). They were carrying out routine sweeps of the area they made a sound contact on sonar, 25 miles southwest of the port. They conduct a five-hour search that yields no results the submarine must have detected them and run for it. Tank Landing craft LCT-277 is hit and damaged by flying shrapnel from a near miss bomb at Anzio's anchorage during another air raid.

We hear on the grape vine that a U-Boat possibly U-371 off Algeria. Attacked a convoy bound for Naples SNF 17. US Liberty Ship freighter Maiden Creek was hit by a torpedo attack. The ship was abandoned initially but then was re-boarded by her crew who say that she wasn't going down without a fight. The ship's crew worked hard for an hour preparing for a tow but U-371 torpedoed her again. The resulting explosion killed six merchant seamen, two armed guards and sent her quickly to the bottom.

We had another thrilling night of sights and sounds at Naples. We could see the fierce furnace within the mountain reflected in the night sky. There were red clouds of vapour above the crater reflecting the angry glow in the caldera. The mountain sat there ominously with luminous streams of melted lava streaking down its sides. We were ordered to get some rest and we were told the duty crew on shift would alert the ship. If we came under air attack we would defend the ship and the anchorage. If the threat from the volcano became too dangerous we would have to help in the evacuation of Naples.

Or we would move the ship to a safe distance watching the destruction being not able to do anything. So we were told to sleep in our coveralls with our shoes ready to slip on. Some of us had a restless night, as we were awestruck with the sights and sounds from the mountain. It roared tremendously all through the night, off and on vibrating the ship.

18th March

On Sunday night, the roars became more frequent and it grumbled like a lion's roar. Every now and then there was a tremendous roar, which rattled and shook the whole ship. Streams of fire were shooting thousands of feet into the air. Like tendrils of some god-awful monster, and the countryside was lit up for miles around. Often at times the entire top of the mountain looked as if it was on fire in a blazing inferno. It's really uncanny, yet amazing to look at a phenomenon like this and truly uncomfortable as well. We didn't know on the ship that several of the lava flow's being emitted was slowly advancing down the mountain. The larva was going toward villages like a crawling dragon spraying puffs of black smoke from its edges. The smoke contained poisonous gas enough to choke a living soul to death.

19th March

Submarine chaser SC-545 was on patrol west of Anzio doing a routine sweep for submarines and E-boats. SC-545 engages and sinks a German E-boat with only minor damage to their boat from machine gun fire.

I learned from one of the officers who had been ashore. The streams of lava that were flowing down the mountainside were advancing towards Naples. He said it was one of the most phenomenal things he had ever witnessed. He saw a huge mass of fiery viscous, molten rock some 20 feet high and 200 yards wide. That creeps or ooze's along destroying everything in its path. It was moving slowly enough that people could move out of the way of the encroaching danger. Everything that is in the path of an advancing lava flow will be knocked over, surrounded or buried by the lava. Also everything would be burnt to a crisp ignited by the extremely hot temperature.

In the evening the northern flows reached the villages of San Sebastiano and Massa di Somma. The villages were 1.5 kilometres from the mountains crater. As the first houses start to burn up and collapse the mass evacuation began. Many people evacuate their homes giving them up to this fire-eating beast. But some of the people being devotedly Christian brought their religious icons onto the streets. They stood the statues and icons up in the path of the lava, believing that the white-hot flow would be stopped by religion before taking their homes.

Of course the lava just rolled on, so they moved their statues a few yards down the road! This continued until at last they collected them in before they all were burnt. Such is faith! The lava flow eventually swallowed and destroyed the village. Thankfully most of the people escaped and took refuge at the next village down the road.

233.

20th March
    There were many people evacuating their homes before and as the advancing larva was destroying them. Utter fear and anxiety echoed through the littered streets and out into the polluted atmosphere. The reeking smell of burning stench got spread on the wind out passed Napels to reach us on the ship.
    Other dangers from larva flows are: if it enters a body of water. The water may boil violently causing explosions, throwing showers of molten splatter over a wide area, taking people by surprise. A lot of methane gas is produced as lava buries vegetation. The gas can travel under the ground migrating in subsurface voids across many hundreds of yards. It can explode unexpectedly out of nowhere or ingress in to homes asphyxiating the occupants.
    At night the sky and countryside was bright for miles around. Flames were shooting into the sky for thousands of feet like tendrils. There were roars almost unexplainable in intensity. Tonight there is a lot of lightning around the summit and infrequent blasts like massive bomb explosions.

21st March
    Eruptions changed to explosive activity with a succession of eight lava fountains. Each lasting for 30 minutes or so, boiling and shooting from the crater into the sky. The lava fountains create a sustained ash plume, which reached about 5 Klm above the crater rim and spread the countryside with ash and cinders. The lava fountains were followed by a formation of small pyroclastic flows on the flank of the volcano.

Pyroclastic flows are fast moving current of hot gas and rock particles that flows down the side of a volcano reaching tremendous speeds. The hot gases and high speed make them particularly lethal, as they have been known to incinerate living creatures like humans instantaneously.

The effects of the eruption caught the air force at Pompeii airfield near Terzigno by surprise. The volcano showered the airfield with tons of hot volcanic ash and brimstone. The B-25 Mitchell aircraft from 340th Bomber Wing were covered with hot ash cinders. That burned the fabric control surfaces and melted the Plexiglas's portholes and cockpit windshields. Some were just cracked and glazed over opaque in colour so the pilots could not see through them. Some of the aircraft tipped onto their tails from the weight of the ash and tephra that had built up on the fuselage. Nearly all of the 88, B-25's were damaged in some way 76 planes were un-recoverable. Despite a major effort by the 12th Air Force to repair and salvage the damaged planes. There were a few casualties when a water tank exploded due to a lava flow that invested into the camp.

The camp suffered significant damage to its maintenance and accommodation facilities. When the eruption had finished the camp was not recoverable so it was abandoned. The Air Force dismantled everything that could be saved and relocated to Paestum Airfield.

22nd March 1944

Mount Vesuvius is about 9 miles from Naples and it is 4,190 feet high. The mountain measures about thirty miles around its base.

Geologists estimate it to be 17,000 years old. Vesuvius has erupted numerous times during its life; Six times in the eighteenth century, Eight times in the nineteenth century and then again in 1906 and1929, it is not a peaceful giant.

The most intense fountain of lava was witnessed from the ship this day. The fountains were emitting from the crater like a giant flamethrower shooting up in the air. It threw a burning spout of fire into the air reaching heights of 1,000 meters. With the fountains huge clouds of red-hot cinders were belching up then they both would fall and crash onto the mountainside, before turning into streams of fire running down its sides. The cinders are so deep that all traffic was stopped on the roads in Naples. About noon the wind changed and the cinders began falling on Torre Annunziato. Everything had a coat of black in Naples and out at the anchorage, just like light snow or dust. You could run your finger along any surface of the ship and see that you had drawn a line down to the battleship grey paint. Lads could not help writing their names or humorous graffiti.

27th March

Destroyer USS Livermore (DD-429) provides gunfire support at Anzio. Motor Torpedo boat PT-207 is damaged by artillery gunfire off the beachhead. British Coastal Forces laid on the excellent plan called "Operation Gun".

Operation Gun obtained the use of our British LOG's 14, 19 and 20. Which are Landing craft guns with numerous 4.7-inch guns aboard manned by Royal Marines.

The plan was to utilize the best boats from each unit of the British Coastal Forces and the American PT boats. The main battery in our LOG's would attack the German coastal convoys blasting them to smithereens. The American PT's had better radar and were used as scouts and screens for the force. While the British MTB's and MGB's due to their better torpedoes and heavier guns were the main force.

The force would travel up the coast from Anzio and intercept and destroy any convoys it would come across. As the force patrolled north along the coast the northern PT's scouting ahead. PT-212 and PT-214 picked up a German convoy at 22.00 Hrs. 150 miles from Anzio and they reported that six Flak-Lighters. (Marinefährprahm a large German landing Craft) Were proceeding southward in convoy with two Destroyers along the coast. The main force moved into position to intercept them at 23.30 Hrs. The scouting group engaged the Destroyers hoping to: destroy them, drive them off or distract them away from the convoy.

The scouting group fired three torpedoes at the Destroyers at less than 400 yards range. Then they retired at a fast rate of knots behind a smoke screen as they did this they were immediately under heavy fire from the enemy. The enemy got a lucky hit with a 37mm shell; it hit PT-214 in the engine room. Luckily their engineer kept the engines running even though he was wounded and they made it behind the smoke.

237.

As the PT's retired they witnessed a large explosion in the direction of the second of the two Destroyers. But because of the smoke that they had laid they could not estimate the extent of the damage. Damaged or not the destroyers reversed course and ran away up the coast.

As soon as the PT's delivered their attack the commander of the LOG's ordered opened fire at the convoy of Flak-Lighters. The first shells fired were star shells, fired blindly on bearings and ranges given to the gunners from the control group. They illuminated the target perfectly for the Task force. The Flak-lighters were taken by complete surprise and mistook the star shells for aircraft flares. They fired erratically and furiously straight up in the air for aircraft that were never there. This unintentional distraction gave the Royal Marine gunners on the LOG's all the opportunity they needed. They relay their guns on to the new visible targets and reload and fired. Within ninety seconds one of the Flak-Lighters blew up with a tremendous explosion and within ten minutes three others had been set on fire. The LOG's reversed course to pass the convoy on the way out and caught the last two Flak-Lighters as they tried to retire from the action.

Of the six Flak-Lighters destroyed two of them were carrying petrol judging from the impressive explosions. Two others were carrying ammunition judging from the off shooting pyrotechnics. One of the other two was suspected of carrying both petrol and ammunition. As this went up extremely well in huge fireballs the sixth one sank without exploding. The results of this action in its success were to display the outstanding features of combined operations and lead to many more in the future.

The eruption of Vesuvius seems to have abated very slowly during the past few days. Cinders and ashes that had been falling down over all the villages seem to be slowing down. The smoke from the crater is apparently changing from the intense black to white again. The Italians seem to be making a start to recover from this natural disaster. Bulldozers were ploughing the cinders to the side of road in huge banks like snow. Practically all the gardens and vineyards are covered in a tremendous depth of ash. All the way from Vesuvius to Salerno people are saying it won't do the grapes any harm it will help them grow. Many people are homeless and without food. But they seem to be taking it in their stride. Even though four villages were destroyed and 26 people lost their lives.

HMS Delhi was finally released to sail to Palermo for rest and recuperation but as usual this changed we only got a few hours in port. Then we received orders to return to Malta. We arrived on the 28th ready for her next mission on the 30th.

CHAPTER FOURTEEN
HMS LAFOREY AND CONVOY UGS-37

29TH March 1944
British Destroyers: HMS Ulster (R83), Laforey (G99) and
Tumult (R11) of the 14th Flotilla, were carrying out routine
Anti-Submarine Asdic sweeps. They were fifty nautical
miles northeast of Palermo, Sicily. Within the tremendous
range of actions carried out by the Royal Navy in the
Mediterranean. U-boat hunting was still recognised by
most as a "piece of cake a bit of a milk run". Destroyers:
HMS Blencathra (L24), Quantock (L58), and Hambledon
(L128) joined them in the hunt at midday. Soon the
metallic clang of the Asdic's (Anti-Submarine detection
Equipment) indicated they had located their quarry.

Attack after attack, the U-boat was heavily depth-
charged. But it managed to carry out many evasive
manoeuvres in an attempt to evade destruction. The
Destroyers failed to bring the U-boat to the surface. But as
darkness fell, the asdic team on Laforey was confident.
That during the night, lack of air and battery power would
bring her to the surface. HMS Ulster had to retire for
another mission and was replaced with HMS Wilton
(L128). All the gun crews on the six destroyers were eager
to deliver the coup de grace if the U-boat surfaced. They
were constantly traversing their arcs of fire scanning for
any sign of it.

30Th March

Shortly before 01.00 Hrs the asdic watchmen aboard all the ships sent messages to their bridges. They could hear the U-boat blowing her tanks. The order was given to prepare the gun crews for star shells to illuminate her and get ready with high explosive rounds.

On board the Laforey, Captain Armstrong for some strange reasons best known to himself. He had decided not to sound off full action stations aboard his ship. The crew were therefore at defence stations with only half the armament manned. None of the watertight doors were sealed with many of the crew stood down. Some of the crew were getting sleep in the mess-decks others were relaxing unawares of the drama unfolding. Suddenly the order was given to the gun crews to open fire. Within seconds night became day as the star shells illuminated the whole area. Especially Where the U-boat would break the surface as some of the gunners saw its bubbles rising out of the sea.

The submarine surfaced and was engaged by all the ships with surface gunfire, at a range of about 1,500 yards. HMS Laforey's 4.7-inch guns were straddling the U-boat within seconds. All the gun crews firing on the submarine was determined to ensure that the U-boats deck was raked with fire. The crew were trapped and condemned, denying any resistance from their deck gun. As the star shells burnt out their white phosphorous they started going out turning the night back to black.

241.

Laforey's captain decided instead of firing more star shells he would switch on his spotlight. This turned out to be a more of a double-edged hindrance than assistance and was a terrible and deadly decision. The spotlight highlighted the exact position of the ship to the submarine. The U-boat commander could not believe the opportunity given to him. It was all he needed to fire a salvo of three GNAT torpedoes within seconds. They already had them loaded in their tubes ready to fire just in case. They fired them in the general direction of the ship with luck. Suddenly there was a deafening explosion the Laforey was struck, almost instantaneously by all three torpedoes, the ship was fatally hit. The rest of the destroyers didn't notice the Laforey had been hit as they were concentrating on the submarine. The explosion's instantly put the Laforey in complete darkness, knocking out all her electrics the other ships thought she had just turned off her spotlight. The explosions were lost with the amount of gunfire flashes in the darkness. The flashes of the guns blinded all the lookouts on every ship so they did not notice the confusion.

The Laforey was going down fast. Some of the crew were thrown into the sea as soon as she was hit. They were gagging on fuel oil trying to swim or cling on to any debris they could find. As she was breaking up in her death throws, the remaining crew left aboard, started to throw anything they could find that floated overboard. But it was just mere seconds before she was going down. They thought it was now or never and frantically threw themselves over the side.

242.

As soon as they hit the water their arms were wind milling working like pistons propelling them away from the ship starting her final plunge into the deep. They were trying to get clear of the inevitable whirlpool of suction following the ship beneath the waves. Gradually the cacophony of gunfire died from all the Destroyers. HMS Tumult and Blencathra had sunk the U-boat. The black silence was broken with cries of sailors dotted around. They were like a bunch of corks bobbing in the sea. Oil fuel fouled their mouths and stung their eyes as they tried to survive. They were clinging on to anything and trying to help others to stay afloat while calling out to be rescued. There were a few blowing whistle's on the life preservers they had managed to find.

The destroyers sent out boats to pick up survivors from the U-boat, as they still did not realise the Laforey was lost. To the seamen in the sea it seemed an eternity before the first boats started to appear in the darkness as dark shapes. Suddenly there were cries of "Swim you German bastards, swim!" The rescuers were taken aback when they was answered back in English. As they were convinced the survivors were German sailors from the U-boat. Their fellow seamen they had rescued were treated to doses of morphine and cleaned up. The morphine was topped up with a tot of Nelson's Blood (Rum) to add to the pain relief. Most of the rescued sank into the peaceful safety of sleep. One hundred and eighty two of the crew of Laforey was lost that night with sixty-nine being saved. Seventeen German crew from U-boat U-223 were saved but two died later from their wounds.

30th March 1944

On leaving Malta we were tasked with getting to Gibraltar as fast as we could to meet up with UGS-37. We were tasked with convoy protection duties to Tunisia and through the Mediterranean. The convoy had sailed from Norfolk, Virginia, USA and we were to meet them in the straits. A little way into our trip it was reported to us that Destroyer HMS Laforey had been sunk at Anzio. It hit the crew hard, that she was gone and she had lost so many of her crew. We had been sharing the same stomping ground with her for a while and most of the crew knew someone aboard her. Later on we came across some wreckage floating about with survivors clinging on to it barely alive. An American sloop had been attacked and sunk by a submarine a few days before. Only a few living survivors were recovered, as most of them were already dead in the water when we got there. It was a case of recovering the bodies to gather their ID's off their tags gruesome but it had to be done. So we could inform the admiralty who in turn would inform the Americans of the casualties and let their poor families know. Then we gave them a funeral at sea to honour them as we did not have enough cold storage for the bodies.

We had an update on our duties at Anzio to try and raise our spirits. Whilst we were there we had suffered 291 attacks totalling 2,500 sorties of enemy aircraft. The Anti-aircraft fire our ship and all the other ships in the anchorage had fired amassed a grand total of 204 planes destroyed and 133 planes probably destroyed or damaged.

244.

We got to Gibraltar on the 2nd April. We were given a few days R&R whilst the ship got fitted for ASW (Anti-Submarine Work) as the convoy was delayed with bad weather. We had a depth charge rack fitted angled off to the port stern quarter at last we could hit back at the U-boats. When the captain gave the order to fire the depth charges, the crew would remove the brake pins off the rack. The depth charge would roll down the rack under gravity and drop into the water. The captain would then yell "Full ahead, full steam, both engines!" We would jump from zero to 10-20 knots. The depth charges would sink in the water until they reached their set barometric pressure for a certain depth and would explode. The force of the explosion would shoot the water up about 50 to 60 feet in the air. If a ship did not go fast enough for the run at full steam it would most likely be caught in its own depth charger explosion. If a ship was in the close vicinity of the explosion it might have its screws damaged or even lost or the propeller shafts might jump its bearings. So it was essential the boiler room staff and engine room staff was at their best game.

6th April
We were waiting for convoy UGS37 to arrive in our area. UG convoys were a series of eastbound trans-Atlantic convoys. Travelling from the United States escorted across the Atlantic by the Americans to Gibralter. They mostly carried: food, ammunition, military hardware and troops.

245.

We eventually got some good news from our boys back at Anzio. They had finally had some good luck against "Anzio Annie". One of Anzio Annie's shells proved to be a dud, as it landed it punched an 18-inch hole deep into the ground for a length of nearly forty-seven feet. A crew of bomb disposal dug down to it and recovered the shell. Finally they had a good idea of what type of gun they were up against. However inaccurate intelligence about the K5-E guns was still a problem. Some experts estimated the range of these guns was far more than they actually were. This meant that the aircraft searching for the guns now had a much larger area to cover so it still was a problem to find them.

7th April
The war in Tunisia is changed considerably when, the Americans from the west and the British 8th Army enters Tunisia from the East. There overall goal is to link up in Gasfsa, Tunisa.

9th April
Finally we get the call that our convoy is approaching Gibraltar. So we all get the ship ready loading last minute stores, double checking everything is ready to go and wait to join up with it. UGS-37 turned up several hours later and we joined them with four extra U.S. Destroyers that were waiting at Gibraltar with us. Also there were two British rescues tugs: HMS Mindful, HMS Vagrant and Frigate HMS Nadder. HMS Jonquil a Corvette completed the strong escort contingent that had been put together.

The Americans with convoy UGS-37 had crossed the Atlantic with six Destroyers', sixty merchant vessels and six LST's. As the escorts refuelled at Gibraltar we were joined by a further 44 merchant ships. So in total there were 108 merchants of which; 37 of them had Armed Guard contingents aboard for protection. There were 14 troop carriers with a total of 5,693 troops in amongst the merchants.

10th April
Finally UGS37 and all the escorts left the Straits of Gibraltar on our slow moving huge convoy. Unknown to us our entry into the Mediterranean was well publicized by German reconnaissance aircraft and by coast watchers in Spain.

11th April
With a clear sky, descending moon and a calm sea we were some 35 miles east of Algiers off Cape Benegut. We were in formation around the merchant ships that were in 12 column lines of 9 ships. We were making just over 7 knots with the convoy spaced fairly tight together for protection. As we all passed into the Tunisian War Channel we all knew it demanded full alertness as it was a danger area. The Destroyer escorts were on the perimeter, three to port with one of them being USS Lansdale carrying the glide bomb jamming equipment and three to starboard. We had USS Holder and USS Forster ahead of the columns by 3,000 yards.

247.

We were positioned off the port quarter between the escorts to provide AA cover. The rest of the destroyer contingent was astern as a reserve force so they could react and interdict any approaching ships.

Enemy reconnaissance planes had been following the convoy for most of the day and all the crews of the ships were on full alert. An enemy aircraft was spotted by our lookouts just before 23.00 Hrs at high altitude approaching the convoy. They were still far enough away not to cause us any problems. It was reported up the chain of command to the convoy leader. Soon enough at 23.15 the single aircraft was joined by up to ten more enemy planes this was detected on radar. Suddenly just a few minutes later a pathfinder flare appeared ahead of the convoy. With that marker flares began to dot the port flank at 23.30 Hrs. The escort Destroyers on command made smoke to try and obliterate the convoy from sight. As flares now completely illuminated the entire force a flock of planes that were in the immediate vicinity swarmed towards us. Practically all the escort ship's guns spoke up at that time and our guns on Delhi opened up. The amount of flak was extremely heavy creating an umbrella of shrapnel over the convoy. Thirty bombers and torpedo planes a mix of JU-88's and Dornier-217's commenced a well-coordinated attack.

All the ships started zigzagging at high speed to spoil the aim of any torpedo bombers. The Liberty ship SS Horace H. Lurton had bombs fall close enough to shake the ship and worry the crew. She was then just missed by a torpedo that crossed her stern between her and the next merchant.

248.

Within seconds of that happening the Horace H. Lurton was struck by a bomb from a dive-bomber that had slipped through. It exploded on the boat deck ripping her lifeboats to bits, with shrapnel ricocheting everywhere. The shrapnel flying about wounded four armed guards, at least the damage was minimal to the ship. One Armed guard was hit by flak aboard SS James E. Howard he fully recovered from his injuries on return to the States. Three of the crew of Liberty ship SS John C. Breckenbridge were hit by 20mm anti-aircraft fire by mistake from another ship. It was firing on a plane (blue on blue friendly fire) the same thing happened to SS Gideon Welles. Six of her crew were wounded and the SS Sarah J. Hale was hit by flak and 20mm shells from another of her sister ships.

HMS Delhi's gun crews spotted a JU88 strafing the convoy with machine gun fire on its approach. This gave Delhi's gunners the perfect aiming mark to let rip with everything they had. Every gun that could come to bear on the target opened up. The planes starboard side engine caught fire never the less the plane kept on coming full pelt. The sweating gunners kept up their fire relentlessly pumping lead into the air and enemy aircraft. Each one of the gunners was trying nervously to swallow the lumps in their throats as the enemy got closer. They were willing their bullets to hit the plane before it was too late. Finally just as the plane could drop her torpedoes or bombs it seemed they had been hit. The plane slid over with the cockpit shot up in a swerve out of control and crashed in flames into the sea.

About midnight USS Lansdale detected some sort of radio gliding bomb control signal and started jamming the signals. Seconds later she was straddled by a stick of bombs as she radically manoeuvred. Shrapnel from Flak landed on the deck of SS Harry Lane. It was not a surprise with the amount of fire that was being put up. Some of it had to come down on the ships eventually. As they say what goes up must come down and during war the amount of bullets fired into the air at aircraft or in celebration I am surprised that there is not more casualties as they come down. SS Hamlin Garland had another lucky miss when a torpedo exploded only 45 feet from her hull. Several bombs fell close to the SS Edward P. Costigan without damaging her.

12th April

At 23.30Hrs Destroyers: USS Holder (DE-401) and USS Forester were both stationed in front of the convoy in vanguard position. A plane of a type not positively identified was sighted off the port beam to them. They opened up with all their guns that could be brought to bear on the target. But the plane got through the flak and approached USS Holder at 23.39Hrs, flying very close to the water. It was observed to launch two torpedoes at a range of 300-400 yards virtually point blank range as this was spotted, flank speed was ordered and full left rudder. The torpedoes wakes were clearly visible and running straight at them.

At 23.40 Hrs before the change of course and speed had taken effect on USS Holder's course. The torpedoes struck amidships on the port side below the water line with two distinct heavy explosions. They were a fraction of a second apart and seemed of almost equal intensity a yellow flash accompanied the explosions. The ship settled and took on a four-degree list to starboard almost instantly. The torpedoes explosion's blasted open three of her four engine rooms slightly below the water line; she lost 17 men as the torpedoes exploded. The attack finished as the last flare went out about half an hour after midnight. Twelve wounded were transferred to the USS Forester from USS Holder. Without any propulsion of her own USS Holder was towed by HMS Mindful to Algiers. Where emergency repairs were carried out and U.S. Fleet tug Choctaw got her back to the States.

The destroyer USS Holder could attest to the ferocity of the air attacks in the Mediterranean off the coast of Algeria. The Luftwaffe used Cape Bengut on the coast of Algeria, as a rendezvous point before attacking passing convoys. Convoys passing the point could expect to receive the full attention of the enemy bombers flying from Italian air bases. The enemy planes were flown by experienced crews well trained in anti-shipping raids. Our escort force had done its job and no merchant ship was badly damaged in this raid and we cruised on at full alert.

15th April

We were on a flank carrying out a patrol for submarines whilst on lookout for enemy aircraft. We all had forgotten that we had deployed the CAT in tow just in case. Suddenly there was a big explosion astern of the ship and we thought oh no the aircraft were back from last night. So we were all looking in to the sky but there was no sign of any aircraft. Then somebody said maybe it's a shore battery they can fire this far can't they. So we waited to see if any other shells came flying in but no nothing happened. All of a sudden the skipper remembered the CAT, so we hauled the CAT in and it was blown apart. It was a sub that had fired off a gnat torpedo which homed in on our CAT and blew it all to bits. That's when we knew there had been a U-boat in the area and we were being hunted. So we started irregular erratic manoeuvres to throw them off. Our sonar operator was on full alert attempting to try and pick them up on ASDIC. After a few hours of this finding nothing we gave up and increased speed to catch up with the convoy and warn them. After we had caught them up the whole convoy was on full alert for submarines for four hours. After all the ships reported nothing found the convoy relaxed back to regular convoy routines.

16th April

At sunset the convoy was 15 to 20 miles east of Derna, Libya. U-407 fired a spread of three torpedoes at three overlapping steamers in the convoy. Two of the torpedoes struck home hitting the Meyer London and Thomas G. Masaryk.

252.

One of the torpedoes hit the Meyer London on the port side in number five hold the explosion blew a large column of oil and water over the stern. The explosion threw two of her armed guard over the side of the ship it also demolished the gun crew's quarters and injured the men standing watch on the aft gun. The damage was extensive to the ship it blew off the screw and rudder and left the fan tail hanging at a 15 degree angle. The ship now out of control, nearly collided with the Thomas G. Masaryk missing her by only 20 feet. The merchant ship HMS La Malouine a Flower-class corvette came to the rescue of the two seamen that were thrown overboard. The rest of The Meyer London's crew: 8 officers, 37 crewmen and 27 armed guards abandoned ship in four lifeboats eight of them were wounded. The fatally hit ship sank in a little more than an hour slipping beneath the waves. The crew in the lifeboats were picked up by HMS La Malouine an hour later when things started to calm down.

The torpedo that hit the Thomas G. Masaryk was in the side of hold No.3 setting fire to her cargo. She was carrying drums of acetone and they burnt bright blue and extremely hot. The flames spread rapidly and the brave crew fought the fire to try and save the ship and her cargo. She was taken in tow to try and beach her in shallow water at Meneola bay in the Gulf of Bomba, Libya. There she was scuttled to extinguish the flames. Remarkably not a life was lost on either ship.

A skeleton-armed guard was placed on board Thomas G. Masaryk to protect her and her cargo. They defended of a German plane who tried to strafe and bomb the ship on the 27th May before the ship was recovered on the 28th May.

17th April
UGS-37 arrives at Bizerte after defending the convoy the anti-Aircraft fire scored 7 Junkers-88's belonging to III & I KG/77 and one Dornier from 5KG/100. These loses demonstrated the strong defences of the escort group and their anti-aircraft shield. HMS Delhi returned to Gibraltar temporarily to refuel, rearm and re-supply and receive orders for convoy UGS38.

CHAPTER FIFTEEN
UGS-38

19th April
It was late in the day when UGS-38 arrived and we joined the convoy.

UGS-38 consisted of 105 merchant ships of which there were 28 troop ships carrying 12,378 troops. There were also 21 escort ships in total so it was well protected. USS Lansdale and two other Destroyers had the equipment to jam remote control glider bomb transmissions; the Americans called them Jig ships. Our ship HMS Delhi with Dutch Cruiser Heemskerck was used primarily for AA defence.

The enemy could strike suddenly and effectively against our large convoys. The most dangerous period was when dusk was melting into darkness. Lansdale and Heemskerck were posted on the port side of the convoy inter mingled with the escorts. We were posted on the starboard side mixed with the escorts. We had two British minesweepers HMS Speedy ahead of the convoy and HMS Sustain on the beam to starboard of the convoy. We had a British rescue tug HMS Aspirant travelling with us in the pack. There was also U.S. Coast Guard Cutter USCGC Taney as part of the escort group. Hidden within the convoy we had 3 of our British submarines: HMS Sickle, Spirit and Stratagem. Travelling on the surface trying to get to Malta unseen in amongst the merchants another reason we was travelling so slow.

The collection of ships proceeded at about eight knots along the North African coast. We knew from experience and intelligence that the Straits of Gibraltar was watched. The enemy knew when the convoy had passed and at what speed. We also knew they were keeping an eye on us from high flying reconnaissance planes from afar. As we would pick up a blip on radar occasionally but we never saw them.

20th April
All through the day there were several reports of enemy planes shadowing the convoy. But none of these planes were actually sighted they were just seen on radar. Apart from one unidentified plane flying at an extremely high altitude in a westerly direction, showing a vapour trail that gave it away. Although several alarms had been raised during the day the convoy was still untouched as it approached and passed Cape Bengut. The light was beginning to fail as dusk was coming on, all of the officers and crew were on stand to just in case.

19.40 Hrs
We were off the Algerian coast getting on 5 miles to the east of Cape Bengut. An action station was called for air raid red because radar indicated 2 to 6 enemy planes were near. But nothing was seen by the lookouts in the darkening sky.

19.50 Hrs

Unfortunately the weather conditions did not favour our attacking forces. It was a clear sky and we had a calm sea, flat as a mill pond and you could see for miles. As there were no mistral winds bringing in the bad weather and clouds. USS Sustain reported detecting enemy radar transmissions but no enemy aircraft were spotted by eye or radarscope.

20.30 Hrs

USS Lansdale signals Sunray the convoy commander on U.S. Coast Guard Cutter Taney. Explaining why he considered an attack was imminent and probable. the convoy commander put us all at stand too an alert position all guns loaded and made ready.

20.45 Hrs

USS Sustain reports glider bomb transmissions and Lansdale and HMS Speedy confirm it. Lansdale immediately starts to jam the signals and the other two Jig ships commence their music jamming.

Lansdale and the other Jig ships unknown to them had detected the German remote control signals for their glide bombs. The signals came from an attack on a French convoy passing one hundred miles north of their location. They're jamming even at that distance frustrated the Germans in their attempts to use their weapons and the unseen convoy benefited from ours.

257.

20.50 Hrs

Unknown to the convoy and us U-boat U-969 had been trailing us all. She had tried to set up for an attack but due to technical problems had to retire unsuccessful. German torpedo planes a mix of Junkers 88's and Heinkel 111's approached the convoy from the east in the growing darkness. The Junkers 88's and Heinkel 111's approached from the landward side of the convoy. They used the shadow of the landmass to cover their silhouettes in the sky. This made the escort's radar useless because of the echo from the land causing a static shadow on the radar screens. The attackers came in low and fast, with no flare announcements giving them away. They used the moonlight to the west as a horizon to outline their targets which was of course our ships.

20.53 Hrs

USS Pride, USS Lowe, USS Joseph and the E. Campbell were stationed in front of the convoy as vanguard. USS Pride intercepted a conversation in German on her VHF radio. Her SC radar at the exact same time momentarily made contact on a bunch of planes bearing 050° about 40 miles out. She assumed the aircraft was hostile as there was considerable radar jamming coming from their formation. The convoy Leader quickly ordered the escorts to make smoke and begin evasive manoeuvres. On receipt of the orders the Pride, Lowe and Campbell started up their smoke generators. They began to lay a dense smoke screen across the exposed front of the convoy.

21.01 Hrs

The big Junkers JU-88's of the first wave skimmed the water and then turned tightly to approach the convoy from head on. USS Lowe in the vanguard reported radar contact on five enemy planes. They came from dead ahead through the smoke screen.

It just goes to prove smoke screens can be a double edged weapon. They can provide cover for your ships from the enemy. But they also let the enemy know where you are and block the enemy from sight for your gunners.

All of a sudden the radio was a blaze with reports Campbell's radio operator sent in panic "They are all around me, they are all around me" and a split second later "They are the enemy, they are the enemy. Something like twenty-four JU-88's and Heinkel 111's armed with aerial torpedoes struck in three waves. Each wave struck with less than a minute apart, right on top of each other. On the port side Lansdale's SC and SG radar picked up planes bearing 140° at a range of 15,000 yards interference and jamming made radar identification difficult.

2103 Hrs

All the escort ships on the Starboard side of the convoy including Delhi commenced firing as targets came into arcs of fire. The effect was amazing with the tracer's criss crossing the sky like fireworks with streamers attached. On the port bow of the convoy Lansdale SG radar picked up another contact bearing north 5,000 yards range. Lowe reported at the same time another attacking group from the port bow.

259.

They were coming in a pincer type attack on both sides to separate the fire from us. Lowe reported sighting five enemy planes flying low over the water. Lansdale took aggressive strafing fire from a low flying plane on the starboard bow. Seconds later a torpedo hit SS Paul Hamilton a merchant in the convoy. The Paul Hamilton was carrying 501 troops and a cargo of 7,000 tons of high explosives. The torpedo set of an instant chain reaction and the entire cargo exploded. Paul Hamilton was blown to bits, and every person on board a total of 580 was killed apart from one Armed Guard. The explosion created a huge fireball that leaped several hundred feet in the air illuminating the convoy like daylight. The explosion creating a mushroom cloud rising up rapidly skyward it went thousands of feet in the air that could be seen for miles. She quickly broke up and went to the bottom of the sea in bits within a matter of minutes.

21.04 Hrs
Luckily by the light of the explosion and fireball other ships sighted four more planes coming in on the starboard beam. Instantly they were engaged in fire by machine gun and AA batteries aboard all the ships. The second wave about seven JU-88s came on the heels of the first almost to the minute. They split up some taking starboard and some port of the convoy. The SS Stephen .F. Austin was under attack one torpedo passed twenty feet from her stern lucky for them. Unluckily the rouge torpedo in amongst the convoy struck the SS Samite.

Two bombs fell within a few feet of the SS Stephen F. Austin and she hit back at the aircraft with anything she could throw up at them. Her armed guards fired everything from small arms (rifles and pistols) through .30 and .50 browning machine guns to a pompom. Stephen F. Austin armed guards hit the Ju-88 that fired the first torpedo destroying it. They then switched fire on to the second plane but she only managed to fire one round. Before the Ju-88 launched a torpedo at them the torpedo struck her badly damaging the ship. She began to take on water and the captain ordered abandon ship. She was abandoned but after the air attack had finished the crew re-boarded and saved the ship. The only casualties the crew received were two armed guards wounded by strafing fire. She received assistance from British rescue tug HMS Hengist and proceeded to Algiers. The SS Samite was damaged but stayed afloat and remained with the convoy. The enemy's second wave also hit the SS Royal Star that sank within forty minutes but by chance all the crew survived with minor injuries.

The third wave bore down on the port bow of the convoy they had five JU-88's. At the same time coming in from the starboard bow was another five but this time it was Heinkel 111's. The JU-88's went running through the convoy to set up a coordinated attack directly against Lansdale. The JU-88's were engaged in fire from the antiaircraft guns of every ship they passed. The USS Newell identified JU88's passing astern of the ship. She engaged them with a withering amount of machine gun fire hitting the aft plane.

The JU-88 was seen to explode in to bits to the port side of USS Newell. Lansdale's main battery opened up on planes that were off on her port side. They were still at a fair distance away, estimated at 3,000 yards from the ship. She fired three full salvos of all her guns. The second and third salvo's made direct hits on planes. One was confirmed seen crashing into the sea and one exploded in mid-air. It seemed briefly that Lansdale was taking the brunt of the attacks like they were singling her out. Lansdale was holding her own against over whelming odds but the swarms of attackers would prove to be too much.

All the ships in the convoy fired whenever planes were visible in the growing darkness. The Lansdale narrowly missed disaster as a torpedo passed her bow by feet. But yet again another rogue torpedo hit the SS Paul Hamilton she exploded hurling steel and fuel oil into the air. The cocktail of fuel oil and seawater rained down and fell in a deluge on the decks of nearby ships. The oil was coming down like a cloudburst with flying steel intermingled with it. SS Fitzhugh Lee's entire gun battery was knocked out of commission hit by flying shrapnel. Three of her armed guards were severely wounded and some army personnel aboard her were minor casualties.

There were numerous reports of ships that had thought they had taken a plane down, many of them trying to claim the same plane at once. But in total thanks to the heavy AA fire disrupting the attack five x JU-88's and 2 Heinkel 111's were shot down and four enemy fighters from their escorting squadron also got knocked out of the sky.

262.

21.05 Hrs

All of a sudden the coordinate torpedo attack against Lansdale worked to a T. Both sets of aircraft, two on the port side and three on the starboard attacked. The commanding officer had just gone out on to the port wing of the bridge. He watched the planes on the port quarter setting up for a run. When he heard the junior officer who was looking through binoculars on the bridge call out. "Torpedoes approaching from the port". Luckily these missed the ship by only a few feet.

The commanding officer knew that the planes on the starboard side were coming in on approach to drop their deadly load. So he ordered right full rudder and increased speed to 15 knots. The group of planes on the starboard dropped a bunch of torpedoes most missed. But one struck the ship in the forward boiler room it had a 600lb warhead. The explosion broke her keel and the main deck over the forward boiler room was ruptured. The explosion ripped right through the ship to the port side. Creating a massive hole below the water line as well as in the starboard side where it entered. The forward stack was knocked over by the shock wave that radiated through the ship by the explosion.

Lansdale inclinator meter on the bridge that shows the angle of the ship in rough weather showed a 12° list to port virtually immediately. The ships structure of the hull at the point of explosion was twisted drastically and she was visibly lower in the water at the stern. The explosion ruptured the forward bulkhead of the boiler room, which flooded the I.C. Room, the ships office, and the aft deck mess hall.

263.

HMS Lansdale's rudder was jammed at 22° to the port and power was lost to the steering engines, as well as all power was lost to the forward engine room. The aft engine room made turns for 22 knots on the port screw to try to maintain the ships speed of 15 knots. All power and lights were out forward of the impact area. The bridge had no communication with the aft of the ship past the damage. The cables to the steering control on the bridge were damaged and parted at the explosion point, so steering was lost. All telephones aft were out except for a sound powered phone circuit between the aft engine room and the aft boiler room. Lighting functioned aft until the ship was abandoned. All power was lost on the main battery guns and the 40mm anti-aircraft guns so they were useless. The single 40mm mounted guns and the twin port side 40mm operated in manual. So they could be hand traversed and elevated to fire. Lansdale had her back broken; rudder jammed, and was listing to port.

The destroyer steamed in a circle at thirteen knots un-controlled. Lansdale's crew refused to quit the fight despite all the casualties. With the single 40mm mounted guns, twin port side 40mm and machine gun battery's they kept planes under fire. The plane that had dropped the torpedo that hit her came over the forecastle and then down the port side. The enemy plane was hit by the starboard machine gun battery, and raked with fire from the port 40mm guns. It received direct hits from the port 20mm's, and by the port 40mm gun mount. The enemy's plane was absolutely riddled and one of its motors burst into flames. It lost control and crashed into the sea not far from Lansdale.

Lansdale's forward boiler room was still on fire burning ferociously. There were copious amounts of smoke being emitted and this made the ship a conspicuous target. Two more JU-88's attacked the ship one plane came in on the port bow and the other on the port beam amidships. They had no qualms and launched torpedoes at the stricken ship. One torpedo went past the bow only just clearing it by 15 feet. The other torpedo passed astern by twenty feet. Both planes were taken under fire by the port machine gun battery and the single 40mm on the main deck. The 40mm on the main deck continued to fire with its crew up to their knees in water. After being riddled with fire one of the planes was seen to crash into the sea a few miles away.

21.15 Hrs

The captain thought the ship could be saved and could be kept afloat. He ordered the crew remaining to lighten the ship as much as possible in the hope this would help. The three remaining crew of the forward repair party started jettisoning weight from the forward section. The torpedo tubes were jammed fore and aft and it was impossible to jettison the torpedoes without power to the winches. All the shells from the upper handling room of gun turret No.1 were jettisoned just literally thrown by hand over the side. Then the crew went on to No. 2 guns upper handling room to empty it, as the guns were useless. The gun crews then commenced to jettison the main magazine, but the winch was damaged and had to do it by hand. All the heavy equipment was impossible to get over the side so had to be left.

While all this was happening every effort was being made by the engineers and stokers to free up the rudder and try and put out fires. Some of the crew searched the ship to find casualties and relocate them to a central spot on the ship and provide first aid. But to no avail the work on the rudder was going nowhere it just wasn't going to happen without a bit of peace and time to send divers over the side.

21.22 Hrs
With the inclinometer on the bridge reading 45° and it was continually increasing every minute. The commanding officer was of the opinion that the ship was in danger of rolling completely over. He therefore gave the order to abandon ship. As there was no way to communicate with the aft part of the ship, the crew in the stern did not get the order straight away. They only started to abandon ship when they saw personnel forward of the damaged area jumping clear abandoning ship.

Because of the utter chaos aboard and due to lack of communication, the aft boiler room was not abandoned. The stokers started to see water starting to come down the escape hatch so they decided enough was enough time to go. Both boilers were secured before abandoning to prevent a boiler explosion as seawater entered the red-hot furnace. This would give the crew more time to get clear. They went up the escape ladders to the machine gun deck. The aft engine room was the same it was only abandoned, when water started to come down from the main deck hatch high on the starboard side.

266.

The port side single mount 40mm anti-aircraft gun crew eventually abandoned their gun, when it was submerged and they were unable to fire it. The machine gun crews only abandoned their post when they found they were suddenly firing standing in water on the machine gun deck. The port battery abandoned when they could not get their guns to bear on the enemy planes due to the list. All the bridge personnel went over the starboard wing windshield and climbed down the side. They went via the first superstructure deck to the forecastle deck before going over the side. Efforts by the crew to launch the starboard forward life raft were unsuccessful, as it was thoroughly jammed in its pulley mechanism.

21.30 Hrs
The list had continually increased to a rough guess of 55° and the ship began to creak and groan as it began to break up. Five minutes later, with agonising ripping of metal sounds she broke in half. The stern section of Lansdale went to the bottom quickly. The bow section remained afloat for 20 min to give a final fanfare before sinking to the depths.

USS Menges and USS Newell came to the rescue and picked up the survivors. Out of a crew of 282 officers and men 234 were rescued within a few hours. Seven bodies were recovered and 42 were recorded as missing in action "may they rest in peace".

267.

This fierce and brief action indicates how strong the defence of convoys had become. This attack on the convoy UGS-38 marked the last major action by the Germans against convoys in the Mediterranean. It might have turned out a lot harsher, but for the fact that the enemy air squadrons involved in it. Had earlier that evening attacked another convoy? When they struck at UGS-38 they were either out of radio-controlled bombs or were fed up with the control signals being intercepted. I believe the Germans were aware of the presence of the jamming ships. They specifically targeted USS Lansdale as five to seven torpedoes were fired at her. That alone indicates she was a specific target rather than a target of opportunity.

CHAPTER SIXTEEN
CONVOY GUS-38

We waited at Port Said to join US-bound convoy GUS-38. Initially this was made up of 80 merchant ships on the 24th April. Initially it was going to take a route through the Mediterranean picking up ships as it went along to Bizerte, Tunisia. But it was soon to grow to be 107 merchant ships in 16 columns of six or seven by the time we got to Gibraltar.

GUS stood for Gibraltar to United States. Some of the merchant ships seemed to enjoy the muscular presence of our British cruiser. We joined the American escort screening vessels to give them an extra punch in AA defence. The same general procedures prevailed in this convoy as we had learned to expect with the Americans. They had adopted the Royal Navy's operating procedures as we had been doing the job for longer. Manoeuvring instructions i.e. changes in route came from the convoy commodore/ commander by flags hoisted up the signals mast. The daily change of positions throughout the convoy at noon came by flag signals as well. At night a system of coloured lights was used instead of flags for emergency course changes. These were mounted on a small mast on the flying bridge, affectionately known as the "Christmas tree". Of course the escort ships had the freedom to race around the convoy to various positions. Radio signals from the commander's vessel were used when in contact with the enemy to speed up reactions.

269.

3rd May 1944

U-boat U-371 a type VIIC submarine was on patrol and spotted our convoy approaching. Captain Fesski ordered his boat to submerged to let the convoy pass and to set up for an attack. After all the ships had passed overhead he ordered the submarine to surface to attack the convoy from behind. USS Pride (DE-323) stationed 3,000 yards of the port beam of the last ship in the port column. USS Pride reported at 21.39 Hrs that her lookouts spotted a small yellow flickering light on the surface, at a distance of one and a half miles bearing 2600°. The Escort commander ordered them to investigate the light source by circling the light at a range of 500 yards and observing. The pride reported the light was a flare bobbing about, although the sea was calm. She was unable to determine the exact identity or type of flare. So the Pride returned to her station around the convoy and carried on with routine.

22.50 Hrs

Convoy course 270° speed 8 knots Destroyer USS Menges (DE-320) who was stationed astern of the convoy. She reported a surface target contact on radar astern of the ship on course 290° it was 10,000 yards away from the convoy. She was commencing a plot to keep an eye on the strange contact.

23.00 Hrs

Hrs Menges reported the target had reversed its course and was approaching the convoy.

23.14 Hrs

USS Menges reported she had lost the target it had just disappeared at 3500 yards and they were going in for a sonar search. The U-boat had fired an acoustic torpedo at the closing destroyer and quickly submerged to escape the Destroyer's wrath. The torpedo homed in on the noise from the Menges screw hitting her. The explosion was so violent that the aft third of the Destroyer was a mangled wreck.

23.34 Hrs

Menges reported by flashing Morse spotlight that she had been torpedoed. Although seriously damaged the Menges remained afloat the explosion killed 31 of the crew and wounded 25 others. The commander refused to give the order to abandon ship as long as there was a chance of saving her. Several of the crewmembers heroically jumped astride torpedoes, which had broken free from their secure storage locations. The torpedoes were loosened in the blast and were endangering the ship rolling about. They quickly disarmed them and secured them on to the deck and other equipment which they could tie them off to.

23.36 Hrs

US Coast Guard manned Destroyer USS Pride was sent to assist Menges. While USS Campbell searched for the submarine they located it with sonar and attacked it with depth charges.

USS Campbell made wide zig-zags in a circle pattern to the north of Menges. They positioned themselves in order to have the moon light between themselves and the Menges and Pride. This assisted in keeping an eye out for surface contacts. While approaching the area about 4,000 yards from Menges, Campbell dropped two depth charges. Set at 100 feet with an interval of about one minute, so as to disconcert the enemy submarine. Hopefully it would also distract any acoustic torpedoes, which might have been fired in the direction of the disabled Menges.

4th May 1944
At 00.35 Hrs as USS Pride moved in to assist Menges her (SL) radar picked up a highflying aircraft. The aircraft circled over Menges, Pride and the Campbell. At the same time lookouts reported seeing the same type of yellow flickering light that was seen earlier. It was on the port bow the distance was undetermined.

00.47 Hrs
USS Pride picked up a sound contact while manoeuvring near Menges at a depth of 1,500 fathoms. She rolled one depth charge set at 100 feet as an offensive defence measure against possible torpedo attack. USS Campbell ordered her hedgehog manned as she detected the submarine bearing 150° at a range of 1200 yards.

01.00 Hrs

Campbell passed directly over the submarine, her Fathometer indicated disturbance over the entire dial. As she went to fire the hedgehog it failed to fire. Quick checks on the system could not determine the fault so its use was abandoned. Contact with the submarine was held at 100 yards to try and prevent a counter attack as it was too close for a torpedo to arm.

01.04 Hrs

Suddenly the radar picked up a small blip within 700 yards for a split second then it disappeared. Campbell decided to roll a depth charge set at 100 feet as an offensive counter measure against a torpedo. HMS Aspirant rescue tug snuck in and took Menges in tow to Bougie, Algeria, for temporary repairs. Whilst this was happening five of our ships continued to try and hunt down the U-boat.

HMS Blankney (sub chaser), FFS Senegalese (Free French Destroyer), French DD Alycon, USS Joseph e. Campbell and USS Pride tried to hunt down U-371. The hunt went all through the next day into the night. They had countless sonar contacts and had carried out a multitude of depth charge attacks whilst systematically searching for the submarine. The submarine did some fancy manoeuvring and fish tailing to avoid them.

4 May 1944

01.20 Hrs Finally French destroyer Senegalese reported a submarine on the surface bearing 230° at a range of 2 miles in the Gulf of Bougie.

273.

French destroyer Senegalese went immediately to General quarters. Set flank speed on a course of 2700° to try and get to the north of the sub. They did this in order to cut it off from escaping north away from the other ships. Trapped between the ships and the north coast of Africa there was little the U-boat could do to escape.

01.26 Hrs
USS Pride commenced plotting the submarine at a range of 6 ½ miles bearing 230°. FFS Senegalese began directing heavy fire at the submarine it was only a matter of time before the sub was cornered. Senegalese was quite evidently doing a fine job with the sub.

01.55 Hrs
FFS Senegalese got a little too confident in her abilities and got a little too close for comfort. The U-boat saw their chance to retaliated and fired off a torpedo.

01.59 Hrs Senegalese reported a torpedo had hit her. Thou damaged she managed to send the location of the submarine. Senegalese reported the submarine was trying to submerge, and she gave the other ships her course bearing and range. She then sailed clear of the area out of danger to carry out emergency repairs. But the U371 submarine had been mortally wounded with water leaking in to the hull from the pummelling she had received from Senegalese. The exhausted Captain Fenski and his crew came to a decision.

With her batteries almost flat Oberleutenant Horst-Arno Fenski ordered the U-boat to remain on the surface. Whilst the crew abandoned the submarine he would scuttle his boat sending her to the bottom. With three dead crewmembers aboard at least he had saved 49 crewmembers.

02.35 Hrs
The Pride remained to seaward as protection. The German survivors were located and picked up by the rest of the ships. After the rescue they were all transferred to the USS J.E. Campbell who took them to Algiers. The Menges was safely towed into port and later returned to the States. In the States Menges received a new stern off another destroyer USS Holder that had her bow destroyed. She re-joined the fleet in record time within a couple of weeks.

We continued with the routine convoy duties until the late morning when we had an air raid red pipe up. There was a massive barrage of anti-aircraft fire given by our ship and the others. Until we found out it was a false alarm given off because a lone German plane was flying past the convoy. The German plane was at a high altitude, in fact too high to hit with any of our guns. The rest of the day went by without incident but what we didn't know was that we was about to lose another of our destroyer escorts.

5th May
02.30 Hrs
Our convoy was about 120 miles northwest of Oran,
Algeria steaming west in calm seas with little wind. The
Destroyer screen up front made radar contact 16 miles
ahead. The Destroyer USS Laning (DE-159) was
dispatched to investigate at high speed. It soon radioed
back to us the contact had disappeared, indicating that it
was probably another U-boat hunting the convoy. We
found out much later after the war the U-boat was the U-
967 commanded by Abrecht Brandi. He was one of the
only two U-boat commanders to receive the Knight's Cross
with Oak Leaves, Swords and Diamonds, the highest
German military decoration.

The commander of the escort ships sent an additional
three Destroyers including the USS Fechteler and our ship
to assist USS Laning in finding the submarine. After a short
while we were re-ordered to return to the main body of the
convoy. Our primary role for this convoy was AA defence
not sub-hunting our depth charges were for defence not
offence.

03.45 Hrs
A heavy explosion detonated between the screening
Destroyers out in front and the main body of the convoy.
The escorting commander assumed that the explosion was
from an acoustic torpedo. That had been set off by the
sounds of the ships screws at the end of its run, as it did not
hit a single ship.

The U-boat hunting us must have fired the torpedo with blind hope. It was too far of a range and it must have got to its limit of run and detonated. The Destroyer escorts were quick on the game, they did a sonar sweep of the area and quickly confirm the presence of a submerged contact. The commodore of the convoy ordered an emergency turn to starboard. For the convoy to take evasive action as the Destroyers went in to hunt the U-boat down.

04.41 Hrs
USS Fechteler and Laning moved in to attack an echo located outline of a U-boat. Laning closed in quickly with a depth charge attack. USS Fechteler's crew readied their depth charges to do a parallel run alongside. This was to double their chances of hitting the damned submarine. Lookouts suddenly spotted the unmistakable track of a torpedo running in the water heading directly for USS Fechteler. The captain immediately ordered evasive manoeuvres. The Fechteler was in the process of executing an emergency turn to port when the GNAT torpedo homed in on her engine noise. The torpedo struck the destroyer directly amidships on the bottom of her hull. It seemed like she was lifted clear of the water by the force of the explosion, the impact was catastrophic. The Fechteler's hull and keel were broken as she slammed back down on the surface and quickly began to wrench apart. As the ship wallowed taking on water writhing as the extra weight ripped her apart.

The USS Laning stood by to assist as the Fechtelers captain realised she was going down fast and ordered abandon ship. As his ship was tearing in two and breaking apart the surviving crew made their escape.

Assisting in the rescue of the crew was the British ocean tug Hengist. That had come up from her position at the rear of the convoy as the convoy turned away. The rescue tugs were known to be the guardian angels of the convoys as they rescued so many of the sailors and ships in distress. Both parts of the Fechteler sank shortly after the majority of the crew got off. Twenty-nine of the crew lost their lives sadly, twenty-six injured out of the one hundred and eighteen crewmembers that survived the tragedy. The saved crew were transferred to the USS Laning who took them to Gibraltar. U-967 escaped despite a furious counter depth charge assault. She sneaked away to fight another day.

Shortly after the attack we were all dumbfounded. As a sailing schooner flying the Spanish flag sailed unmolested through the convoy. It was an odd and unsettling feeling as we watched this majestic yacht sail through our numbers with neutral colours flying. The sight of this sailing vessel immediately conjured up images of pirates on the Spanish mane for the most of us. The nervous officers aboard all thought it was full of enemy agents and that we should have challenged her. As the convoy passed Gibraltar we were assigned to put into port as we were not needed for the trans-Atlantic crossing.

28th May

Anzio Annie's secret is out.

We found out what had happened at Anzio and there was a delighted feeling going about the ship. All the men that had been under fire from those brutal guns were extremely overjoyed. In a lapse of discipline and complacency there was a super mistake by the Germans the guns were out of sight in their tunnel as usual. Several of the gun crews went outside to sun themselves near the tunnel entrance as it was a nice day. One of our spotter planes suddenly appeared at a low height buzzing them taking photos it was following the train lines in hope of catching the guns.

The gun crews panicked and some of them ran towards the safety of the tunnel entrance. The aircrew noticed the movement of the soldiers and pin pointed a possible location. The commander of the guns captain Borcher decided to expend half of his remaining ammunition that night just in case of an attack.

This only infused the Allied command to strike at that possible location. At dawn on the 29th eight P-40's arrived carrying a 1,000lb bomb each. They struck at the tunnel entrance and luckily one bomb fell just into the tunnel destroyed the gun crew's kitchen and admin rail car sadly there was no damage to the guns.

It was clear that the Allies knew where to find the guns and the Germans could expect more air raids to destroy the guns. The Germans would have to move them or lose them either to air attack or by the advancing troops from the beachhead.

279.

That night they fired off their last 16 massive rounds. They then loaded up their equipment and moved the gun trains steamed to the north as fast as they could. Unfortunately there were no working rail tracks to the north, as our Air Forces did a grand job in demolition obliterating them. The Germans had to take the guns to the port of Civiaveccia in a hope Naval forces could evacuate them. But the German Navy could not get their barges through to help them. The Germans were forced to make the guns unusable and abandon them to be captured by our troops.

Quite a few cheers went up when we heard this and the captain ordered an extra tot for everyone in celebration.

June
Was a quite month for us at Gibraltar with shore leave and essential maintenance was done to the ship. Over the next few days the dockworkers could clean the hull off and give it a coat of antifouling paint. Then it was our time to do a boiler clean and catch up on our own admin. The crew did vital maintenance on the rest of the ship like greasing the working parts of the ship and repainting, oiling the working parts of the guns and ram rodding out the barrels. The ship was a hive of activity all working and resting in shifts to get the ship spick and span and operating at a high standard. We missed a lot of action on the D-Day landings on the 6th June mores the pity we were all looking forward to taking part in it but the orders never came for us.

CHAPTER SEVENTEEN
OPERATION DRAGON

July 1944
We were nominated for duty with Task Group 88.1 of the Carrier Task Force 88. We were to provide support during the planned landings in the South of France Operation Anvil. Later the name changed to Operation Dragon.

Task Force 88.1 consisted of
HMS Pursuer Carrier, carrying 881 Naval Air Squadron with F4F Grumman Wildcat's,
HMS Searcher Carrier, carrying 882 Naval Air Squadron with F4F Grumman Wildcat's,
HMS Attacker Carrier, carrying 879 Naval Air Squadron with Seafire's the naval version of the Spitfire,
HMS Emperor Carrier, carrying 800 Naval Air Squadron with Grumman F6F Hellcat's,
HMS Khedive Carrier, carrying 899 Naval Air Squadron with Seafire's,
HMS Hunter Carrier, carrying 807 Naval Air Squadron with Seafire's,
HMS Stalker Carrier, carrying 809 Naval Air Squadron with Seafire's,
HMS Royalist dido class light Cruiser (Flagship),
HMS Delhi (our ship) light Cruiser,
HMS Caledon and HMS Colombo, Both light Cruisers,
6 British Destroyers HMS Troubridge, Tuscan, Tyrian, Teazer, Tumult, Wheatland,
1 Greek Destroyer HMS Echo renamed to HHMS Navarinon.

The operation was controversial from the time it was first proposed. Due to arguments between Eisenhower's American military leadership and our British High command. Churchill argued against it saying it diverted military resources that were better deployed elsewhere. The French Leaders pressed the Americans for an invasion to happen. Finally on The 14th July the Allied Combined Chiefs of Staff authorized the operation. The operation was delayed for a few weeks for final preparations and for improved weather conditions. The chief objective of the operation was to capture the important ports of Marseille and Toulon.

1st August
All the ships going to be involved with Operation Dragon got under way to our rendezvous points. Ours was at Naples Italy where we joined up with the rest of Task Force 88.1. Then we would be under overall command of the US Navy "some of us had our trepidations about this".

Efforts were made to soften up the whole coast in the days and weeks before the invasion. Of course there was a deception plan with bomber pilots doing their best to disguise the real targets by heavily bombing sites from Genoa, Italy to well past Marseilles to the west. The preceding bombing for the Operation together with resistance sabotage acts hit the Germans heavily. To disrupt the railways, damage the road and rail bridges and disabling the communications network. This would also block the Germans chances to reinforce after we had started the landings.

13Th August

At about 18.00 Hrs all the separate convoys and task forces left their independent rendezvous points. They were at various ports throughout the Mediterranean and they all headed for the operation area on separate routes. This was to distract and confuse the enemy so they would not know the exact location of the landing. Until the last moment and it was too late for them to pre-empt the landing.

Prior to the main invasion, the Hyeres Islands of Port-Cros and Levant, had to be neutralized. The Germans had large gun emplacements on both Islands. The guns could reach the proposed Allied landing areas and the sea-lanes the troop ships would take to the beachheads. The First Special Service Force (SFFS) was made up of 3 regiments of American and Canadian troops. They were specially trained for this sort of operation. SFFS would do this mission as they were trained up in amphibious assaults and mountaineering. Their missions would be called Operation Sitka.

It should be remembered that Operation Dragon was primarily a US one with a significant number of French forces also employed. The main British involvement was in the Naval forces with some 350 Royal Navy ships involved just over one third of the whole of the naval force and over half of the aircraft that were used also came from British aircraft and Carriers.

14th August

After 22.00 Hrs the men of 2nd and 3rd regiments transferred to their rubber assault rafts off Levant. The 1st regiment did the same off Port-Cros. Upon arriving ashore both assault teams had to scramble and climb cliffs surrounding the Islands from 40 to 50 feet high. On Levant the 2nd and 3rd regiments faced sporadic resistance that became more intense toward the port area. As the Special Forces gained the upper hand on the Island it was found that the coastal defence batteries were just well camouflaged dummy gun positions. This left a bad taste in the mouths of the troops that had worked so hard to capture them. A right old slagging off of the intelligence gatherers ensued right up the rank structure from Privates to Majors.

On Port-Cros the 1st regiment drove the German defenders across the island where they made a last stand in an old fort. The battle continued for two days until HMS Ramilles took aim. Training her heavy guns on the fort where the Germans were barricaded. She opened fire with all her guns giving them a good hammering. The German garrison surrendered on the morning of the 17th battered and bruised.

Before the main invasion happened one more operation took place named Operation Span. This was a deception plan, aimed to confuse the German defenders with fake landings and fake parachute drops. This would aid in dispersing the enemy troops to cover an even larger area away from the actual landing zones. Even during the night and on the morning of the attack this went on.

Also a squadron of aircraft dropped aluminium strips to confuse German radar, over Marseilles and Toulon areas. Another Squadron of aircraft parachuted hundreds of booby-trapped dummies north of the cities. The German troops abandoned their positions and raced to confront this supposed threat. American aircraft were used to drop another three hundred dummy Para troops just north of La Ciotat with explosive devices that simulated rifle fire. German casualties from this drop were never found out but total confusion was caused within the German troops adding to the mayhem.

At the same time as the actual landings went in another decoy happened simultaneously. American PT (Patrol Torpedo) boats further confused the German radar operators by roaring in and out of various harbours. Landing craft and other amphibious vessels were employed with inflatable tanks and dummy soldiers on board them. Their task was to approach likely landing areas elsewhere in southern France and along the Italian coast. This tied down German troops and prevented their deployment against the real beachheads.

15th August
The sunrise revealed a clear Mediterranean morning. With the autumn storms and the French mistral winds still weeks away. It was perfect weather for D-Day in Southern France. With lessons learned from previous landings, the Allied minesweepers and frogmen cleared the approaches and the areas off the beachheads of underwater mines.

The minesweepers and frogmen stealthily cleared, under cover of darkness during the night. Then at 06.00 Hrs two hours before H-hour, One thousand three hundred Allied bombers began blasting the coast with saturation bombings. Then once the bombing was going inshore at 07.15 Hrs they used radio controlled Apex drones to deal with the threat of coastal obstructions. These were radio controlled LCVP's (essentially old expendable landing craft).

The LCVP's were filled to the brim with high explosives. They were designed to blast holes in the concrete coastal obstacle barriers the Germans built. They were closely followed by rocket firing LCT(R). Their job was primarily intended to detonate the land mines on the beach above the water line that had not been cleared with their incredible firepower. A second equally important side effect was to shred any barbwire that was set up on the beach.

As well as our task force of Carriers and aircraft the invasion force was supported by heavy gunfire from five venerable Battleships: USS Nevada, USS Texas, USS Arkansas, HMS Ramillies and the French Lorraine. They began firing at 07.30 Hrs on specific targets detected by aerial surveillance.It was a meagre contribution by the two American escort Aircraft Carriers compared to the British seven Aircraft Carriers. In support of the landing force was nine: Royal Navy light Cruisers and 14 Destroyers. To the Americans two heavy and 4 light Cruisers and fifty Destroyers.

The Free French navy provided five light Cruisers and seven Destroyers. During the first 64 hours of the invasion ninety four thousand troops there about were landed. They had with them twelve thousand vehicles and forty six thousand tons of stores. Most of the men and vehicles were landed by the end of the first day.

German resistance was found to be patchy and relatively poor. The previous landings in Normandy, France, had drawn many of the experienced troops and units there, away from our landings. The Allies found their advance was restricted by the lack of supplies, particularly petrol and diesel rather than the fighting. The unexpectedly overwhelming landings caused the Germans to effectively abandon southern France. They retreat as quickly as possible, under constant Allied attack as far as the Vosges Mountains. The air superiority with the British seven Escort Carriers was paramount to this and was possibly the greatest winning contribution. With land operations rapidly advancing it quickly outran the range of land-based aircraft this was fully taken on by our carrier force. They racked up a formidable tally of German vehicles and equipment destroyed and flew almost 1,000 sorties in the first eight days of the operation.

Overall the landings were an overwhelming success the casualties at the landings were mercifully very light. With only ninety-five killed and three hundred and eighty five wounded. Forty of these casualties were caused by one of the only few air raids that managed to sneak in to attack the beachhead.

287.

On the first day the 15th at 21.00 Hrs two Dornier DO-217's crept in, between the air cover patrols and delivered a Henschel Hs 293(anti-ship rocket powered missile) that sank the USS LST-282.

27th August
We were released from Operation Dragon Task Force 88.1. For strategic reasons we returned to Royal Navy control and returned to Gibraltar. This was for further Operations in the western Mediterranean.

13th September
Our ship was present at the formal re-entry of the free French Navy. This happened officially at the naval base at Toulon. This is where HMS Delhi and I split up as I received orders to return to England. It was a sad moment for me as the ship and I had been through a lot.

28.

29.

30.

31.

32.

33.

34.

290.

35.

36.

291.

CHAPTER EIGHTEEN
FAIRMILE B MOTOR LAUNCHES
ML-149

I was posted to HMS Hornet the base for Coastal Forces
Training. It was the home for the fast motorboats and
launches. They used to speed in and out of Portsmouth
during the war to harass German shipping. They were also
used as Air Sea Rescue for downed aircrew, Mine
sweeping duties, Mine laying duties, Navigational Leaders
or escorts for convoys, Coastal Raiding, Patrol boats,
Ambulance Launches, Anti-submarine patrols and
Clandestine landings on the coast of France. Everything
was buzzing with sailors going here there and everywhere.
*Reference picture 28.

I was to be trained on the Fairmile B Type motor
Launch. An excellent sea-keeping vessel it was built from
prefabricated wooden kits. The kits were sent to various
small boat yards around the UK and around the world to be
assembled. Each kit was made up of six packages, and each
package was designed to fit in a standard 15-ton lorry for
ease of transportation. Two American Hall Scott petrol
engines were chosen to power this versatile vessel. Because
pre-war searches for suppliers of high power diesel engines
suitable for marine use had proved fruitless. The petrol
engines of course represented a much greater fire hazard
than diesel engines.

With the fuel capacity of 10,478 Litres this was sufficient to give the boat a range of 1,500 miles at 12 knots. At the maximum speed of 20 Knots the range would be significantly cut down to around 800 miles. On occasions extra fuel tanks were fitted to the deck to significantly extend their range for long sea passages.

Length- 112 feet,
Beam- 18 feet 3 inches,
Draught- 4 feet 10 inches forward 5 feet ½ inches aft,
Engines- two Hall Scott Defenders, each 600 bhp max,
Displacement- 67 tons to 85 tons dependant on type of armament,   Normal crewmembers;
2 Officers, 2 Petty officers,
1 Chief Stoker, 2 Stokers,
2 Gunners, 1 Signalman,
1 Asdic Operator
1 Telegraphist,
1 Torpedo Rating, (If fitted with torpedo tubes),
1 Leading Seaman Coxswain,
3 Ordinary Seamen,
1 Cook.

These boats proved to be excellent sea keeping vessels in most weather conditions, which I was, thank full for. Though they did begin to broach in seas of force eight and above, rocking dangerously. This made most of the crew seasick even the most experienced sea hand. Our crewmembers and I suffered badly in severe weather up to force ten. We was thrown about continually and soaked to the skin.

293.

The boats could be reconfigured for different roles within forty-eight hours. As the decks were fitted with steel strips, that had tapped holes all the way along. Different types of armament could be bolted to the strips. In this way the boats could be fitted with a multitude of different equipment. Different types of armament that could be used were: Torpedo tubes, mines, depth chargers, various types of guns and other specialized equipment. As well as the crew's ad hock small arms whatever they could get hold of. It was also common practice to keep a bunch of hand grenades in a steel box bolted to the deck on the bridge. All the boats were fitted with ASDIC (sonar) as standard for submarine chasing so the Fairmile B became a veritable any task, any job, work horse of the Coastal Forces described in many a book as "maids of all work".

Armament variations;
Convoy escort
One 3-pounder Mk1 aft, Two 303" Lewis guns, Twelve depth charges, One Holeman projector or 2"rocket, flare launcher, Smoke generator.

Submarine chaser
One 3-pounder Mk1 forward, One single 20mm Orelikon amidships, One twin 20mm Orelikon aft, Twin 303" MG's on sides of bridge, Fourteen depth charges in chutes, One Y Gun with four reloads,
One, Holeman projector or 2"rocket flare launcher,
Smoke generator.

Mine Sweeper
40mm Bofors Mark III forward, one single 20mm Orelikon amidships, one twin 20mm Orelikon aft
Twin 303" MG's on sides of bridge, One Holeman projector or 2"rocket flare launcher, Smoke generator.

Mine laying
One 3-pounder Mk1 forward, one single 20mm Orelikon amidships, one twin 20mm Orelikon aft
Twin 303" MG's on sides of bridge, Nine moored contact mines or Eight ground influence mines were carried, One Holeman projector or 2"rocket flare launcher,
Smoke generator.

Torpedo boat
One 3-pounder Mk1 forward, Twin 303"MG's on sides of bridge,
One Holeman projector or 2"rocket flare launcher,
Two 21" Torpedo tubes, One Holeman projector or 2"rocket flare launcher,
Smoke generator.

Other equipment fitted for various tasks;

An A frame for sweeping acoustic mines in shallow waters, Additional generator and batteries were carried for magnetic minesweeping with a Mark VIII LL sweep with an acoustic SA towed box, The Mark V Oropesa sweeps, The Mark VII Oropesa sweeps.

Other equipment continued;

Type QH2 radar Royal Navy Type 970 Echo sounder,
Asdic recorders, Pitometer or Chernikeef log recorders and
direction finding loop control,
Ex-destroyer 2 pounder Mark II Mounted gun with its 200
rounds per minute firepower, Six pounder manually
operated gun, Hedgehog Anti-submarine projector.

Holeman projector.
This was an anti-aircraft mortar type weapon. It launched
an explosive projectile at an enemy aircraft. The projectile
was a type of mills bomb or grenade with a 3.5 second
fuse. Similar to a 3" mortar round with stabilizing fins.

Y gun.
This was mounted on the centreline of the deck with the
arms of the "Y" pointing outboard. Two depth chargers
were cradled on shuttles and inserted into each arm. An
explosive propellant charge was detonated in the vertical
column of the Y-gun to propel the depth charges to either
side of the launch. Range was about 41 meters over and out
from each side of the launch.

The Hedgehog (also known as an Anti-Submarine
Projector).
Was a forward throwing anti-submarine weapon. It fired a
number of small spigot mortar bombs from spiked fittings
on a launch plate fitted to the forward deck of the launch.

The Hedgehog bombs exploded on contact with the submarine, rather than using a time or depth fuse as depth charges did. They achieved a higher sinking rate against submarines than depth charges did. The device was named for the way the rows of empty spigot spikes resembled the spines of a hedgehog.

The Fairmile B and A were known as Motor Launch's or ML's for short. They put in the longest hours of sea time for the Coastal Forces compared to the rest of the little vessels used. Though little is ever heard of them, they had ploughed up and down our coastal waters around the country all through the war. Escorting convoys all year round winter and summer foul come fair weather. Once our land forces had pushed the Germans away from the coasts that face our country. The threat of enemy contacts diminished in the channel so our ML's had to do their work without so much as a smell of the enemy.

15 December 1944
I was attached to Fairmile B Motor Launch ML-149 at Falmouth; Cornwall. The Commanding officer was TLt William Hamish Mitchell a potato farmer from Jersey. We had T/S.LT Donald Clement Lefever as first Lieutenant. It was configured in the Anti-submarine role. It was built by Vospers in Portsmouth and completed in February 1941. She was re-numbered ML (A) 3 in July 1945 and was sold in 1946.
* Reference Picture 28.

297.

The Navy had taken over parts of Falmouth when they established it as a naval base at the start of the war. They gave it the name of HMS Forte. There were four principle bases to HMS Forte and they called them, 1 Fort, 2 Fort, 3 Fort and 4 Fort. Which made them sound impressive but they really were nothing like that impressive. By calling them Forts it gave an impression that they were military strong houses surrounded by barbed wire. Protected by machine gun positions in sand bag sangers and pill boxes. But they were nothing like that at all.

The working area for the ships and Motor Launch's was part of Falmouth Docks and coastline towards Pendennis Castle. This was given the name Fort 4 and was protected with fences and sentries and a cliff to back on to. The other three Forts were ordinary places; Membley Hall Hotel on Cliff Road on the sea front was Fort one, Imperial Court Hotel was just outside the docks on Bar Road was Fort two, and the two old Customs bonded warehouses on the site of the now Trago Mills was Fort three. The Forts 1,2,3 were all used for accommodation for the crews on shore leave whilst their ships and ML's were in port. The attractive and not so attractive Wren's were in Fort two with the Warrant Officers and Petty Officers. The Officers were in Fort one and lower ranks were billeted in the warehouses at Fort 3. Rank does have its privileges I suppose.

298.

First off there was getting used to life aboard a Motor Launch with runs seaward on these trim little vessels. We had to get used to manoeuvring around the Motor Launches at nineteen knots in good weather. With the breeze of the wind and the utter feeling of controlled power that acted as an elixir on both mind and body.

Then came the firing practices in the open sea out in the bay we had to get used to all the guns firing aboard the small Motor Launches. Firing all the guns with their sharp crack of cordite filled the small Launches with noise and this could be a distraction to those of us who had jobs to do. The living tongues of flames shooting from the muzzles of the guns could also affect the handling of the small craft. With the screams of the shells flying off then suddenly the white splashes with thunderous impacts. Occasionally you had a ricochet whizzing off into the distance. The acrid smell of cordite mixing with the high-octane petrol smell of the boat and the fresh salt sea breezes is a smell to remember.

There were five launches on duty at a time, and their crews had to be instantly ready day and night. One of the duty boats was used almost exclusively for the conveyance of pilots. Out to beyond Pendennis point, Black rock and St Anthony Head. We used to convey the pilots at high speed to and from the stream of shipping from the convoys. It was a pleasant duty, which entailed occasional races at high speed. Going half-a-mile a minute through the darkness and spray to the moving leviathans of the ocean was thrilling.

299.

Also one of the duties of the pilot launch was the morning and evening mail, message, and signals runs, collecting and delivering to the ships lying out in the bay at anchor. Another regular duty for some of the ML's was the regular standing patrols. Up and down the sheltered waterways along the Cornish and Devon coast both at night and day. Examining the permits of the fishermen by day and preventing the movement of small craft during the hours of darkness.

Our main role was anti-submarine work it was to chase down any hostile submarine and attack them where possible. Possible hostile submarines get reported to us from: aircraft, other ships and coastguard or had been detected by us whilst out on patrol. We would hopefully engage them and destroy them or chase them off. For anti-submarine work these wonderful fast ML's were great for the job. When the message came stating that a vessel was under attack or a submarine had been spotted or suspected. A number of us were instantly released from the leash. We would speed out to perhaps twenty miles from the coast to engage them. We would do it in a fraction of the time taken by larger vessels. We were on the scene with all the guns loaded and made ready for a surface attack. We would prepare and arm the hedgehogs and depth charges for submerged assaults on the offending U-boats. Part of our anti-submarine work was to escort convoys we would pick them up in the western approaches and bring them in to safer waters.

300.

The number of vessels composing a convoy varied, but often exceeded twenty big cargo ships. Some convoys would be carrying 100,000 tons of merchandise. Often the convoys would have troopships with some 20,000 troops on board. The escort flotilla with the convoy consisted most of the time by a light Cruiser acting as flagship and six Destroyers. The Destroyers were spread out ahead and on the flanks of the convoy able to move faster than the merchants and troopships. They were slow compared to our ML's. By using our greatly superior speed we were able to zigzag and circle round the whole convoy in a very short time. Trying to detect and deter the enemy in its hunt of the slow moving convoys.

When all is said and done, Anti-submarine warfare is very like big game hunting. Success depends entirely on the initiative, skill and resource of the individual hunter. There are several recognised methods of attack and defence employed by surface ships in naval warfare. The principle danger zones for England are the North Sea, the English Channel, the Irish Sea and the eastern portion of the North Atlantic i.e. the Western Approaches. It was through these waters that every hostile submarine must pass through on its voyage out to its hunting grounds and back through to get back home. This geographical factor restricted the Germans and their major operations to some 150,000 square miles of sea. The fact Germany possessed a large submarine fleet and a number of bases only along her own North Sea coast and temporary ones on the Flanders Littoral.

This insured we had to have a concentration of Allied anti-submarine craft made available in the narrow seas (English Channel). The Germans limited access to the hunting grounds helped our Coastal Forces to restrict their movements. The 150,000 square miles of sea formed the theatre of operations for the Coastal Forces.

We had special charts, divided into areas comprising a few hundred square miles of sea. Each area of the submarine danger zone was given a distinctive number. These were allotted to individual bases for anti-submarine patrols and minesweeping fleets for protection. The areas themselves were again subdivided on special charts into squares or sections ridded off. Each square covered a few leagues of sea (league equal to 3 nautical square miles) and allotted a letter. This then was the chessboard on which the game of submarine warfare was played. Between adversaries of the U-boat submarines against the concentration of fast ML's and other coastal motorboats of the coastal forces. Of course the Flotillas changed in their duties like tours around the different areas. Our Flotilla did its tour at Falmouth. Then moved on to Great Yarmouth, HMS Midge and then on to Lowestoft, HMS Mantis. Then it was back to Falmouth like a round robin exercise.

The wintertime was grim on board the ML's. Often we had to put to sea in appalling weather with the wind blowing a gale and high seas. But when you had a U-boat flap on there was little you could do. You were always soaked to the skin with no place to dry out. Apart from us lucky ones that worked most of the time in the engine room where it was dry and warm.

302.

Darkness and the moaning of the wind, driving snow and the lash of the sea whipping clouds of icy spray sweeping high over the mast. This was the ultimate challenge calling for all the qualities of dogged endurance of a good seaman. Inherently this was in all the British Sailors and military men from birth. There was always the slow, monotonous routine of night patrols to get you down. It was a continuing battle of nerves and will power not to get bored and complaisant. The patrols would consist of minutes dashing through the blinding, stinging spray. Then engines were shut off to listen out for the engine noise of U-boats on the hydrophones and a scan with the ASDIC and radar. Most times more than most of all there was no result, only the ceaseless wash of the sea and the low moaning of the wind. Then it would be another mile or so pounding through the waves to stop again with engines off drifting. All the eyes of the crew on deck watching the horizon for the enemy. The crew members below deck were listening and monitoring the consoles of the asdic and radar. Only to be brought back down to earth with the same discouraging result nothing.

The stinging frost of the night slowly became the numbing cold of early morning. The first dim light of a winter dawn broke over the grey tumbling sea as another night patrol was over. The long hours in the icy spray had left its mark on all the crewmembers their limbs were stiff and sore. The edges of wet and half-frozen sleeves on our uniforms rasped swollen wrists and necks. With our faces red from the windburn and eyes ached.

But little was ever said in the way of complaint for men grow hard on the challenge of doing their duty on the sea. Or else they would succumb to the hardships and withdraw into themselves. As the light of a new day strengthened in intensity and stated to warm us up slightly. Away to the westward the blue outline of land became visible and the cheering thought came to us all. That soon the welcome warmth and shelter of the homeport would be upon us. With its accommodation and a bed that didn't rock with every wave would embrace them. For however brief a visit it was home for us until the next patrol, operation or mission. Whilst we rested we were safe in the knowledge others kept watch upon the seas.

14th February 1945
The Ostend Disaster
On this date the greatest single loss of men and boats of the Coastal Forces happened in a catastrophic accident it took place at Ostend in Belgium. The 29TH Motor Torpedo Boat (MTB) Flotilla mostly manned by Canadian sailors had been operating. They had been in continuous action in the English Channel since D-Day (6th June 1944). During this time, it had fought a series of running battles with German E-boats (S-boats) the enemy's version of the MTB's.

On the morning of the 14th, the Flotilla was in the Belgian port of Ostend to rearm and refuel. They were in preparation for the night patrol along the Belgian coast that was to come that night. The crews were draining the bilges of the small craft and the crew of MTB-464 drained a considerable amount of water from its central fuel tank.

In the process, they inadvertently pumped 190 litres of fuel into the water around them. The fuel of course sat on top of the seawater and emitted an explosive vapour across the whole of the port. About 4pm the volatile fuel slick ignited by possibly a spark from one of the boats electrical systems or a passing sailor's discarded cigarette end. Sailors rushed to extinguish the blaze and help any trapped crewmembers. But the wooden MTBs quickly caught fire as the blaze turned to an inferno. The ammunition and fuel tanks aboard some of the MTB's exploded with a deafening roar. The concussive sound reverberated through Ostend shattering virtually every window.

The catastrophic disaster claimed thirty-five Royal Navy lives and twenty-nine Royal Canadian Navy lives. Numerous others were injured and burnt from the Flotillas personnel and the port workers. It had destroyed: five of 29th's MTB's and seven of the Royal Navy's MTB's. Because of the effect of this event in the numbers of operational boats in the Channel. The Germans made several incursions with E-boats across the Channel making the most out of our misfortune. They came to harass our shipping near Great Yarmouth and Lowestoft. Our Motor Launch and others were re-deployed to that area.

At times we were operating from HMS Mantis and HMS Minos at Lowestoft and HMS Midge at Great Yarmouth. Our shallow draft is a great asset, for rendering us more or less immune from torpedo attacks from the submarine's we hunted and from the E-boats.

305.

We would even hide and observe the sea from the shallow inlets in the fens. We hoped to scare off the enemy even though they were faster than us and better armed and armoured. We had the advantage of being on our turf with greater numbers.

Considering the size of our Motor Launch's the interior accommodation is very good but cramped. There is no waste of space every conceivable nook and cranny is used. Right at the Aft is a small compartment for the steering gear. Then alongside this came the officer's quarters with a sleeping cabin containing two bunks and a wardroom. The wardroom was no bigger than a family's dining room table with a small room to the side of it with the officer's toilet in beside this room was their own companion way to the main deck. Then came the petrol tanks sealed off from the rest of the interior of the boat containing 10,478 Litres of high-octane fuel. The engine room is amidships, with the chart-house just forward of it. The magazine comes after this and adjoins the mess deck lobby, which contained the main access to the upper deck. Opening off the lobby were four small compartments. On the port side for the Petty officers' was a cabin with space reserved for the coxswain and engine room chief and the boats main WC. On the starboard side the radio room and galley forward of this occupying most of the forward third of the hull was the mess deck. Where the crew sleeps and have their meals with six folding bunks along each side.

It would be make-believe to deny that certain days of patrol work in the summer months with the sunshine are pleasant. With the exhilaration of speed over the water on a heavily armed motor launch. The spice of danger and adventure was to save it from becoming too monotonous. This made it feel like a great adventure right out of the pages of a classic pirate story. With the rise in the threat from German attack boats many Fairmile's were up-gunned and the number of depth charges reduced. Our boats lacked the speed and armour to deal decisively with the fast E-boats. Our ML's packed heavy firepower and we provided a significant deterrent to the German raiders.

We had two flotillas of 8 ML's at Lowestoft and our number was sometimes supplemented by MGB's joining us. Our jobs were two fold we either formed part of the escort's for northbound or southbound coastal convoys. Or we would be allocated with another boat to operate in pairs on the 'Z' line. This was an imaginary line beyond the convoy channel out in the middle of the English Channel to intercept E-Boats, U-Boats and other trespassing enemy patrols.

So when we were attached to a northbound coastal convoy for protection. The convoy would be temporarily waiting for us in a holding position off the coast of Lowestoft. We would join the convoy an hour before dusk and the convoy would set sail an hour after the sun had gone down. When the convoy was safely in line with Hull we would separate from the convoy. We would cruise into the Humber and stay in Immingham Docks before leaving to join a southbound convoy back to Lowestoft.

When we were on the 'Z' line we would cruise out to our allotted position to arrive before dark. We would be holding in position for Twelve hours. After radioing our arrival we would immediately cut our engines and lower a Hydrophone to listen for incoming Jerries. If there was much sea running i.e. bad weather this could be very uncomfortable. If we had a sound contact we would make note of the bearing and start our engines. We would run at 18 knots for 3 minutes then stop and listen again. If there was still a contact the procedure was repeated until we could pinpoint their location. We would then radio in to HQ with a report and attack the enemy with depth charges. If we discovered the sound contact had disappeared on us. We would remain in position listening for a determined number of minutes past the hour before regaining our original position on the 'Z' line. We would also listen out for reports from convoy ships, HQ and aircraft about any cross Channel raiders that had been spotted. If there was any we would intercept them and usually the sight of us approaching fast would make them turn back to safer waters. At dawn we would return to Lowestoft to get some rest before the next mission.

Our ML's (Motor Launches) used Hamilton Dock at Lowestoft. We would set out frequently for "E-Boat Alley" off the East Coast to engage the German E-Boats. Officers were billeted at the Royal Hotel and the crews were mainly billeted in requisitioned houses in the Grove Road area of the town. E-Boats have been over several times and have been successfully engaged and repelled by our ML's.

308.

Whilst our crew were on leave while the boat was refitting two of our flotilla made contact with an E-Boat. It was a very dark night, but at 2.20 am the ML's sighted the Phosphorescent bow wave some 500 yards away on their starboard bow. They knew their maximum speed was so much slower than the E-Boats. They used their instinct to immediately come to the decision to ram. It was their only chance to sink the E-Boat as the enemy could outrange his guns in a few seconds. They hit him with a terrific crash just forward of the bridge with a rendering crunch. The E-Boat bounced clear off the ML with loads of smoke pouring out from it. The port gunner on the bridge of the ML got to his feet manning his gun and got a full magazine off into the enemy boat. The E-Boat tried to vanish into the darkness behind a cloud of smoke. But the other ML plunged into the engagement with all the guns blazing away that they could get to bear on to the enemy. The E-Boat was returning fire fiercely, but she was too badly damaged to escape the ML's.

There were some minor explosions within the E-Boat and the crew abandoned ship. Within minutes the enemy boat disappeared amid a shower of sparks and smoke beneath the waves. One of our boats lost everything forward of the bridge and was towed to Lowestoft stern first. The other ML had all of one side riddled with bullet holes smashing everything on the bridge to smithereens on that side. They had rescued the German crew and brought them in as prisoners.

Our flotilla then comprised of only six boats and this resulted in it being split up for various unexciting duties. Our ML-149 was dispatched to Fleetwood and based at Heysham harbour. We were attached to the Fleet Air Arm for general duties. This included crash boat when they were practicing deck-landing practice on to Aircraft Carriers or when they had bombing exercises. We also had to escort submarines on the surface in the Western Approaches. They were vulnerable if alone as they could easily have been considered enemy. A mistake by an over enthusiastic aircraft that did not first establish their identity happened occasionally. Accompanied by a surface ship they were considered safer. We operated out of many harbours that were not normally used for military vessels.
*Reference picture 31.

We celebrated the end of the War in Europe at Glasson Dock. With the ML dressed overall with all flags flying and quite a few drinks. The building on the right of the photo was the Caribou pub/ hotel. The owners did rather well out of the crew during our stay!!

Note from author.
"To this day the first officer of ML-149 T/S.LT Donald Clement Lefever. Who is 90 years of age living in a care home with mild dementia remembers my Grandfather Eric Levin. He remembers Eric was on cookhouse duty one day and made a wonderful rice pudding. It was in a large oblong metal tray and had a lovely baked brown crust apparently it was called Chinese Wedding Cake!"

Our motor launch was re-rolled to be a minesweeper and minelayer. An A frame was constructed on the aft of the motor launch as an experiment. This was to see if it would aid in deploying the minesweeping gear and with the launching of the mines when we was laying them. I believe that was when the name changed from ML-149 to ML (A) 3.

1st April 1946
We were instructed to proceed to Queenborough (Sheerness) to 'Pay off'. Where we had to retire the ML and the Navy would eventually sell her off.

CHAPTER NINETEEN
FAIRMILE B MOTOR LAUNCHES
ML-919

10 April 1946
I was transferred to ML-919 it was still a Fairmile "B"
Motor Launch.
*Reference picture 32.

She was built by JAS. N. Miller at ST Monance in Scotland
and was completed 09/10/1944. The Commanding officer
was T/Lt. B. Foxlee with First Lieutenant T/S.Lt. A.M.
Clark and Third officer T/A/S.Lt. P.O. Ledingham. She
was primarily used for mine laying operations and then she
was refitted for minesweeping operations after the war she
was re-designated ML-2919 and sold in 1953 private owner
in England.
*Reference picture 33.

The next picture is of my new crew I don't know where
this was taken. But it was one of the many small ports we
called at.
* Reference picture 34.

Coastal Forces operated out of many bases around the
country the one at Ramsgate was called HMS Fervant. Our
boat operated out of this harbour for a short time.
 * Reference pictures 35.

The set of photos were Taken at Ramsgate harbour in 1946. The tall sailing ship in the background was called the "Alastor". She was renamed the "Bounty" as a tourist attraction. She was a three-masted iron Barque built by "Mounsey and Foster". She was used as a floating restaurant with amusements and exhibitions. It was not alas a commercial success and it was decided the vessel was to be towed to London in 1951. It was the hope of keeping the Cutty Sark, company in the next dock. But when it reached the Thames Estuary "Bounty" broke adrift and ran aground causing extreme damage to her. Due to the damage and no funds for repair it was decided to scrap her and she was broken up in 1952.

The buoy/ torpedo shaped bit of kit in front of me at the bottom with my crewmates trying to throw me over board. Is a blimp float part of the Orpesa mine sweeping equipment.

In the next picture taken at Ramsgate I was loading equipment during a re-supply stop in harbour. I have no idea what I was loading up with now but I am sure it was important.

* Reference picture 36.

One of the weapons seamen feared most was the sinister sea mines that lay hidden until an unlucky ship came upon them. It didn't matter who's mine it was, friend or foe. The mines could not tell the difference all was susceptible to them.

The Royal Navy carried out various types of mine laying during the war from defensive minefields. That acted as barriers with anti-submarine traps at focal points for convoy routes. To offensive mining, that disrupted movement of enemy shipping in the enemy's coastal waters. Primarily our Motor Launches carried this out covertly. As they could race over the channel to lay their mines under the noses of the enemy at night and race back to safe waters.

Now came the time to clean up our waters and the French coast. We were to make it safe for our shipping to safely traverse the Channel. Without the constant fear of being sunk! By our mines or the enemy's mines, that we all had laid in war time. You had various mines and minesweeping kit to combat them. The old fashioned sort of mine you see at the seaside used, as a collection box was a moored mine. This was anchored by a cable to the sea floor with an anchor or dead weight on the end. This type of mine would float just below the surface of the water. Most of them had horns and if a ship hit one of these horns it went off.

The method of detonation was quite simple for these mines. The horns on them were a semi-soft metal like Lead and they contained a file of acid. When a ship hit the horns they would crush and the acid file would break. It would then run through tubes to collect in a primary central compartment. The acid would react with metal filaments creating an electrical current like a battery. This would set off the electrical detonator setting off the main charge.

314.

The skill had to be mastered in minesweeping these type of mines safely. The equipment most often used was the Orpesa sweep. We would tow the sweep behind the Motor Launch through a pattern of a grid in the area of the suspected minefield. The Orpesa sweep consisted of a long cable to a blimp. Then the sweep with a cutter positioned near to the end, where a shaped float supported the end off the seabed. The sweep would either explode the mine's or cut the cable forcing them to the surface. On the surface they could be destroyed by gunfire. If the gunfire hit a horn it would explode if it didn't then eventually the mine would get pumped full of shells. The holes in it would make it fill with water causing it to sink to the bottom. Powerful winches and davits on the stern helped to deploy and recover the complex equipment. We routinely practised sweeping; it was a challenging operation that required endless drill to perfect.

Another type of mine used was known as a ground-mine. They were used in relatively shallow water and lay on the seabed. They were activated either by magnetism or the sound of a passing ship. Our wooden ML's were obviously immune to the magnetic threat with their wooden hulls. They didn't put out enough of a magnetic field we just had to be careful not to make too much noise.

With this type of mine we had what was known as the "Double L" sweep it consisted of two cables fastened together. One of the cables was about two hundred and seventy four meters long the other was four hundred and fifty meters long.

On the end of each cable was an electrode. They produced a magnetic field between the two of them behind the Motor Launch. As the ML's were made of wood we could go over the mines and they would not detonate. But the magnetic field being towed behind us simulating a ship and would detonate them. You used to get this violent explosion behind you about three hundred and fifty meters away with no warning. The sudden explosions would sort of shock and shake you up a bit.

The sound activated mines were called acoustic mines. To deal with them we had a large bucket shaped container and inside this was a Kango-Hammer mechanism. Like the pneumatic hammer that road workers use to dig holes in the road with. We used to lower this below the boat and it used to make this awful clatter enough to wake the dead. When we activated the air compressor on the deck it was attached to it with air hoses. You would just hope it made a lot more noise than the Motor Launch's engines. With a bit of luck it would set the mine's off before you got too close.

The Germans became quite sneaky towards the end of the war they would fit the ground mines with a delay actuation mechanism. That could count anything from one to fourteen ships passing the mine before it went off. So of course you never really knew when an area was clear. You could sweep with all the types of kit you had and it wouldn't go off. Until you or some other unlucky sod passed it on the fifteenth time. Suddenly it would go off making it virtually impossible to declare an area safe.

316.

The Germans came up with another variation to their mines known as an Oyster mine. These sat on the bottom under the sea like an oyster in the sand. These had a sort of little set of bellows inside of them like air bladders. When a ship passed over the mine the displacement of the ship altered the pressure on the seabed and this activated the mine.

The sweeping procedure for oyster mines involved dropping a pattern of standard hand grenades into the water. The grenades separated by cylindrical wooden blocks were loaded into a tube. The tube had a slit down one side to help with the removal of the pins from the grenades. Once the tube was full you would pull the pins arming the grenades. But as they were in a tube the fly off levers could not be released to go off. The grenades would be discharged in to the water as your boat went along at fifteen knots.

The motor launch would travel thirty meter sand we would dispel the grenades as we went along. We would do thirty meters in the four seconds before the first grenade exploded. So it was thump, thump, thump, thump, as you went along Whilst of course you prepared another set of grenades in another tube to go again in the set pattern you was following. It worked out to be one tube every forty to sixty seconds. This would build up enough of a pressure wave to explode any oyster mines. Hopefully they went off in the area away from the launch. The only protection for ships from this type of mine in un-cleared areas was to move very slowly.

The speed depended on the depth of water and the displacement size of the ship. For example a ship weighing one thousand tonnes was to do seven knots in ten fathoms of water. A Battleship approximately fifty thousand tonnes was only allowed to do three knots making them an extra slow sitting duck for enemy planes.

Of course there were other complications affecting the minesweeping. Weather played a big part, too rough and you just could not sweep. Let alone the risk of the weather breaking loose mines from their anchors. Causing a hazard to shipping every-where, floating free and drifting off. The Germans would also put in there moored mine fields sweep cutting obstacles rather like the anti-tank spikes, like they would put on beaches made of girders welded together. So we would end up losing our sweeping gear or end up with it entangled, all making it rather difficult. But as they say practice makes perfect and of course the seven P's came in to play:" Prior Planning and Preparation Prevents a Piss-Poor Performance".

In our Motor Launch flotillas there were a superior influential heavier number of "Wavy-Navy" officers and "Hostilities Only" veteran ratings. We were all thrown together with Fleet reserve officers and ratings. Because of the experience us veterans had we had the respect given to us from the reserve officers. All of us working in very close proximity sharing the tedium of patrolling and escort duties. That was only very occasionally relieved by bursts of action or out of normal special takings. We all worked together like a well-oiled machine a very tight band of men Together like a family.

In the majority of boats the wardroom and mess decks had a closer and friendlier atmosphere. Than would have been possible on the bigger ships. Discipline was more democratic with people getting to know each other's little ways and foibles. A well-run boat has mutual respect up and down the chain of command from the highest rank to the lowest. A family ambience could exist, which could enhance the overall effectiveness of the crew. (Note from author; most modern military units could use this advice to run smother with respect and cohesion up and down the rank chain learning and working together with individual's talents and experience to benefit the team).

4 Sep 1947
Discharged from Royal Navy I re-enlisted into the Royal Fleet Reserve. I went on to serve on several ships around the world until 1955 then it was time to concentrate on my family and be with them. I had experienced my excitement and action it was time to relax a bit now.

Author's epitaph

My Grandfather always said he enjoyed his life in the Royal Navy. But only on a few very occasional times did he talk about his experiences to me. When he did it was usually after a couple of beers and it was after I had joined up. I have always found it a great travesty that the stories of HMS Malaya, HMS Delhi and the Royal Navy Coastal Forces has not been told more widely in books and on TV and film.

Especially the men who served in the Coastal Forces whose men went out night after night and day after day. Taking the fight to the enemy over and over again risking their lives for their comrades in arms. All through the war in every theatre of operations around the world. Their boats were frail wooden craft, either: Motor Torpedo Boats, Motor Gun Boats or Motor Launches. All with similar hulls with different armaments loaded with high-octane petrol. They never expected to come back unhurt. They went into enemy waters to seek and destroy at close range and they kept the shipping lanes clear. Fighting close engagements with E-boats and U-boats, clearing and deploying mines and landing commandos and special operations operatives on occupied territories to carry out sabotage and reconnaissance raids. They achieved a remarkable success totally disproportionate to their numbers and the size of their vessels.

I have to say that I have a strong impression of a small group of courageous, determined and dedicated men with strong bonds of camaraderie and esprit de corps.

320.

I understand some of what they went through from my own service in the RAF Regiment during the 1980's, 1990's, 2000's with tours to Saudi, Kuwait, Iraq, Afghanistan and exercises all over the UK, Europe, Cyprus and Middle East. To the present day I am now serving in the Army in the (MPGS) Military Provost Guard Service protecting our Forces Bases. I hold my Grandfather's ships and crewmembers in the highest esteem in my thoughts and to one and all I would like to say a huge thank you for the dedication and sacrifice they gave.

They shall grow not old, as we that are left grow old.
Age shall not weary them, nor the years condemn,
At the going down of the sun and in the morning,
We will remember them.
PER ARDUA.

Ode to a Stoker

When the bugle sounds ACTION, The foe is in sight,
Then who is it takes you hotfoot to the fight?
Who gives you the speed to keep up the pursuit?
Without which you wouldn't be able to shoot?
Why, who but the stockers,
Those thrice cursed stockers,
Who fight their fight blind,
And the odds never known,
For they are the blighters who make the ship go.

Danger always alongside, unheard and unseen,
From wondering mine to a stray submarine,
And should it occur that the ship is going down,
They've a chance to be scolded to death or drown,
Small hope for the stokers,
The batten down stokers,
Whose manner of passing you never know,
For they are the mucky boys,
The unlucky boys,
The plucky boys,
They are the blighters that make the ship go.

Printed in Great
Britain
by Amazon

The Hope of Glory

Exceeding Expectations

Gordon C Methven

DEDICATION

I dedicate this book to my wife Lesley and our daughters Gillian and Amy
for their love, patience and understanding during the writing.

SPECIAL THANKS

I would like to thank Deborah and team for helping me exceed my
expectations and also appreciate her, Mike and Barbara for taking the time
to read the manuscript and providing useful recommendations.

CONTENTS

INTRODUCTION

In the 1980's I was on duty in Aberdeen on the night the Piper Alpha platform blew up in the North Sea. Tasked with keeping an eye on the accident and emergency department at Aberdeen Royal Infirmary, I watched helplessly as the injured and dying were brought in by ambulance from the helicopter pad. There was chaos all round due to the large number of relatives frantically searching for news of their loved ones, as well as reporters, photographers and camera crews wanting as much information as possible in order to get the story of the disaster out as soon as possible. Hardened police officers had tears in their eyes and I too found myself welling up but needed to stay focussed in order to be of any help. I desperately wanted to reach out to those in distress but the only way open to me was to be there for them.

I felt hopeless….

Sometimes I watch the news on television, read a newspaper or webpage and hear about a tragic event and am reminded of that terrible day.

Yet I no longer feel the hopelessness I felt back then. 'Time is a great healer' I hear you say, however, I now have something else to help me deal with tragedy, something in my life that enables me to have hope when the storms of life strike. There is hope rather than hopelessness.

We are bombarded with news broadcasts from all over the world these days. It is therefore difficult for anyone to go any length of time without hearing of a disaster or tragedy that has taken place somewhere. The media loves to report on the dead and dying, or how someone in public office has been exposed as a liar or a cheat etc.

We all have storms in life that we need to walk through. It is difficult enough to do so without hearing more news stories about someone else's tragedy. This endless catalogue of despair has an effect on people.

They feel hopeless….

What is it that I have that enables me to cope better with the storms of life? What gives me and millions of others hope for situations when all hope seems gone? What is this mystery, this secret that is being kept from the masses?

To answer this I need to quote the words of a convict, the Apostle Paul in his letter to the Colossians:

> 'I now rejoice in my sufferings for you, and fill up in my flesh what is lacking in the afflictions of Christ, for the sake of His body, which is the church, of which I became a minister according to the stewardship from God which was given to me for you, to fulfil the word of God, the mystery which has been hidden from ages and from generations, but now has been revealed to His saints. To them God willed to make known what are the riches of the glory of this mystery among the Gentiles: which is Christ in you, the hope of glory.' (Colossians 1 verses 24 to 27)

The answer to the mystery is, 'Christ in you, the hope of glory' .

When you have Christ in you, you receive the 'hope of glory'.

This is the reason I have written this book. There is definitely an acute necessity for more teaching materials on the subject of biblical hope. My express desire is to provide material for pastors and leaders that contains the information required but, more importantly, also gives inspiration and hope to the people who read it. There is a need for the 'hope of glory' and my hope is that this book will in some way help reveal that mystery.

I am not a theologian and so my understanding is based on experience learned from the school of life and also what I have gleaned by listening to people whose lives are full of this 'hope of glory'. However all of us should be ready to give an account for the hope that is in us, in answer to those who ask us. As the fisherman Simon Peter said:

> 'But in your hearts set Christ apart as holy [and acknowledge Him] as Lord. Always be ready to give a logical defence to anyone who asks you to account for the hope that is in you, but do it courteously and respectfully.' (1 Peter 3 verse 15b - Amplified Bible)

The gospels were written by ordinary men whom had spent time with Jesus, therefore I am encouraged to provide my own logical defence to those who ask me.

This then is my account of 'the hope of glory'.

Gordon C Methven
April 2013

FOREWORD

Hope is one of the most under taught topics in the Bible. One of the most read passages is 1 Corinthians verse 13, known as the love chapter and it concludes with these words, 'and now these three remain faith, hope and love. But the greatest of these is love'. It is true of course that love is the greatest because God is Love and it is also true that without faith it is impossible to please God but the Scripture says these three remain not these two. There are so many books that have been written on love and faith compared to hope, but without hope, faith doesn't have a foundation to draw on as it says in Hebrews 11 verse 1 'Now faith is the substance of things hoped for, the evidence of things not seen'. I have taught on the subject of hope for many years and have seen that vision and destiny are seen through hope, released through faith and administered through love.

In this book Gordon Methven, through simple biblical teaching and heartfelt personal testimony, opens the reader's eyes to see, that beyond the circumstances of life, hope will anchor the soul. When the flesh cries hopelessness, the believer's heart can soar with hope.

I have known the author for many years as a man who inspires hope in his family, friends and church, and as much of his life is revealed in these pages you will receive, not only knowledge, but impartation. You will find as you read, as said by the prophet Isaiah, that those who hope in the Lord will renew their strength, they will soar on wings like eagles; they will run and not grow weary, they will walk and not faint.

A story is told of a balloon salesman in the streets of New York City that when business slackened he would release a balloon to fly away above the heads of the crowd, up through the skyscrapers, to catch their attention. Sometimes he'd let a red one go followed by a blue or a white.

Watching this with intrigue was a little African American boy who came up to him and asked, 'Mister, if you let a black one go, would it fly?' 'Sonny', the old man said, 'it's what's inside that makes it fly.'

All too often our potential is limited to our upbringing, ethnicity, education and by what's in our thinking, instead of being unlimited by a hope that God can put in our hearts.

In natural thinking hope is usually used in the context of the probability or chance, It is frequently expressed in terms of a whim or a wish, e.g. I hope the sun will shine today. Biblical hope is far more definite and tangible. A more accurate Biblical definition is, hope is a firm expectation, accompanied by a deep desire in our hearts, to see the realization of promised things come into being for God's glory and our good; In other words, a futuristic absolute.

If you are just beginning your Christian journey or have walked as a Christian for some time, this book will cement in you a foundation that will help to renew your mind and keep you focused on that which is important.

The scripture says in 1 Peter1 verse 3 "Blessed be the God and Father of our Lord Jesus Christ, who according to His great mercy has caused us to be born again to a living hope." Hope is inseparably linked with our salvation.

In a time when the earth is groaning, the economy is shaking, the kingdoms of this world are faltering and moral absolutes are being challenged, governments as well as church leaders are searching for answers to these complex issues. As these things occur individual lives are shaken, resulting in hopelessness for many. This book is timely.

Let hope arise!

Tony Fitzgerald
Apostolic Team Leader
Church of the Nations

CHAPTER 1
WHAT HOPE IS

'Hope is the word which God has written on the brow of every man' –
Victor Hugo

As young parents Lesley and I experienced a crisis that shook us to the core. I was around 27 and still in my probationary period with Grampian Police Service. One day, my Sergeant called me back to the office and informed me that I was needed at home. Gillian, our two year old daughter, was taken sick with suspected meningitis and needed to be taken to hospital. As I drove home, my heart was racing and I was absolutely frantic. I had heard of meningitis - the killer disease, and just couldn't believe that this was happening. It felt like a nightmare but it wasn't. This was real life.

On arrival home, I ran indoors where Lesley tearfully explained that Gillian had been very ill that day with flu like symptoms and a rash. She also complained of feeling dizzy and had been bumping into things. Two doctors had attended and advised Lesley that it was just a flu bug but she just knew it was something far more serious and had called the doctor a third time. The last doctor had taken one look at Gillian and knew straight away something was wrong. He had called for an ambulance but there were none available and Lesley had therefore called the police station for me to come home and be with them.

I picked up Gillian and we ran out to the car. We drove to the local children's hospital where we explained the situation to the staff. They immediately took Gillian from us and rushed her to another area to assess her condition. A while later as we waiting to hear what was happening, a doctor appeared and told us to prepare ourselves for the worst. Gillian had all the symptoms of meningitis and they did not think she was going to pull through.

At that moment all hope was gone. We sat speechless as the doctor explained matters further. He said that they still had to carry out a lumber puncture, where a sample of cerebrospinal fluid (CSF) is taken from the lower region of the spine and checked for the presence of bacteria or viruses. If this was clear then it wasn't meningitis. We were completely stunned. What could we say or do? We gave them the permission and then sat and waited; absolutely void of hope and desperate for someone to say something that would give us hope for the situation or something to happen that would change things for the better.

Sitting there, my thoughts turned to God and at that moment I realized that He was our only hope for the situation we were in. I had been brought up to attend church but over the years had drifted away until the only time I attended was at special events such as weddings, funerals, Easter and Christmas. I did believe in God but seldom prayed and only occasionally read the bible.

However, a friend at work had given me a book about the healing power of God through faith in Jesus. I knew that a lot of people with far more faith than I had lost children but that book gave me hope that Jesus could heal Gillian. I had a faith of sorts from my 'Christian' upbringing in the Church of Scotland and my time in the Boy's Brigade, which is a similar but older movement to the Scouts with more emphasis on faith.

I thought of the Boy's Brigade motto, 'Sure and Steadfast'. It had something to do with hope I remembered. Whatever happened, I was determined to be 'sure and steadfast', for Gillian and for Lesley.

I prayed aloud to 'Our Father who art in Heaven', it was how I had been taught to pray, and asked him to heal Gillian and give her back to me. I said that if he decided it was time for her to go home to heaven then I would understand but asked Him to please give me another chance to tell her about Him and give her the same opportunities I had been given as a child to learn about Jesus.

After praying the prayer, I had peace in my heart and I knew that whatever happened, Jesus was going to look after her, either on earth or in heaven. We waited for the doctor to return and when he did, he told us that the lumber puncture test they had carried out had come back clear.

The doctor seemed surprised by this turn of events and said that Gillian was a little better. He told us that she might pull through after all but that she was still critically ill. She was taken to an isolation ward and Lesley was given a bed nearby so she could stay with her. I had to go back to work and due to my shifts could only pop in to see them from time to time but my Sergeant was brilliant. He said I could go to the hospital any time I wanted provided there were no ongoing emergencies. Every time I saw Gillian she was a little better and after a week she was allowed home.

The doctors did not know what the disease had been. They said that it wasn't meningitis as the lumber puncture had come back clear. I asked what else it could have been and was told it must have been a meningitis type flu virus.

Whatever it was, I just knew that God had moved on our behalf and had given Gillian back to us. I wouldn't say that I had more faith than anyone else but what I did have was a belief that God could heal Gillian and a little bit of hope (expectation) that he would do so. I believe to this day that the Holy Spirit visited that hospital ward and brought healing to Gillian.

When I speak to people about hope, they think of hope as being like wishful thinking. They hope they will be married one day. They hope they will have children. They hope they will have grandchildren. They hope their families will be safe and well. They hope to get a good job or run a business. They hope to have a nice holiday. They hope to receive nice gifts for birthday and Christmas.

As I learned in that hospital ward real hope is far more. It relates to something that a person carries deep within their soul. It's the precious thing that enables us to go on every day, that which helps us walk through the storms of life, the wings that help us fly above the clouds and stay positive no matter what's going on around us.

Lesley and I had endured a real storm that day but after what happened we had more hope in our lives than we ever had before.

I don't know what would have happened to us if Gillian had died that day but we would have needed something to give us hope, something to lift us out of despair.

So what is hope? To find the answer, I decided to look various dictionaries which define hope as follows:

> **Hope (verb)** - to want something to happen or to be true, and usually have a good reason to think that it might
>
> **Hope (noun)** - something good that you want to happen in the future, or a confident feeling about what will happen in the future

So, hope is a reason for, or a feeling about something good happening in the future. It is about an expectation for the future in a positive form, whereas despair, the opposite of hope, is an expectation for the future in a negative form. In that hospital ward, Lesley and I experienced both in a way that we hoped we would never have to face again.

I am absolutely convinced we all need hope in our lives. It is one of the things that make life worth living. To try and explain, without hope my life would be like a journey without a destination, a ship without a harbour, or summer holidays without sunshine. There would be no real reason for living.

I have noticed that people can live without faith, however if they have no hope they often give up on life altogether. Very often, the way the world is today, hope is frequently dashed, leading to great sorrow and anguish. There is so much information being fed to our minds these days through television, the internet, the media etc. that our minds are awash with false expectation of what the future may hold.

With regard to relationships, we watch movies and read novels that have no basis in reality. Marriage has become a romantic novel with a dashing hero as the groom and a beautiful damsel in distress becoming the blushing bride. They will have a fairy tale wedding and live happily ever after. Really?

In my experience, the reality of course is totally different and often people don't live, 'happily ever after'. We see adverts of gorgeous families where the husband has rippling muscles and hair you would die for. The wife wouldn't look out of place in a Miss World contest and the children are well behaved and very happy. They then sometimes look at their own families where the husband has a pot belly and has lost his hair. The wife is totally exhausted and sometimes looks like she has been dragged through a hedge backwards and the children always seem to be complaining about what they don't have. Why isn't our family like the ones we see on television? Rather than living in hope for their future they fantasize about it. Then when the fantasy doesn't become reality they become disillusioned with their own lives. What a shame!

There is of course another problem where people have seen too many soap operas, where disaster follows every family that appears in it. We also watch the news and read newspapers that constantly report on the tragedies that have been happening somewhere around the world. This can cause people to believe that nothing good will ever happen to them. Rather than living in hope for their future they live in a constant state of fear, worrying about what the future may hold.

In both scenarios, disappointment invariably follows and I see people growing ever more confused and totally dissatisfied with the realities of what real life has to offer.

Hope is a very powerful thing. When hope is dashed, it can lead to despair, depression, anger, bitterness, envy, jealousy and the like. I saw the results every day in my job as a police officer – thoughts of suicide, depression and every negative emotion on open display. When I spoke to people as to why they were feeling the way they were, it usually transpired that their expectations had been sunk in some way.

Someone close to them had badly let them down and their hope for the future was gone.

They had expected to get a job or a promotion and it had been given to someone else.

They had expected to pass an exam they needed to find the job they had set their hearts on and had failed.

No wonder they were in a state. People really need something solid to base their hopes on, something or someone they can rely on not to let them down in times of trouble.

There is an incredible amount of searching going on all over the earth as people look for something or someone to pin their hopes on.

Furthermore, there is a passage in the bible that actually speaks of a person that the Gentiles (non Jews) shall put their hope in.

> And again, Isaiah says: "There shall be a root of Jesse; And He who shall rise to reign over the Gentiles, In Him the Gentiles shall hope."
> (Romans 15 verse 12)

The root of Jesse speaks of a descendant of Jesse, the Father of King David. It is actually speaking about Jesus, who is a descendant of King David. This scripture then goes on to say:

> Now may the God of hope fill you with all joy and peace in believing, that you may abound in hope by the power of the Holy Spirit.
> (Romans 15 verse 13)

I thought to myself, 'this is what people are searching for! People are looking for real hope and the peace and joy that go along with it!'

In studying hope though, I have found that biblical hope is different from the normal human hope described in the Chambers dictionary. There is more depth to it!

I looked at the subject in more detail and read Hebrews 11 verse 1, which is a famous passage of scripture, much used to encourage people to have more faith.

> Now faith is the substance of things hoped for, the evidence of things not seen.
> (Hebrews 11 verse 1)

From this scripture it became clear to me that biblical faith and hope relate to things not seen. They are not something that can be sensed in the natural. They are spiritual things.

I then looked at 1 Corinthians chapter 13 which mentions hope as one of the three graces.

> And now abide faith, hope, love, these three; but the greatest of these is love.
> (1 Corinthians 13 verse 13)

From this I understood that hope and faith are actually two different aspects of the grace of God. One is not more important than the other, but they are very much connected. On checking my Strong's Concordance I found the word used in Hebrews 11 verse 1 for faith described as:

> Faith - Greek 'pistis' - (Strongs Concordance 4102) persuasion i.e. credence; conviction (of religious truth, or the truthfulness of God or a religious teacher), especially reliance upon Christ for salvation; abstract - constancy in such profession; by extension the system of religious (gospel) truth itself - assurance, belief, believe, faith, fidelity.

Therefore, I saw 'Faith' as being a conviction, an assurance or a strong belief. I then looked up the word translated as 'Hope' in the above bible verse and my Strong's Concordance described it as:

> Hope - Greek 'elpis' - Strongs 1680 (to anticipate, usually with pleasure) expectation or confidence.

Therefore, I understood 'Hope' as being a joyful expectation. Great news! I now understood the difference between faith and hope. Faith is a conviction, whereas hope is an expectation. Both are equally important in my spiritual walk.

As I studied this scripture, I realized that faith is the 'substance' of things hoped for. How often do we hear people say of a politician that there is no 'substance' to what they are saying. We have no real expectation that what they are saying will ever be put into practice.

It also says that faith is the 'evidence' of things not seen. As a retired police officer I have had many experiences of giving evidence. In a court of law, evidence is that which gives substance to an accusation, or alternatively that which gives substance to a person's innocence. So when the bible speaks of faith giving substance to things hoped for and evidence to things not seen, it is really speaking of a conviction that is substantial, a faith that provides real substance for hope.

We can say then, that faith is what gives substance to our hope and hope is what gives joy and peace to our faith.

I believe that what people are really searching for but maybe don't know it, is faith. They are looking for something, or someone of substance to put their hopes in.

There are those who laugh at people of faith and say that their own philosophy makes more sense to them. One thing that stands out to me in my life though, is that I have never heard anyone say, 'It was my atheism that helped me through that situation', or 'My communist philosophy gave me the strength to carry on', or 'It was my agnosticism that gave me the hope I needed when life was tough'. Substitute any 'ism' you like and it is unlikely that you will ever have heard anyone say such a thing. Substitute the word 'faith' and it is likely you would have heard it said numerous times.

I have heard many people attacking faith in the media through publishing books and producing CD's and DVD's promoting their view that the world would be a far better place without religion. They always focus on the negative aspects of religion such as bigotry, sectarianism and prejudice. However, I have found that when speaking of the positive aspects of religion such as faith, hope and love, they have no legitimate answer to give other than to mock and hurl insults.

In my opinion, what a person believes directly affects the hope that they have. That's why faith is so important. People need hope far more than they need an intellectual mindset. They need something to hope in and hope isn't based on intellectualism. Hope is something that stirs the heart of man at an emotional level. It is one of the things that make life worth living and I believe that there is nothing, in this world, that stirs up the hope in a person's heart more than the love of God and faith in Jesus Christ.

I have found that having faith in Jesus Christ, has given me someone of substance to put my trust in and a faith that provides substance to my hope.

The poet Emily Dickinson said that, 'Hope is the thing with feathers that perches in the soul, and sings the tunes without the words and never stops at all.'

An unknown author said, 'Hope sees the invisible, feels the intangible, and achieves the impossible.' The poet Alexander Pope said, 'Hope springs eternal in the human breast'. The bard Robert Burns, said, 'Hope springs exulting on triumphant wing'.

So what do you do when all hope seems gone? My answer to that question is, 'put your hope in Jesus'.

SUMMARY

1. Hope relates to our expectation.

2. Faith relates to our conviction.

3. Faith gives substance to our hope.

4. Hope gives joy and peace to our faith.

CHAPTER 2
CHRIST IN YOU, THE HOPE OF GLORY

'Hope is the companion of power and mother of success; for who so hopes
strongly has within him the gift of miracles'- Samuel Smiles

I have heard Christians speak of, 'hoping in Jesus'. Although I have felt
that some of them are merely repeating words that they have heard and
have no real understanding of what they are saying, I believe many are
speaking about having a joyful expectation that is in their hearts because of
their hope in Him. I used to look at them and wonder how they could be
so happy, especially when everything seemed to be falling to pieces around
them. Then I would see them later on and notice that the storm they were
facing in their lives had passed and they were still very happy. What I
believe they have that other people don't is hope.

It seems to me that it is this hope, this joyful expectation that makes a
true Christian's life richer in the things that really matter, like, love, joy,
peace, patience etc. Isn't that what people are really looking for?

I watch people as they go about their daily lives. They all want to be
happy but most of them really don't know how. Whether it's money,
relationships or success, many find that the thing they are striving for
doesn't really cut it. They can't find the happiness they are truly searching
for.

This used to be a complete mystery to me as well. What is it that really
makes a person happy?

I started reading the bible looking for answers and found something very interesting to me. I noticed that the apostle Paul wrote about this very thing in his letter to the Colossians, where he spoke of a mystery that God would reveal to the Gentiles (non Jews).

> I now rejoice in my sufferings for you, and fill up in my flesh what is lacking in the afflictions of Christ, for the sake of His body, which is the church, of which I became a minister according to the stewardship from God which was given to me for you, to fulfil the word of God, the mystery which has been hidden from ages and from generations, but now has been revealed to His saints. To them God willed to make known what are the riches of the glory of this mystery among the Gentiles: **which is Christ in you, the hope of glory**.
> (Colossians 1 verses 24 to 27– emphasis added)

My understanding of this passage of scripture is this. When Paul spoke of the riches of the glory of this mystery, he was speaking about something real, something that people were searching for. A mystery that had been hidden from ages and from generations but that had now been revealed to His saints. I saw that this mystery was also being revealed to me as I read the scripture - 'Christ in you, the hope of glory'.

I read on as Paul described the purpose behind a person hoping in Jesus.

> Him we preach, warning every man and teaching every man in all wisdom, that we may present every man perfect in Christ Jesus. To this end I also labour, striving according to His working which works in me mightily.
> (Colossians 1 verses 28 to 29)

Hope rose in my heart as I understood what he was saying - the 'hope of glory' is that people that believe in Him will become like Jesus.

I needed to understand this better as I knew that I wasn't perfect. I believed in Jesus but there were and still are, many areas in my life that are far from perfect. Yet Paul was saying that I could be like Jesus.

I had to investigate further. What does that mean? What does becoming like Jesus really mean?

As a child I was given a mental picture of Jesus that wasn't really true. A man dressed in brilliant white robes that walked around carrying a lamb on his shoulders. He looked like a film star and never smiled because he was so concerned about the little lambs. He always looked very sad in all the pictures I saw of him and didn't seem to be very happy.

I needed to know what Jesus was really like. I read further and discovered that, according to the Bible, Jesus was full of joy. He was really happy. Okay, I don't think he was smiling when they nailed him to the cross but other than that, when you read the bible, you see that he wasn't sad at all, he was full of joy.

> These things I have spoken to you, that My **joy** may remain in you, and that your **joy** may be full.
> (John 15 verse 11– emphasis added)

> But now I come to You, and these things I speak in the world, that they may have My **joy** fulfilled in themselves.
> (John 17 verse 13 – emphasis added)

As I studied this, hope rose in my heart and my understanding of the bible changed. I realized that the gospel itself is a message of hope to the world. I saw that Jesus, when He was with His disciples, was not only their teacher but also their example. He was, and is, full of hope, full of faith, full of love, full of joy and full of life. It's so exciting for me to appreciate that when he wrote of 'Christ in you the hope of glory', Paul was expecting people to also be full of these things, that those who follow Jesus will become like Him, that they would also be full of the 'hope of glory'.

Like many people, as a young person, I was told that I would never amount to anything. Yet, according to the bible, those who walk in faith with Christ will become like Him. That's something to hope for isn't it?

In actual fact, when I look at Ephesians Chapter 4, I see that the growth of the church itself is in regard to it becoming Christ like.

> And He Himself gave some to be apostles, some prophets, some evangelists, and some pastors and teachers, for the equipping of the saints for the work of ministry, for the edifying of the body of Christ, till we all come to the unity of the faith and of the knowledge of the Son of God, to a perfect man, to the measure of the stature of the fullness of Christ; that we should no longer be children, tossed to and fro and carried about with every wind of doctrine, by the trickery of men, in the cunning craftiness of deceitful plotting, but, speaking the truth in love, may grow up in all things into Him who is the head —Christ— from whom the whole body, joined and knit together by what every joint supplies, according to the effective working by which every part does its share, causes growth of the body for the edifying of itself in love.
> (Ephesians 4 verses 11 to 16)

I therefore perceive that the 'hope of glory' is not only for people as individuals but also for society as a whole. For isn't that is what the word church really refers to, society being impacted by the Kingdom of God through faith in Christ?

There is then, in my view, obviously a lot more to the measure and stature of Jesus Christ than simply speaking of the hope and joy that he had. I see the 'hope of glory' as people becoming like Jesus through having faith and putting their trust in Him and that those that are like Him also start hoping for and hoping in the same things He does. They begin to love and believe in the same things Jesus does.

As Paul prays for the Ephesians:

> Therefore I also, after I heard of your faith in the Lord Jesus and your love for all the saints, do not cease to give thanks for you, making mention of you in my prayers: that the God of our Lord Jesus Christ, the Father of glory, may give to you the spirit of wisdom and revelation in the knowledge of Him, the eyes of your understanding being enlightened; that you may know what is **the hope of His calling**, what are the riches of the glory of His inheritance in the saints and what is the exceeding greatness of His power toward us who believe, according to the working of His mighty power which He worked in Christ when He raised Him from the dead and seated Him at His right hand in the heavenly places, far above all principality and power and might and dominion, and every name that is named, not only in this age but also in that which is to come.
> (Ephesians 1 verses 15 to 21 - emphasis added)

I believe that it's important for Christians to know the hope of His calling, that they receive wisdom and revelation and that their understanding is enlightened as they get to know Him better. Also, that they realise the greatness of His power that's available to those that believe in Him.

Through years of listening to Christian teaching I have come to understand that there are different ways that the Father teaches us.

> We learn through our experiences, through living our lives and making mistakes. This is sometimes called the 'university of life' or the 'school of hard knocks'.
> There is also the way of teaching in school and college, where we learn by studying rules and principles and completing tasks presented to us by a teacher or by reading text books and manuals.
> Mentoring is another way to teach, as a parent to a child or a master

to an apprentice, where we learn by following the example they set to us.

Then there is the most exciting of all, where we receive inspiration direct from the Father. This not only gives us head knowledge but, more often than not, changes our heart for the better as well.

An example of divine inspiration is found in the book of Matthew.

> When Jesus came into the region of Caesarea Philippi, He asked His disciples, saying, "Who do men say that I, the Son of Man, am?" So they said, "Some say John the Baptist, some Elijah, and others Jeremiah or one of the prophets." He said to them, "But who do you say that I am?" Simon Peter answered and said, "You are the Christ, the Son of the living God." Jesus answered and said to him, "Blessed are you, Simon Bar-Jonah, for flesh and blood has not revealed this to you, but My Father who is in heaven.
> (Matthew 16 verses 13 to 17)

I can imagine Jesus being really excited. He has been teaching His disciples about the Kingdom of Heaven and suddenly Peter announces something that he hadn't been taught by normal human methods but something he had heard directly from the Father.

This 'hope of glory' I am describing is about a walk of faith, a promise of the divine, a journey where the destination is glorious. As we walk with Jesus He uses all four ways to teach us. He uses our experiences and also uses other people such as parents, teachers and mentors to teach us. As we walk with Him we also receive inspiration direct from the Father through listening to the Holy Spirit. Becoming like Jesus is therefore surely something to hope for.

I found another scripture where the apostle Paul speaks of this walk of faith in his letter to the Philippians:

> Not that I have already attained, or am already perfected; but I press on, that I may lay hold of that for which Christ Jesus has also laid hold of me. Brethren, I do not count myself to have apprehended; but one thing I do, forgetting those things which are behind and reaching forward to those things which are ahead, I press toward the goal for the prize of the upward call of God in Christ Jesus.
> (Philippians 3 verses 12 to 14)

The prize is the 'Hope of glory', of becoming like Jesus.

I have sometimes heard this passage of scripture used in such a way that pressure is put on people to be more like Jesus. Preachers can sometimes try to force people to be more like Him. This is often done with the best of motives but if pressure and force of will were enough to make people have a nature like Jesus, there would have been no need for His sacrifice on the cross.

It is my opinion that there needs to be a proper balance in everything we do and that includes our spiritual life. Everyone makes mistakes and nobody should feel pressurised into being like Jesus. No-one can achieve this in their own strength. It's more about walking in faith and being led by the Holy Spirit.

However, I also realise that people do need to be encouraged in their faith. That's why ministers of the Gospel need to have such wisdom. Christian leaders have to be fathers and mothers as well as being managers. Their role is to mentor and not to control, to encourage people in their walk of faith, so that faith, hope and love increases and their congregation experiences true joy, peace, patience and other virtues in their lives. Motivated by such grace in their lives they then become a blessing to others.

I'll sum it up like this:

As people walk with the King of Glory in faith they find themselves changing on the inside so that they become more like Him, in the way they do things and in the way they relate with other people.

It's about people having a faith that enables them to hope that they can change; that they and their families have a future and a hope. They have a person of substance that walks beside them and helps them live their lives. They put their hope in Jesus.

That's why Paul says, 'Christ **in you** the hope of glory'.

SUMMARY

1. The hope of glory is that we become like Jesus.

2. That means we feel the same way about things as He does.

3. We behave the way He would.

4. We have faith in the same things.

5. We hope in the same things.

6. We hope for the same things.

7. We love the same things.

8. We are not perfect but become more like Him as we walk in faith with Him.

9. We cannot do this in our own strength but only through the leading of the Holy Spirit.

CHAPTER 3
THE FATHER HEART OF GOD

'Until you grasp whose you are, you'll never know who you are. You'll
spend your life searching for something you already have in Him.'
– Tony Fitzgerald

It's impossible for me to speak of the 'hope of glory' without sharing my
understanding of God's heart. For to walk in faith with Jesus, I believe that
really you need to know Him well and understand that He has the same
nature as His Father.

The Apostle John spoke of God's nature in his first letter and the
importance of really knowing him:

> He who does not love does not know God, for God is love.
> (1 John 4 verse 8)

This scripture tells me that the Father's heart is full of love. His very
nature is love. How do I know that Jesus has the same nature as His
Father? Let's look at the gospel of John Chapter 14 where Jesus is speaking
to His disciples:

> 'If you had known Me, you would have known My Father also; and
> from now on you know Him and have seen Him.' Philip said to
> Him, 'Lord, show us the Father, and it is sufficient for us.' Jesus
> said to him, 'Have I been with you so long, and yet you have not

known Me, Philip? He who has seen Me has seen the Father; so how can you say, 'Show us the Father'?'
(John 14 verses 7 to 9)

From these scriptures it is clear to me that when you know Jesus you know the Father as well, for their natures are identical. They have the same heart for people. Later in the chapter he goes on to say:

'If you love Me, keep My commandments. And I will pray the Father, and He will give you another Helper, that He may abide with you forever — the Spirit of truth, whom the world cannot receive, because it neither sees Him nor knows Him; but you know Him, for He dwells with you and will be in you. I will not leave you orphans; I will come to you.'
(John 14 verses 15 to 18)

In verse 18 Jesus makes a statement that I find very interesting, 'I will not leave you as orphans, I will come to you'. There was obviously a danger that the disciples would be fatherless if He left them. However, He said that he would ask the Father to send someone in His place to be with them. He was speaking of the Holy Spirit. He speaks more about this in John Chapter 16.

I have still many things to say to you, but you are not able to bear them or to take them upon you or to grasp them now. But when He, the Spirit of Truth (the Truth-giving Spirit) comes, He will guide you into all the Truth (the whole, full Truth). For He will not speak His own message [on His own authority]; but He will tell whatever He hears [from the Father; He will give the message that has been given to Him], and He will announce and declare to you the things that are to come [that will happen in the future]. He will honour and glorify Me, because He will take of (receive, draw upon) what is Mine and will reveal (declare, disclose, transmit) it to you. Everything that the Father has is Mine. That is what I meant when I said that He [the Spirit] will take the things that are Mine and will reveal (declare, disclose, transmit) it to you.
(John 16 verses 12 to 15 the Amplified Bible)

From this I understand that the Holy Spirit takes what he hears from the Father and discloses it to us. He doesn't speak his own message but only what he hears from the Father.
Let's look at another passage of scripture about the Holy Spirit.

For as many as are led by the Spirit of God, these are sons of God. For you did not receive the spirit of bondage again to fear, but you received the Spirit of adoption by whom we cry out, 'Abba, Father'. (Romans 8 verses 14 to 15)

According to Romans 8, the Holy Spirit is the 'spirit of adoption'. It is by Him that we cry out 'Abba (father)'. He speaks to our hearts and confirms that we are children of God. He has the Father's heart. It is therefore clear to me that He has the same nature as Jesus and the same nature as the Father.

The bible speaks about something called spiritual warfare, which is a battle fought in the spirit realm over who controls the minds and hearts of mankind.

For we do not wrestle against flesh and blood, but against principalities, against powers, against the rulers of the darkness of this age, against spiritual hosts of wickedness in the heavenly places. (Ephesians 6 verse 12)

Much of this spiritual warfare relates to how we see our heavenly Father and how we see ourselves. The powers of darkness seek to give people a twisted mindset about His nature, causing us to act in ways that are not His will, believing we are actually doing the right thing.

This spiritual warfare can so affect people that they can sometimes be so sure they are right that they end up arguing with God even when He sends someone to speak to them. This is especially true when it comes to who our spiritual father is.

I saw this in action in John Chapter 8 where Jesus was debating with some Jews.

'I know that you are Abraham's descendants, but you seek to kill Me, because My word has no place in you. I speak what I have seen with My Father, and you do what you have seen with your father.' They answered and said to Him, 'Abraham is our father.' Jesus said to them, 'If you were Abraham's children, you would do the works of Abraham. But now you seek to kill Me, a Man who has told you the truth which I heard from God. Abraham did not do this. You do the deeds of your father.' Then they said to Him, 'We were not born of fornication; we have one Father—God.' Jesus said to them, "If God were your Father, you would love Me, for I proceeded forth and came from God; nor have I come of Myself, but He sent Me. Why do you not understand My speech? Because you are not able to listen to My word. You are of your father the devil, and the desires of your father you want to do. He was a murderer from the beginning, and does not stand in the truth, because there is no truth in him. When he speaks a lie, he speaks from his own resources, for he is a liar and the father of it. But because I tell the truth, you do not believe Me. Which of you convicts Me of sin? And if I tell the truth, why do you not believe Me? He who is of God hears God's words; therefore you do not hear, because you are not of God.' (John 8 verses 37 to 47)

Jesus was teaching people in spiritual bondage, seeking to set them free, which was what His Father wanted. Although they initially believed in Him they didn't like being told that they could be free. They believed that because they were the physical descendants of Abraham they were already free.

During the discussion they actually accused Jesus of being illegitimate. This was controversial but Jesus answered them just as controversially by telling them they were of their father the devil because He was teaching them the truth, what He had learned from His Father and they were refusing to listen to Him.

They were not accusing Him of sin but they were still refusing to listen to something that could liberate them spiritually. They believed their religion was what could make them free, even though what they were doing was not the Father's heart for them.

If we look at this passage of scripture in relation to the time these people were living it becomes clearer as to why they were so annoyed with Jesus.

There was an amazing expansion of the Jewish religion taking place at the time and people were converting to Judaism all over the Roman Empire. Many people in Israel were very excited about this and expecting the coming of the Messiah who would drive the Romans out of Israel. They were very proud that their religion was spreading and obviously believed they were carrying out God's will.

Although their religion was being relatively successful, it did not mean that they were living in accordance with God's will and following His plans and purposes for Israel.

When I read the bible it is apparent to me that Jesus didn't come to Earth simply to start another religion, because if the Jewish religion had the ability to set them free then these people would already have been spiritually liberated.

Jesus actually came to reveal His Father's heart and to begin establishing the Kingdom of Heaven upon the earth through the sons of God.

There is another facet to this passage of scripture that I find interesting. When Jesus told them that they were of their father the devil He was referring to their spiritual ancestry. The way I see it, mankind can be descended spiritually from one of two fathers. Either they are descended from Abraham or they are descended from satan. Those who are spiritually descended from Abraham are also spiritually descended from our Father in heaven and therefore have the right to call Him 'Father'.

> There is neither Jew nor Greek, there is neither slave nor free, there is neither male nor female; for you are all one in Christ Jesus. And if you are Christ's, then you are Abraham's seed, and heirs according to the promise.
> (Galatians 3 verses 28 to 29)

> For the kingdom of God is not eating and drinking, but righteousness and peace and joy in the Holy Spirit.
> (Romans 14 verse 17)

From reading these scriptures it is clear to me that those who have faith in Jesus Christ are the children of Abraham and therefore the heirs of the Kingdom of Light. The book of Colossians tells me that the saints are those who have been called out of darkness and into the Kingdom of light. This Kingdom is righteousness, peace and joy in the Holy Spirit who reveals to us the Father's love and His way of doing things. That's what sets people free!

> Giving thanks to the Father who has qualified us to be partakers of the inheritance of the saints in the light. He has delivered us from the power of darkness and conveyed us into the kingdom of the Son of His love, in whom we have redemption through His blood, the forgiveness of sins.
> (Colossians 1 verses 12 to 14)

Therefore, when it comes to the spirit realm, we can only have one of two fathers. We are either the sons of God (and I use the word son for both male and female) or we are the sons of the evil one. If we have neither then we are fatherless, orphans in the spirit realm and easy prey for the principalities and powers of darkness and those who follow them.

There are other religions that believe in God and have followers that worship Him. They believe that their religion has the power to set them free but no other faith, apart from Christianity, teaches people to call Him Father. If we make Christianity just another religion, among many that worship God, then I feel that we miss the point completely. True Christians are those who are adopted into God's family and become the sons of God.

I think many of us would be very surprised if we could look at planet Earth with the eyes of the Father and see the true sons of God. You see, being spiritually free is not really about what religion we belong to but actually about who our spiritual Father is. Romans 8 tells me that the sons of God are those who are led and controlled by the Holy Spirit, the one who reveals the Father's heart to us.

I will go over this again to make it as clear as possible in case there is anyone confused by what I am saying:

1. The Father's heart is full of love.
2. He sent His son Jesus to die for us.
3. Jesus revealed the Father's heart.
4. Jesus then asked His Father to send the Holy Spirit.
5. The Holy Spirit also reveals the Father's heart.
6. The sons of God are those who are led and controlled by the Holy Spirit.
7. The sons of God are adopted into His family.
8. The sons of God are those who reveal the Father's heart to other people.

There are those that take the word of God and use it in such a way that it causes hurt and damage to other people. That is not the way of the Kingdom and it is not God's will, for as I've said earlier, 'God is love'. When we take what is written in the bible, listen to the promptings of the Holy Spirit and thereby accurately interpret it from the Father's true nature, then we will be more able to help set others free.

Just as there are two fathers in the spirit realm there are also two rulers over the domains of light and darkness. Jesus the King of Glory who rules over the Kingdom of Light and satan who rules over the powers of darkness.

The second chapter of Ephesians describes how people are set free from his influence.

> For by grace you have been saved through faith, and that not of yourselves; it is the gift of God, not of works, lest anyone should boast. For we are His workmanship, created in Christ Jesus for good works, which God prepared beforehand that we should walk in them. Therefore remember that you, once Gentiles in the flesh— who are called Uncircumcision by what is called the Circumcision made in the flesh by hands— that at that time you were without Christ, being aliens from the commonwealth of Israel and strangers from the covenants of promise, having no hope and without God in the world. But now in Christ Jesus you who once were far off have

been brought near by the blood of Christ. For He Himself is our peace, who has made both one, and has broken down the middle wall of separation, having abolished in His flesh the enmity, that is, the law of commandments contained in ordinances, so as to create in Himself one new man from the two, thus making peace, and that He might reconcile them both to God in one body through the cross, thereby putting to death the enmity. And He came and preached peace to you who were afar off and to those who were near. For through Him we both have access by one Spirit to the Father. (Ephesians 2 verses 8 to 18)

It is through Jesus that we are delivered from the influence of satan and transferred from darkness into the Kingdom of Light and therefore have access by the Spirit to the Father. Jesus speaks of this matter during His answer to a question put to him by the disciple Thomas.

Thomas said to Him, 'Lord, we do not know where You are going, and how can we know the way?' Jesus said to him, 'I am the way, the truth, and the life. No one comes to the Father except through Me. If you had known Me, you would have known My Father also; and from now on you know Him and have seen Him.'
(John 14 verses 5 to 7)

According to the bible I realize that I cannot call God my Father unless I approach Him through faith in Jesus Christ. If you are one of those that find it difficult to call Him Father then there is no need to despair for as the Apostle Peter says.

But, beloved, do not forget this one thing, that with the Lord one day is as a thousand years, and a thousand years as one day. The Lord is not slack concerning His promise, as some count slackness, but is longsuffering toward us, not willing that any should perish but that all should come to repentance.
(2 Peter 3 verses 8 to 9)

The will of almighty God is that all men call Him Father but we can only do this with authority when we have faith in Jesus Christ.

The 'hope of glory' is therefore not only that we will become like Jesus but that, through the leading of the Holy Spirit, we would also become the sons of God.

It is the sons of God that reveal His true nature to the world and who have the amazing right to call Him Father.

Now, isn't that something to hope for?

SUMMARY

1. The Father's heart is full of love.

2. He sent His son Jesus to die for us.

3. Jesus revealed the Father's heart.

4. Jesus then asked His Father to send the Holy Spirit.

5. The Holy Spirit also reveals the Father's heart.

6. The sons of God are those who are led and controlled by the Holy Spirit.

7. The sons of God are adopted into His family through faith in Christ and the leading of the Holy Spirit..

8. The sons of God are those who reveal the Father's heart to other people.

9. If we don't know the Father's heart we can follow the wrong path believing we are doing the right thing.

CHAPTER 4
HOPE IN GOD'S LOVE

'God loves each of us as if there were only one of us.' – St Augustine

When someone is struggling, I often hear well-meaning people use stock phrases like, 'Put your faith in Jesus' and 'God works in mysterious ways'. It's easy to say things like that but it doesn't really help. When everything is falling apart around you and nothing seems to be going right it is harder to have hope for anything. It is more difficult to have hope then because thoughts come against your mind that nothing is ever going to go right for you again. Depression sets in and all hope seems gone.

In such situations we need something to hope in more than ever. For me that is when having real faith in Jesus is such a help. There is something incredibly important though that we really need to believe to have hope in Jesus. We need to believe that God loves us.

This involves knowing the Father's heart and is absolutely paramount to the Christian faith. We really need to know His character and His nature to truly know His heart. Sadly, it is often the case that people don't know His true nature and it has either caused them to reject Him, or to live their lives in fear of being rejected themselves.

If we believe that God is extremely strict and wants to punish us all the time then we will interpret scripture from that perspective. If however, we believe that He is a loving Father who only wants the best for His children then we will interpret scripture completely differently.

When I read the bible, I see God as a loving Father, who only wants the very best for us.

> In this the love of God was manifested toward us, that God has sent His only begotten Son into the world, that we might live through Him.
> (1 John 4 verse 9)

> For God so loved the world that He gave His only begotten Son, that whoever believes in Him should not perish but have everlasting life.
> (John 3 verse 16)

There are many more scriptures that say the same thing and tell us of the nature of the Father. His very nature is love and He knows what is best for us.

Isn't it true that knowing our Father in heaven directly relates to love? I mean, when discussing faith with people, they often ask, 'how do you know that God is real?' For me, I know that God is real because I feel Him in my heart in the same way that I feel love for my wife and children. How do you know that love is real? The answer is, you feel it in your heart. How do you know that God is real? The answer is, you feel Him in your heart.

What I consider to be the most important part of our walk with God, the thing that provides the cement that holds everything in our faith together is this, that we love the Lord our God and that we love each other. As Jesus says in answer to a question about faith:

> 'Teacher, which is the great commandment in the law?' Jesus said to him, 'You shall love the LORD your God with all your heart, with all your soul, and with all your mind.' This is the first and great commandment.'
> (Matthew 22 verses 36 to 38)

Jesus tells us that this is the most important thing. Then he adds:

> 'And the second is like it: 'You shall love your neighbour as yourself.' On these two commandments hang all the Law and the Prophets.
> (Matthew 22 verses 39 to 40)

So the most important thing in the commandments is to love God and love our neighbour as ourselves. We are to

1. Love God
2. Love our neighbour
3. Love ourselves

How can we achieve this? The answer is found in 1 John chapter 1

> We love Him because He first loved us.
> (1 John 4 verse 19)

We love God because He first loved us. This is, I believe, the most important thing in our walk with God, the most important aspect of our faith and where our hope and love for Him really springs from. We must believe that our Father in heaven loves us.

I'm not talking here about a theological discussion because people that read the bible know that it says that 'God is love'. I'm speaking of an issue deep inside a person's heart that causes them to continually doubt that they are good enough to be God's son.

The truth of course is that nobody is good enough. It's the sacrificial exchange that Jesus made on the cross that makes us acceptable to the Father. It's not about works or what we do. The Father is more interested about who we are. He is more interested in our character and in whether or not we reflect His nature.

I have seen people struggling with faith for most of their lives. The issue for them is not that God exists or that Jesus is the Son of God, the virgin birth, or any other theological discussion. The real issue for many people is that they just don't believe that God loves them and don't believe that other Christians love them either.

This can show itself in different ways, a common one being that they refuse to have anything to do with a local church or a ministry, even if they say they believe in God.

Another way this issue reveals itself is when people spend their lives doing lots of different things to try to please God and hoping that He will love them. Then when they mess up for whatever reason (and everyone misses it from time to time) they feel condemned and feel that God can't possibly love them. They then try their best to do something else that they feel will make up for them messing up and then they might feel loved again.

In my opinion, this kind of thinking isn't based upon the faith of God but just a religious version of worry. You see, the opposite of faith is doubt, which produces fear, despair, worry and anxiety instead of hope. This is not the fear of God you read of in the bible, which speaks of putting your trust in Him but a fear that maybe God doesn't really love them.

Perfect love casts out this fear and replaces it with faith and hope. However the scripture also says that, 'he who fears has not been made perfect in love'.

I believe that being made perfect in love relates to our walk of faith. A loving pastor or mentor will see this fear in people and work with them to enable them to get their breakthrough and realise that God loves them just the way they are. It's got nothing to do with works but everything to do with faith, hope and love. It's about being part of a family that cares for each other.

People who have this fear of rejection can sometimes end up in a church group or ministry where being accepted or loved revolves around how much work they do for the ministry. They work their socks off and feel accepted and loved so long as things are going well. Then as soon as things go wrong or they make a mistake, the correction handed out is sometimes way out of all proportion to the mistake that's been made. They then feel rejected and the fear that God doesn't love them returns. They then work even harder in order to feel accepted again and, rather than experiencing the love of God and having hope in their hearts, they eventually end up feeling frustrated, abused and manipulated. If someone was in a marriage that functioned this way, it would be doomed to failure.

Being a Christian is like being in a marriage. We are in a covenant relationship with almighty God. He loves us, we love Him and we love each other. This is a fundamental part of the Christian faith. If a person struggles with believing that God loves them then it is very difficult for them to have hope.

People who live this way are living in doubt rather than in faith. They are struggling with what is sometimes called an 'Orphan Spirit' or a 'Spirit of Slavery'. They have fear in their hearts rather than hope.

There is no need for any of us to live in such bondage. Our Father in heaven loves us and accepts us purely by our faith in Jesus. None of us are perfect but as we walk in faith with Jesus under the guidance of the Holy Spirit, He works on our faults and helps us to become more like Him in nature. As we become more like Him we reveal the Father's heart more and more to other people.

Why is it so hard for people to believe that their Father in heaven loves them? The bible clearly tells us that he is long suffering and full of mercy.

> Therefore know that the LORD your God, He is God, the faithful God who keeps covenant and mercy for a thousand generations with those who love Him and keep His commandments.
> (Deuteronomy 7 verse 9)

> The LORD is merciful and gracious, slow to anger, and abounding in mercy.
> (Psalm 103 verse 8)

I believe that the reason why people find it so hard to believe that God loves them is that there is a battle going on in the spirit realm for their souls. When they make a mistake they feel condemnation. They then put themselves down and feel rejected by God even when he hasn't rejected them. This condemnation comes straight from the accuser of the brethren, namely satan.

You see, where there is sin there is also condemnation. However we were set free from the power of sin by the sacrificial offering that Jesus made on the cross.

> For if by the one man's offense death reigned through the one, much more those who receive abundance of grace and of the gift of righteousness will reign in life through the One, Jesus Christ.) Therefore, as through one man's offense judgment came to all men, resulting in condemnation, even so through one Man's righteous act the free gift came to all men, resulting in justification of life. For as by one man's disobedience many were made sinners, so also by one Man's obedience many will be made righteous.
> (Romans 5 verses 17 to 19)

> There is therefore now no condemnation to those who are in Christ Jesus.
> (Romans 8 verse 1a)

We are not living under condemnation; we are living in the time of a new covenant. As Jesus says, it is a new covenant in His blood, which is shed for us.

> And He took bread, gave thanks and broke it, and gave it to them, saying, 'This is My body which is given for you; do this in remembrance of Me.' Likewise He also took the cup after supper, saying, 'This cup is the new covenant in My blood, which is shed for you.'
> (Luke 22 verses 19 to 21)

When we look at John chapter 3 verse 16, one of the most quoted pieces of scripture in the bible, we see the reason for the shed blood of Jesus.

> For God so loved the world that He gave His only begotten Son, that whoever believes in Him should not perish but have everlasting life.
> (John 3 verse 16)

Jesus then goes on to add that He wasn't sent into the world to bring condemnation but to bring salvation. There is really no need for any of us to feel condemned.

> For God did not send His Son into the world to condemn the world, but that the world through Him might be saved.
> (John 3 verse 17)

There are other scriptures that speak of the love the Father has for us.

> For the Father Himself loves you, because you have loved Me, and have believed that I came forth from God.
> (John 16 verse 27)

> In this is love, not that we loved God, but that He loved us and sent His Son to be the propitiation for our sins. (1 John 4 verse 10)

We can see from these scriptures that the new covenant is based on love; the Father's love for His children and His children's love for Him. If you believe that God doesn't love you and forgives you when you miss it, then you believe a lie.

> If we say that we have no sin, we deceive ourselves, and the truth is not in us. If we confess our sins, He is faithful and just to forgive us our sins and to cleanse us from all unrighteousness. If we say that we have not sinned, we make Him a liar, and His word is not in us.
> (1 John 1 verses 8 to 10)

I know that if I make a mistake and confess my mistake to my Father in heaven and ask for His forgiveness then he will give it. There is absolutely no question of Him keeping it in remembrance to remind me of it later. Once the Father forgives, He forgets all about it.

People can't possibly have true hope for their lives if their hope is based on a falsehood. Hope based on a lie will just cause frustration.

For believers to have true hope in their lives, it is absolutely paramount that their hope is based on a faith that absolutely declares that God loves them.

Our Father's love for us is absolutely unfailing. He's not like you or me on a bad day. He doesn't have grumpy days when he doesn't want to see anybody. He doesn't suffer from mood swings. He doesn't disappear off to the golf course because he can't be bothered with anyone. He doesn't bear grudges or go in the huff with us when we make a mistake. He has a forgiving nature.

The story of the prodigal son reveals much about the loving nature of the Father (see Luke chapter 15 verses 11 to 31).

Our Father in heaven is loving, forgiving and always looking for us to return to Him even when we have majorly missed it. As in the story, it is often the case that it is our brothers that are angrier with us for our actions than the Father is.

King David missed it big style when he arranged for Bathsheba's husband to be killed. (See 2 Samuel chapter 11) yet the Father forgave him. There were obviously consequences for his actions though. Our Father allows us to experience the consequences of our mistakes but He still loves us and forgives us when we show repentance for our actions.

In Psalm 51, King David prayed to God for forgiveness and in this passage of scripture, as in many of the Psalms, we find a description of how David sees the nature of Father God.

> Create in me a clean heart, O God,
> And renew a steadfast spirit within me.
> Do not cast me away from Your presence,
> And do not take Your Holy Spirit from me.
> Restore to me the joy of Your salvation,
> And uphold me by Your generous Spirit.
> Then I will teach transgressors Your ways,
> And sinners shall be converted to You.
> (Psalm 51 verses 10 to 13)

David describes God as having a generous Spirit. This word 'generous' is from the Hebrew word 'nᵉdîybâh', which means generous, magnanimous, free, liberal, noble, willing. This is a far cry from the harsh dictatorial image we sometimes see portrayed when people are describing the Father in heaven.

King David murdered one of his most faithful generals so that he could have the man's wife, yet God forgave him.

We really shouldn't fear that our Father in heaven doesn't love us. His love is perfect and casts out such fear.

We can therefore have absolute Hope in the Father's love, for our own lives, our families' lives and for our future.

SUMMARY

1.   We must believe that our Father in heaven loves us.

2.   It is foundational to the Christian faith.

3.   He wants us to love Him with all our hearts.

4.   He wants us to love Him the way He loves us.

5.   He wants us to love others the way He loves us.

6.   He loves us in spite of our many faults.

7.   He is very forgiving and full of mercy.

8.   His very nature is loving.

CHAPTER 5
THE HOPE OF SALVATION

'Three things are necessary for the salvation of man: to know what he ought to believe; to know what he ought to desire; and to know what he ought to do.' - Thomas Aquinas

Another aspect of hope that comes from my knowing the love of God in my life is, I have also received the hope of salvation.

The bible speaks of putting on a helmet, the 'hope of salvation'. A helmet is a piece of armour that protects the head, where the mind and will is contained. This kind of hope is therefore something that protects my mind and will from fear and despair, which is the opposite of hope.

> For those who sleep, sleep at night, and those who get drunk are drunk at night. But let us who are of the day be sober, putting on the breastplate of faith and love, and as a helmet the **hope of salvation**. For God did not appoint us to wrath, but to obtain salvation through our Lord Jesus Christ.
> (I Thessalonians 5 verses 7 to 9 emphasis added)

The word 'salvation' in this scripture is the Greek word 'Soteria', which relates to deliverance, healing, or to be saved or rescued. It is taken from the root word 'Soter' which refers to a saviour or deliverer. In short, salvation refers to those who have been rescued or delivered by a saviour.

Therefore the thing that I use to protect my mind through every situation is hope in my salvation though the Lord Jesus Christ.

He is my Saviour. He is my Deliverer.

> For our citizenship is in heaven, from which we also eagerly wait for
> the Saviour, the Lord Jesus Christ.
> (Philippians 3 verse 20)

Jesus has the same nature as His Father. In fact there are numerous
scriptures that speak of 'God the saviour'

> Paul, an apostle of Jesus Christ, by the commandment of God our
> Saviour and the Lord Jesus Christ, our hope, to Timothy, a true son
> in the faith: Grace, mercy, and peace from God our Father and Jesus
> Christ our Lord.
> (Timothy 1 verses 1 to 2)

> And Mary said: "My soul magnifies the Lord, And my spirit has
> rejoiced in God my Saviour.
> (Luke 1 verses 46 to 47)

What though, am I being saved and delivered from? I found the answer
in the Old Testament (Old Covenant).

It was an important aspect of this covenant that sin be atoned for in the
form of a blood sacrifice. For people to be righteous before God they had
to make a sin offering. People brought their sin offering to the high priest
who sacrificed the animal and offered it and the blood to God to atone for
sins that people had committed.

> And Moses said to Aaron, 'Go to the altar, offer your sin offering
> and your burnt offering, and make atonement for yourself and for
> the people. Offer the offering of the people, and make atonement
> for them, as the LORD commanded.'
> (Leviticus 9 verse 7)

Once the sacrifice was made, their sins were forgiven for a season and,
for a short time, they were righteous before God. However, when they
sinned again, another sacrifice was required. According to the bible, this
sacrifice made under the law was a mere shadow of things to come. The
blood of bulls and goats had no power to eternally cleanse people from
their sins.

> For the law, having a shadow of the good things to come, and not
> the very image of the things, can never with these same sacrifices,
> which they offer continually year by year, make those who approach

perfect. For then would they not have ceased to be offered? For the worshipers, once purified, would have had no more consciousness of sins. But in those sacrifices there is a reminder of sins every year. (Hebrews 10 verses 1 to 3)

It is clear from this scripture that a greater sacrifice was required. When John the Baptist saw Jesus coming to be baptised he made an interesting statement.

The next day John saw Jesus coming toward him, and said, "Behold! The Lamb of God who takes away the sin of the world! (John 1 verse 29)

Jesus is the 'Lamb of God'. He isn't called that because he carried a lamb about on his shoulders, like pictures I saw at Sunday School as a child, but because He was and is the perfect sacrifice, that had the power to take away the sins of mankind once and for all.

When Jesus was whipped, beaten, nailed to a cross and crucified, He did so as a substitute for the sins of mankind. He became the 'lamb that was slain' that all our sins might be forgiven for ever. He bore our punishment that we all might receive His Father's forgiveness and therefore also receive the blessings that were due to Jesus.

God the saviour sent His son Jesus Christ to be the perfect sacrifice, the 'Lamb of God' that we would be saved but also that Jesus would become the saviour of mankind just like His Father.

So I see this salvation as being three fold in nature:

1.   There is our initial salvation, the hope and faith we receive at the time of our conversion or the hope and faith we receive by being brought up in a loving Christian home.
2.   Then there is the salvation (grace) that is on our lives as we continue to walk with Jesus. This is 'Christ in you, the hope of glory'. It is walking with Jesus and becoming more like Him as we spend time with Him.
3.   Finally there is everlasting salvation when we go home to be with the Lord and take our place in the heavenly realm.

Therefore Salvation is three fold; we are saved, we are being saved and we will be saved.

I can therefore hope in all three aspects of salvation.

Therefore remember that you, once Gentiles in the flesh—who are called Uncircumcision by what is called the Circumcision made in the

flesh by hands— that at that time you were without Christ, being aliens from the commonwealth of Israel and strangers from the covenants of promise, having no hope and without God in the world.
(Ephesians 2 verses 11 to 12)

According to the bible, if I am separated from Christ then I am without hope and without God in the world. This is a difficult matter to comprehend as people in the world do have hopes and dreams. However, according to scripture, this kind of hope is different from the hope of the bible. You see, the hope that comes from knowing the Father brings with it the promise of salvation, the message of the gospel.

The reformer John Calvin sought to explain this matter by introducing a theological concept called the 'doctrine of common grace'. He believed that God had poured out his grace on the whole human race so that they could have a limited measure of His influence operating in their lives. He believed that this explained why the human race could produce art and develop science and music, do amazing works, even help others and be blessed in turn by them without appearing to be influenced by God in any way. However, he also believed that this common grace was different from 'saving grace' which draws people to God.

Whether one agrees with Calvin or not, there is definitely a normal human kind of hope that is common to every man. Every person on the face of the earth has hopes and dreams for their lives, for their families' lives and even for their communities.

However, it seems to me that when a people as a whole draw away from God hopelessness increases in their nation and despite the many wonderful accomplishments they may produce, things like drug abuse, suicide, abortion and the like increase. Their hopes and dreams therefore seem fruitless and despair follows.

In my own life, before coming to know Jesus as my personal saviour, I too had hopes and dreams for my life and for my family, but I also knew that there was something missing. Some people call it the 'God void'.

I knew that there was a spiritual vacuum in my life. It was as if there was an empty hole in my heart and I tried to fill it in a variety of ways. I first tried bowling and was quite good at it. This gave me some satisfaction but certainly didn't fill the void. I then tried golf but that wasn't any help, especially when you're as bad at golf as I am.

I thought marriage would fill the void but although I love my wife dearly, I found that there was still something missing. Then, when the children came along I poured out my love and hopes on them but still there was this unexplainable vacuum.

I then tried investigating the paranormal and looked into spiritualism and the occult but that definitely didn't help and actually made me feel worse. I eventually came to realize that I needed Jesus in my life. This was a big shock to me, as although I had been brought up to attend church and Sunday school I was usually bored and found it all irrelevant.

One night in my bedroom I decided to take what I considered at the time as a huge risk. I decided that I would pray to God almighty and ask Him to take charge of my life. Although outwardly I seemed to have everything, inwardly I was in a mess and void of any real hope for my future.

I prayed and told God I was sorry for doing my own thing and asked Him to forgive me. I asked Him to give me the faith that I knew other people had. I immediately felt a warm glow in my heart and experienced a level of love in my being that just washed all over me. Such was the relief and joy I felt, I cried my eyes out for what felt like hours, totally lost in the Father's love.

Not everyone has the same kind of experience I had but one thing everyone agrees on. When you experience the love of God, there comes a new level of hope in your life that is way beyond any hope you've had prior to that.

After praying that prayer I suddenly had a realization that the Lord was looking after me and my family, no matter what happened. Even if tragedy affected us, we had eternal salvation to put our hope in. At that time, a peace and joy came into my heart that was definitely not there before. I would say that the hope that comes from 'saving grace' is a marvelous thing. It produces a peace and joy in our lives that normal human hopes and dreams can never bring.

There is far more to it than that though. When we have this heavenly hope it causes us to desire other things, heavenly things. We hope to see sinners saved, to see the lame walk, to see blind eyes opened, the deaf to hear, the lost to be found. Our hope is no longer on the things of the world or merely on our personal hopes and dreams but also on the things of God.

As Jesus said when he read from the book of Isaiah in Luke Chapter 4.

> And He was handed the book of the prophet Isaiah.
> And when He had opened the book,
> He found the place where it was written:
> 'The Spirit of the LORD is upon Me,
> Because He has anointed Me
> To preach the gospel to the poor;
> He has sent Me to heal the brokenhearted,
> To proclaim liberty to the captives
> And recovery of sight to the blind,

To set at liberty those who are oppressed;
To proclaim the acceptable year of the LORD.'
(Luke 4 verses 17 to 19)

This kind of hope causes you to look beyond your own problems and think about other people instead. It makes your own troubles seem much less important.

Therefore, the hope of salvation is not only for me. It includes the hope for others to be saved and for them to receive the same hope that I have.

Just as our Father, God the Saviour, mentored His son Jesus Christ to become the Saviour of the world, so also it is in Jesus' heart to mentor other sons and daughters so that they can reveal the Father's heart to other people and so help them find salvation.

This desire for others to find salvation was in the Apostle Paul's heart when he wrote:

Therefore I endure all things for the sake of the elect, that they also may obtain the salvation which is in Christ Jesus with eternal glory.
(2 Timothy 2 verse 10)

Normal human hope cannot sustain a person in times of trouble. It cannot lift their soul, but the hope that comes from strong faith, in relationship with Jesus, can sustain you through anything.

SUMMARY

1. The hope of salvation protects our minds from fear and despair.

2. Salvation is ours through the sacrifice Jesus made on the cross.

3. Jesus is our Saviour and Father God is also our Saviour.

4. Salvation is threefold: we are saved, we are being saved and we will be saved.

5. The hope of salvation enables us to focus on matters concerning the Kingdom of Heaven.

6. The hope of salvation sustains us through times of trouble.

CHAPTER 6
THE GRACE OF GOD

'Grace is but Glory begun, and Glory is but Grace perfected.'
– Jonathan Edwards

I hope that you now realize more than ever, just how much our Father in heaven loves you. It is absolutely amazing that the Almighty God who created the universe and spoke galaxies, stars and solar systems into being, considers us worthy of His love. He sent His only son to die on a cross for us so that we could not only have salvation but be adopted into His family.

It's incredible to think of such an amazing love. Imagine citizens of the United Kingdom were being held hostage by a foreign power and threatened with execution. Suppose the Queen loved her subjects so much that she sent Prince Charles to take their place and be executed on their behalf. Think of His Royal Highness being willing to die for His subjects. Not only that but consider Her Majesty then adopting these citizens by Royal Command so that they became joint heirs of the kingdom, along with her own children!

Nobody would believe anyone capable of such love and such grace but that's exactly what His Majesty, Almighty God, did when He sent Jesus to die for us on the cross. Jesus took our place and was executed on our behalf. An exchange took place on that cross and we were given the right to be adopted as God's own children and become joint heirs with Jesus to the Kingdom of Heaven. All we have to do is believe in Him, accept the Royal Command to join His family and begin the wonderful walk of faith, hope and love in His grace. However, there is even more to this that gives me cause to hope:

> John, to the seven churches which are in Asia: Grace to you and peace from Him who is and who was and who is to come, and from the seven Spirits who are before His throne, and from Jesus Christ, the faithful witness, the firstborn from the dead, and the ruler over the kings of the earth. To Him who loved us and washed us from our sins in His own blood and has made us kings and priests to His God and Father, to Him be glory and dominion forever and ever. Amen.
> (Revelation 1 verses 4 to 6)

When we become members of His family we are also made kings and priests to God. The Apostle Peter makes mention of this same matter in one of his letters:

> But you are a chosen generation, a royal priesthood, a holy nation, His own special people, that you may proclaim the praises of Him who called you out of darkness into His marvellous light; who once were not a people but are now the people of God, who had not obtained mercy but now have obtained mercy.
> (1 Peter 2 verses 9 to 10)

A believer's inheritance includes being part of the royal priesthood. We can be assured that our Father hears our prayers!

> For I consider that the sufferings of this present time are not worthy to be compared with the glory which shall be revealed in us.
> (Romans 8 verse 18)

The hope of glory includes being revealed as priests and kings to our God. The role of a priest in Israel was to minister to God, spend time in His presence and then minister His love to the people.

> "Now take Aaron your brother, and his sons with him, from among the children of Israel, that he may minister to Me as priest, Aaron and Aaron's sons: Nadab, Abihu, Elemazar, and Ithamar.'
> (Exodus 28 verse 1)

> Then Aaron lifted his hand toward the people, blessed them, and came down from offering the sin offering, the burnt offering, and peace offerings. And Moses and Aaron went into the tabernacle of

meeting, and came out and blessed the people. Then the glory of the LORD appeared to all the people.
(Leviticus 9 verses 22 to 23)

Under the Mosaic law, the High Priest was permitted to enter into the Holy of Holies to minister to God Almighty on behalf of the people. However, spiritually Jesus is a High Priest forever after the order of Melchizedek.

So also Christ did not glorify Himself to become High Priest, but it was He who said to Him: 'You are My Son, today I have begotten You.' As He also says in another place: 'You are a priest forever according to the order of Melchizedek.'
(Hebrews 5 verses 5 to 6)

Melchizedek was the priest that blessed Abram (Abraham) after his victory over Chedorlaomer, the King of Elam.

Then Melchizedek king of Salem brought out bread and wine; he was the priest of God Most High. And he blessed him and said: 'Blessed be Abram of God Most High, Possessor of heaven and earth.'
(Genesis 14 verses 18 to 19)

This Melchizedek was not a High Priest of the Mosaic Law but one who ministered to God under the covenant of promise.

And inasmuch as He was not made priest without an oath (for they have become priests without an oath, but He with an oath by Him who said to Him: 'The LORD has sworn and will not relent, You are a priest forever according to the order of Melchizedek' by so much more Jesus has become a surety of a better covenant.
(Hebrews 7 verses 20 to 22)

My understanding of this is that Jesus is the High Priest after the order of Melchizedek. The bible clearly states that Christians are members of a royal priesthood. It therefore follows that true Christians are priests after the order of Melchizedek through their faith in Jesus Christ.

Therefore, brethren, having boldness to enter the Holiest by the blood of Jesus, by a new and living way which He consecrated for us, through the veil, that is, His flesh, and having a High Priest over the house of God, let us draw near with a true heart in full assurance of faith, having our hearts sprinkled from an evil conscience and our

bodies washed with pure water. Let us hold fast the confession of our hope without wavering, for He who promised is faithful.
(Hebrews 10 verses 19 to 23)

Being part of the order of Melchizedek through faith in Jesus Christ, Christians, led by the Holy Spirit, have freedom to enter into the holy of holies to fellowship with their Father in heaven in prayer.

Now, the role of the king of Israel was to rule, to establish godly laws and bring justice, to establish God's kingdom upon the earth.

In fact, when the first King of Israel failed to do things God's way, the Lord sought after another man who was of His own heart to be King over Israel.

And Samuel said to Saul, 'You have done foolishly. You have not kept the commandment of the LORD your God, which He commanded you. For now the LORD would have established your kingdom over Israel forever. But now your kingdom shall not continue. The LORD has sought for Himself a man after His own heart, and the LORD has commanded him to be commander over His people, because you have not kept what the LORD commanded you.'
(1 Samuel 13 verses 13 to 14)

However, when a king followed God's ways it brought blessing and honour to both him and the kingdom.

So King Solomon surpassed all the kings of the earth in riches and wisdom.
(1 Kings 10 verse 23)

And Judah and Israel dwelt safely, each man under his vine and his fig tree, from Dan as far as Beersheba, all the days of Solomon.
(1 Kings 4 verse 25)

It is clearly the role of the king to bring justice and to establish God's kingdom upon the earth.

Of the increase of His government and peace There will be no end, Upon the throne of David and over His kingdom, To order it and establish it with judgment and justice From that time forward, even forever. The zeal of the LORD of hosts will perform this.
(Isaiah 9 verses 6 to 8)

When you read about the priests and kings of the bible there is something else that our Father in heaven gives to them either directly by inspiration, or indirectly through another gifted person and that is the gift of prophesy.

When you speak to people about prophesy it is something that has the ability to freak people out. However, the bible is absolutely full of references to prophets and to prophesy. It is therefore important to realize that Holy Spirit led prophesy is something that the Lord will impart to us as priests and kings of our God.

The psalms of King David are absolutely full of prophesy so it is obvious that he was a very prophetic person. Yet he also had people that held the office of prophet to advise him. The New Testament is also full of prophesy. It is very much a part of the kingdom of heaven.

The bible also speaks about false prophets and this has caused some in the church to totally reject this gift in case the person concerned turns out to be a 'false prophet'.

However the very first subject that the apostle Paul speaks of after his famous faith, hope and love quote in 1 Corinthians 13 relates to prophesy.

> Pursue love, and desire spiritual gifts, but especially that you may prophesy. For he who speaks in a tongue does not speak to men but to God, for no one understands him; however, in the spirit he speaks mysteries. But he who prophesies speaks edification and exhortation and comfort to men.
> (1 Corinthians 1 verses 1 to 3)

I recall something that happened to me as an early Christian which is a perfect example of the prophetic at work.

I had become aware of prophesy and was desperate for someone to give me a prophetic word so I could check out whether they were really hearing from God. The church leaders at the time were obviously aware of what was going on and nobody would do what I wanted.

I got so frustrated that during a personal time of prayer I started shouting at God and told Him that if He didn't give me a 'word' then I wasn't going back to church. A foolish and stupid thing to say I know but that was where I was at back then. I then heard a still small voice in my mind say, 'open your bible'. I picked up the bible and it fell open at Jeremiah 50.

> The word that the LORD spoke against Babylon and against the land of the Chaldeans by Jeremiah the prophet. 'Declare among the nations, proclaim, and set up a standard; proclaim - do not conceal it - say, 'Babylon is taken, Bel is shamed. Merodach is broken in

pieces; her idols are humiliated, her images are broken in pieces.' For out of the north a nation comes up against her, Which shall make her land desolate, and no one shall dwell therein. They shall move, they shall depart, both man and beast.'
(Jeremiah 50 verses 1 to 3)

This made absolutely no sense to me whatsoever and I felt even more frustrated than I did before.

That evening I went to a house church meeting in Elgin feeling absolutely awful. I felt dejected that I hadn't received the 'word' I wanted but also felt so guilty that I had fallen out with God.

When I walked into the room the people there were praying. Without any prompting on my part, the group leader suddenly announced that she had a bible verse for someone in the room. She opened up her bible and read from Jeremiah 50 verses 1 to 3. Now, as you can imagine, this totally freaked me out at the time but I knew that this couldn't be anything else than my Father in heaven speaking to me.

Any time I feel any doubt or unbelief, or fear about the future I can remember what happened. It has given me tremendous hope that God is looking after me however much I may miss it from time to time. However, if the house church leader hadn't bothered to respond to the prophetic leading of the Holy Spirit then I don't know what would have become of me.

The point I am seeking to make is that as priests and kings, we have been given the privilege to fellowship directly with our Father in heaven, receive His prophetic instructions and then to establish justice and truth on the earth in the form of God's kingdom which is righteousness, peace and joy in the Holy Spirit. (Romans 14 verse 17). Therefore where the Kingdom of Heaven is being established there will also be those who are spiritually prophets, priests and kings carrying out His will upon the earth.

In my opinion we should never allow fear to stop the prophetic gift from operating as this would be in direct opposition to the establishment of God's kingdom. As Jesus said:

Beware of false prophets, who come to you in sheep's clothing, but inwardly they are ravenous wolves. You will know them by their fruits. Do men gather grapes from thorn-bushes or figs from thistles? Even so, every good tree bears good fruit, but a bad tree bears bad fruit. A good tree cannot bear bad fruit, nor can a bad tree bear good fruit. Every tree that does not bear good fruit is cut down and thrown into the fire. Therefore by their fruits you will know them.
(Matthew 7 verses 15 to 20)

That is not to say that we should allow people to suffer abuse by those that claim to be prophets. We have a responsibility to ensure that people are not being hurt or damaged in any way. However, the way of the kingdom is not to stop prophets from prophesying but to test them by their fruits. Is the kingdom being established? Are people growing spiritually? Is the area being blessed?

The men and women of the bible were extremely prophetic in nature. It therefore follows that those of our own era will also be prophetic in nature. It's important to understand that positionally we are prophets, priests and kings to our God after the order of Melchizedek. It's from that spiritual position that we receive the immense grace He continues to pour out, because of our faith in Jesus Christ. This gives tremendous hope to those who believe in His word.

According to the bible, there are three elements of God's grace that are constant and unchanging.

> And so faith, hope, love abide [faith--conviction and belief respecting man's relation to God and divine things; hope--joyful and confident expectation of eternal salvation; love--true affection for God and man, growing out of God's love for and in us], these three; but the greatest of these is love.
> (1 Corinthians 13 verse 13 the Amplified Bible)

The bible tells us to earnestly desire the higher gifts and the choicest graces. These three are unchanging and will always remain, faith, hope and love, with the greatest being love. That means we are also to earnestly desire 'hope'. That means that there is hope for you and me today, tomorrow and for our future.

So how does the Father pour out His grace upon us? What means does He employ to carry out His marvelous work?

> In this way [our] witnessing concerning Christ (the Messiah) was so confirmed and established and made sure in you. That you are not [consciously] falling behind or lacking in any special spiritual endowment or Christian grace [the reception of which is due to the power of divine grace operating in your souls by the Holy Spirit], while you wait and watch [constantly living in hope] for the coming of our Lord Jesus Christ and [His] being made visible to all. And He will establish you to the end [keep you steadfast, give you strength, and guarantee your vindication; He will be your warrant against all accusation or indictment so that you will be] guiltless and irreproachable in the day of our Lord Jesus Christ (the Messiah).
> (1 Corinthians 1 verses 6 to 8 the Amplified Bible)

The answer is that He pours out His grace upon us by the power of the Holy Spirit. The Holy Spirit shows us the Father's heart and works with us so that we become more like Jesus.

As I've already said in a previous chapter, the 'Hope of Glory' is that we become like Jesus but we do so by walking with him in faith, knowing beyond all doubt that the Father loves us and being led and guided by the Holy Spirit, who is the means by which the Father imparts His grace to us.

As this grace works in our hearts, the fruits of the Spirit become more evident in our lives.

> But the fruit of the [Holy] Spirit [the work which His presence within accomplishes] is love, joy (gladness), peace, patience (an even temper, forbearance), kindness, goodness (benevolence), faithfulness, gentleness (meekness, humility), self-control (self-restraint, continence). Against such things there is no law [that can bring a charge]. (Galatians 5 verses 22 to 23 the Amplified bible)

Salvation is concerned with faith, hope and love and we are saved by grace in this manner: The Father pours out his love into the world by the sacrifice of His son Jesus Christ. When we make a conscious decision to accept this sacrifice, decide we are going to believe what the Bible says, we experience the love of God and hope rises in our hearts. True faith is not just a belief in God, it is also conviction that grows from the love of God in our hearts and the hope that springs forth does so because of this love. The love is shed abroad in our hearts through the Holy Spirit.

I believe that you can see the three graces in operation in these verses as follows

> **Love** - love, kindness, goodness
> **Hope** - joy, peace, patience
> **Faith** - faithfulness, gentleness, self-control

Where there is true faith there will also be hope and love. If the grace of God is really flowing in our lives then all three graces will be in evidence flowing together.

When I decided I wanted God in my life, I already believed but I didn't know Him. I had friends that were Christians and I could see that they had a peace and joy in their lives that they said came from knowing Jesus.

Although I had no relationship with God, my belief (little faith) in His existence gave me the encouragement to approach Him in prayer and ask him to give me what my friends had. It wasn't faith that came to me at that moment; it was the pure and living hope of God that sprang forth in my heart and gave me the peace and joy that I was looking for. Later, a firm conviction (faith) grew in my soul that was founded upon the hope that 'sprang exulting on triumphant wing' when I experienced the love of God in my heart.

The following scripture speaks of the joy and peace we have when we have hope in Jesus.

> Through Him also we have [our] access (entrance, introduction) by faith into this grace (state of God's favor) in which we [firmly and safely] stand. And let us rejoice and exult in our hope of experiencing and enjoying the glory of God.
> (Romans 5 verse 2 the Amplified Bible)

Peace and joy is a product of our hope. Those who have true hope will be filled with a peace and joy that others find truly remarkable. The bible is full of scriptures relating to hope and when you add the ones about joy peace and patience there is a fount of knowledge on the subject that we can draw inspiration from.

> May the God of your hope so fill you with all joy and peace in believing [through the experience of your faith] that by the power of the Holy Spirit you may abound and be overflowing (bubbling over) with hope.
> (Romans 15 verse 13 the Amplified Bible)

From this scripture I see that hope is connected to our peace and joy in believing. A person that has peace and joy is bubbling over with hope.

> Even though we speak this way, yet in your case, beloved, we are now firmly convinced of better things that are near to salvation and accompany it. For God is not unrighteous to forget or overlook your labor and the love which you have shown for His name's sake in ministering to the needs of the saints (His own consecrated people), as you still do. But we do [strongly and earnestly] desire for each of you to show the same diligence and sincerity [all the way through] in realizing and enjoying the full assurance and development of [your] hope until the end, in order that you may not grow disinterested and become [spiritual] sluggards, but imitators, behaving as do those who through faith (by their leaning of the entire personality on God in Christ in absolute trust and confidence in His power, wisdom, and goodness) and by practice of patient endurance and waiting are [now] inheriting the promises.
> (Hebrews 6 verses 9 to 12 the Amplified Bible)

In developing hope we are to have patient endurance. Therefore patience is connected to our hope. People who have hope are usually very patient. I see the fruits of joy peace and patience as evidence of the grace of God, in the form of hope, operating in a person's life.

When we realise that joy peace and patience are fruits of the spirit that come to us as the result of hope, it opens up other passages of scripture that can provide hope and inspiration, such as one of my favourite passages in the bible, Philippians 4.

> Rejoice in the Lord always [delight, gladden yourselves in Him]; again I say, Rejoice! Let all men know and perceive and recognize your unselfishness (your considerateness, your forbearing spirit). The Lord is near [He is coming soon]. Do not fret or have any anxiety about anything, but in every circumstance and in everything, by prayer and petition (definite requests), with thanksgiving, continue to make your wants known to God. And God's peace [shall be yours, that tranquil state of a soul assured of its salvation through Christ, and so fearing nothing from God and being content with its earthly lot of whatever sort that is, that peace] which transcends all understanding shall garrison and mount guard over your hearts and minds in Christ Jesus.
> (Philippians 4 verses 4 to 7 the Amplified Bible)

Although this scripture does not mention the word hope it is really talking about how to receive hope. Those who fret or are anxious are not manifesting the fruits of hope but the fruit of despair. When we rejoice in the Lord and give our worries over to Him it releases hope into our lives and, as a result, we have peace.

When people find out that their partner doesn't really love them or that the thing they were hoping for was really a fantasy, or the thing they put their trust in was really an idol, it can bring people to the depth of despair. That is why they will often steadfastly hold onto a lie rather than face the awful truth. This is what false hope is, holding onto a lie that you hope is really the truth.

However the faith, hope and love that flows from the throne of God above is none of these things. This is a real, vibrant and living faith that provides real hope and true love. That is why King David was able to say the following words;

> [What, what would have become of me] had I not believed that I would see the Lord's goodness in the land of the living! Wait and hope for and expect the Lord; be **brave** and of **good courage** and let your heart be stout and enduring. Yes, wait for and hope for and

expect the Lord.
(Psalm 27 verses 13 and 14 the Amplified Bible)

The Father is constantly pouring out Grace into the world through the power of the Holy Spirit. He does this mainly through the prophets, priests and kings that are part of the order of Melchizedek.

Now isn't that also something to hope for?

SUMMARY

1.   True Christians are joint heirs to the Kingdom of Heaven along with Jesus Christ and part of heaven's Royal family.

2.   Positionally we are priests and kings in the Kingdom in the same manner as Melchizedek.

3.   We are part of the order of Melchizedek.

4.   The gift of prophecy accompanies the presence of the Kingdom.

5.   We can tell false prophets by the fruit they produce.

6.   God pours out his grace in the form of faith, hope and love.

7.   The fruits of the spirit are related to faith, hope and love.

CHAPTER 7
HOPE IN THE HOLY SPIRIT

'Only when the Holy Spirit comes is there any life and force and power.'
– Charles Spurgeon

It's important for all Christians to understand that positionally we are prophets, priests and kings to almighty God and a part of His royal family. There is however something else that provides tremendous encouragement to every believer in Jesus, the amazing truth that we have been given the Holy Spirit to be our guide and helper. As Jesus said:

> If you [really] love Me, you will keep (obey) My commands. And I will ask the Father, and He will give you another Comforter (Counselor, Helper, Intercessor, Advocate, Strengthener, and Standby), that He may remain with you forever -- The Spirit of Truth, Whom the world cannot receive (welcome, take to its heart), because it does not see Him or know and recognize Him. But you know and recognize Him, for He lives with you [constantly] and will be in you. (John 14 verses 15 to 17 the Amplified Bible)

> However, I am telling you nothing but the truth when I say it is profitable (good, expedient, advantageous) for you that I go away. Because if I do not go away, the Comforter (Counselor, Helper, Advocate, Intercessor, Strengthener, Standby) will not come to you [into close fellowship with you]; but if I go away, I will send Him to you [to be in close fellowship with you].
> (John 17 verse 7 the Amplified Bible)

The hope that comes from knowing the Holy Spirit is something so precious. The peace and wonder, the happiness and joy that comes from truly knowing Him is an absolute delight and is definitely the best part of my walk of faith with the Lord Jesus Christ. I would not trade my relationship with Him for anything.

To truly have hope in the Holy Spirit though we need to learn how to hear Him, to know His voice and experience His ways. The reason for this is because there is a battle constantly being fought in the spirit realm over who controls the hearts and minds of men.

The bible tells us that the sons of God are those who are led by the Holy Spirit. To be led by the Holy Spirit isn't something scary. It's about having the ability to hear what he is saying to us as we live our lives so we are doing what will be a blessing to us and others, rather than do harm.

> For if you live according to the flesh you will die; but if by the Spirit you put to death the deeds of the body, you will live. For as many as are led by the Spirit of God, these are sons of God. For you did not receive the spirit of bondage again to fear, but you received the Spirit of adoption by whom we cry out, 'Abba, Father'.
> (Romans 8 verses 13 to 15)

The bible speaks about two different natures that people can have, one that is of the earth - the flesh, and one that comes from heaven - the spirit man. It is the spirit man that accesses the hope of God. So when the bible speaks about being led by the Holy Spirit, it is talking about hearing God's plan for our lives, through the Holy Spirit, so we can lead a life that brings the Kingdom of heaven to the earth. That is definitely something to bring hope to our lives. So what is, 'the flesh'? Simply speaking, it is the unrighteous human nature that we inherited from our forefather Adam. This nature is hostile towards God, whereas the spirit man is the righteous nature inherited from Jesus Christ that supernaturally draws near to God.

If the flesh is hostile to the things of God, it must be hostile towards hope, because as I've already explained true hope comes from our Father in heaven.

The book of Romans is actually a letter that was written to people living in Rome that believed in God. It wasn't originally meant to be read by unbelievers. It tells them about two minds that they have, one of the flesh and one of the spirit. It therefore follows that there is a danger that even believers can interpret the bible from the human nature rather than by listening to the Holy Spirit.

There is a legalistic way of looking at the bible and spiritual matters that kills hope stone dead. It focuses on the human nature and convinces us that we can somehow overcome sin by our own efforts. Then when we fail (as we assuredly will) we are filled with condemnation at our lack of 'faith' and it results in despair, rather than hope.

Condemnation is that feeling you get when you have done something wrong. You think that you are no good and feel rejected by God and other people. It is totally different from conviction, which is when you know you have missed it but want to change for the better.

The human nature is within every one of us. Yet when we believe on Christ Jesus and accept the sacrifice he made for us on the cross and believe in our hearts that he is the Son of God and that God raised him from the dead, we shall be saved.

> But what does it say? "The word is near you, in your mouth and in your heart"(that is, the word of faith which we preach): that if you confess with your mouth the Lord Jesus and believe in your heart that God has raised Him from the dead, you will be saved. For with the heart one believes unto righteousness, and with the mouth confession is made unto salvation.
> (Romans 10 verses 8 to 10)

As I've already explained, salvation is three fold. There is the salvation, the hope we receive at the time of our initial conversion, or the hope and faith we receive by being brought up in a loving Christian home. Then there is the salvation (grace) that is on our lives as we continue to walk with Jesus. Finally there is everlasting salvation when we go home to be with the Lord and take our place in the heavenly realm.

Therefore, when I speak of the two natures, I am speaking of what happens in our lives during the process of salvation. It is during this process that we may sin as a result of our human nature. This does not mean that we have lost our salvation. It merely means that we have missed the mark on that one occasion.

> And this is the message [the message of promise] which we have heard from Him and now are reporting to you: God is Light, and there is no darkness in Him at all [no, not in any way]. [So] if we say we are partakers together and enjoy fellowship with Him when we live and move and are walking about in darkness, we are [both] speaking falsely and do not live and practice the Truth [which the Gospel presents]. But if we [really] are living and walking in the Light, as He [Himself] is in the Light, we have [true, unbroken] fellowship with one another, and the blood of Jesus Christ His Son cleanses (removes) us from all sin and guilt [keeps us cleansed from sin in all its forms and manifestations]. If we say we have no sin [refusing to admit that we are sinners], we delude and lead ourselves

astray, and the Truth [which the Gospel presents] is not in us [does not dwell in our hearts]. If we [freely] admit that we have sinned and confess our sins, He is faithful and just (true to His own nature and promises) and will forgive our sins [dismiss our lawlessness] and [continuously] cleanse us from all unrighteousness [everything not in conformity to His will in purpose, thought, and action]. If we say (claim) we have not sinned, we contradict His Word and make Him out to be false and a liar, and His Word is not in us [the divine message of the Gospel is not in our hearts].
(1 John 1 verses 5 to 10 the Amplified Bible)

The way out is to confess our sin, ask the Lord for forgiveness and move on. We will make mistakes as we are not perfect, but we have a champion that is on our side, encouraging us as we walk with him.

There is a condemnation that the enemy tries to place on us when we sin. But the bible tells us that there is no condemnation for those who are in Christ Jesus.

Therefore, [there is] now no condemnation (no adjudging guilty of wrong) for those who are in Christ Jesus, who live [and] walk not after the dictates of the flesh, but after the dictates of the Spirit. (Romans 8 verse 1 the Amplified Bible)

Some people try to put a burden on people's lives that they are not able to bear themselves and that burden is trying to force people to live a sin free life by their own efforts, through their human nature. They tell us that if we are really saved then we would be able to do this.

Such people may even use spiritual terms like 'by the power of the Holy Spirit'. They tell us that we can renew our minds (the mind of the flesh) by the power of the Holy Spirit. Both of these sayings are absolutely true, however we need to be careful that we are truly being led by the Holy Spirit and not merely trying to overcome sin by our own will power.

It is clearly possible for some people to obtain victory over any particular sin by their own efforts, by sheer force of will power. However, I have noticed that those who obtain such victories do not experience the joy and peace in their lives that they are looking for. Indeed some people become very judgemental about others and also impatient with those who continue to struggle with that particular sin. They sometimes appear to be thoroughly miserable and have no joy in their lives. We have all experienced those who point the finger and say, 'tut, tut', 'if you were a real Christian, you would have stopped doing things like that by now'.

This is not the way of the Spirit, which brings righteousness, peace and joy into our lives and enables us to have patience with others, showing love and understanding, rather than pointing our fingers at them.

If you are a person that struggles with sin in your life and are unable to get the victory, then realise that you may never be able to do so by your own efforts. The true way to be delivered is to trust the Holy Spirit that he is able to deliver you and give the worry and anxiety over to Him. Stop focusing on the sin and start focusing on the answer.

The proper way to experience victory over sin is by having faith and by believing in your heart that Jesus has the power to deliver you. This causes hope to rise forth in your heart. The realisation that you already have the victory, through the exchange that took place on the cross, will arise in your minds, with the expectation in your heart that you have the victory, will walk in that victory and have future victory.

It doesn't mean that you won't lose the odd battle, but that you will win the war. As you walk with Jesus, you are delivered by the power of the Holy Spirit. It's not by striving, it's not by your own might, or your own power but by the grace of God, by faith, hope and love operating in your heart through the power of the Holy Spirit..

We cannot change the mind of the flesh (the human nature). What the scripture really means when it says that we are to 'renew our minds' is that we are to renew our minds to listen to the spirit rather than follow the desires of the flesh.

> I beseech you therefore, brethren, by the mercies of God, that you present your bodies a living sacrifice, holy, acceptable to God, which is your reasonable service. And do not be conformed to this world, but be transformed by the renewing of your mind, that you may prove what is that good and acceptable and perfect will of God. (Romans 1 verses 1 to 2)

We cannot convert the flesh. We are supposed to nail it to the cross.

> And you, being dead in your trespasses and the uncircumcision of your flesh, He has made alive together with Him, having forgiven you all trespasses, having wiped out the handwriting of requirements that was against us, which was contrary to us. And He has taken it out of the way, having nailed it to the cross. Having disarmed principalities and powers, He made a public spectacle of them, triumphing over them in it. (Colossians 2 verses 13 to 15)

The flesh is hostile to God. It cannot submit to God's will. Stop trying to convert it!

Now the mind of the flesh [which is sense and reason without the

Holy Spirit] is death [death that [f]comprises all the miseries arising from sin, both here and hereafter]. But the mind of the [Holy] Spirit is life and [soul] peace [both now and forever]. [That is] because the mind of the flesh [with its carnal thoughts and purposes] is hostile to God, for it does not submit itself to God's Law; indeed it cannot.
(Romans 8 verses 6 and 7 the Amplified Bible)

The mind of the flesh cannot be converted. It cannot submit itself to God's law.

The way of the Lord is to follow the spirit man. The spirit man is a winner. He is filled with faith, hope and love. He is led by the Holy Spirit. He is a new creation and he lives on the inside of you. He is the, 'real you', that God created you to be. He is a champion.

Therefore if any person is [ingrafted] in Christ (the Messiah) he is a new creation (a new creature altogether); the old [previous moral and spiritual condition] has passed away. Behold, the fresh and new has come!
(2 Corinthians 5 verse 17 the Amplified Bible)

So how do we know when the Holy Spirit is speaking to us?

I don't know anyone who hears the Holy Spirit speaking to them audibly very often. What happens most of the time is that a thought comes to their minds that they believe is from the Holy Spirit.

This sometimes causes problems in that people have a thought that gets them very excited and they believe it has come from the Holy Spirit. They then go off and do something stupid without seeking out a father or mentor in the Lord for confirmation that what they are 'hearing' is correct.

Jesus speaks of these thoughts (voices) in John chapter 5.

I am able to do nothing from Myself [independently, of My own accord--but only as I am taught by God and as I get His orders]. Even as I hear, I judge [I decide as I am bidden to decide. As the voice comes to Me, so I give a decision], and My judgment is right (just, righteous), because I do not seek or consult My own will [I have no desire to do what is pleasing to Myself, My own aim, My own purpose] but only the will and pleasure of the Father Who sent Me.
(John 5 verse 30 the Amplified Bible)

Jesus obviously had different thoughts coming to his mind and he had to discern whether or not they were from His Father. How did He know which thoughts to listen to? The answer is of course that He knew His

Father intimately. He recognized His voice because he knew His Father's nature.

That's how you know when the Holy Spirit is speaking to you. You have a thought and you think, 'that sounds like the Lord'. You then check if what you are hearing fits with what you know of the Father's nature. The Holy Spirit will never tell you to do anything that is contrary to His will and will never suggest anything that is contrary to His nature as a loving Father. We also receive confirmation when the Holy Spirit speaks, from the inner witness from our spirit man.

As Paul said in his letter to the Romans:

> I AM speaking the truth in Christ. I am not lying; my conscience [enlightened and prompted] by the Holy Spirit bearing witness with me.
> (Romans 9 verse 1 the Amplified Bible)

There have been occasions in my life when someone has told me something about members of my family or my friends. They have told me that they have said something wicked about me or done something wrong. I immediately knew that it was a lie because I knew my relative or friend's nature and knew that they would never say or do anything like that.

It's the same with the Holy Spirit. You know there are certain things He would never say or do and can easily discern when the thought is from another source. If there is any doubt then seek confirmation from someone you trust.

Some people get very worked up about whether or not they are following the leading of the Holy Spirit and do stupid things like standing praying in the supermarket asking God whether they should go to the meat counter next or the dairy counter.

In my experience the Holy Spirit is pretty relaxed about how we spend our day to day lives and isn't really interested in minor things like I have described above. He usually leaves the minor details up to us.

After all, Jesus came to set us free not to put us into bondage. The leading of the Spirit is more about when we come to make important choices in our lives and about establishing the kingdom of heaven on the earth.

If He feels you shouldn't be doing something or going somewhere, He will let you know.

That's not to say that we won't occasionally hear the prompting of the spirit to go somewhere or to do something we hadn't planned ourselves but I find that most often I do something that I think is my own idea and realize later that it was the Holy Spirit leading me.

There was one time when Lesley and I were in the supermarket and we both felt that it would be a nice surprise if we bought some shopping for one of our friends. We bought a few bags of shopping and went up to her house and left the groceries on her doorstep.

We found out later that our friend was really short on food and didn't have the money to buy any groceries. She had been praying to God for help with the situation. You can imagine how delighted she was when she found the bags.

We didn't think, 'that was the Holy Spirit'. We just did what we felt was the right thing to do. We never did tell her it was us. She'll know now though, if she ever reads this book.

There was another time when we were having horrendous trouble with a man in the police cells who was fighting with everyone and banging his head off the cell doors. I somehow knew that his behaviour was demonic and therefore went into another room to pray. A few minutes later the man had calmed down and was apologizing for his actions!

Many years ago my mum was worried about my dad as he couldn't stop smoking although he very much wanted to stop. He smoked a pipe quite heavily and we were all really concerned about his health.

One afternoon I felt that the Holy Spirit wanted me to pray about the situation. I got what seemed a crazy idea at the time that I should pray he would get a horrible taste in his mouth every time he smoked and that this would help him to stop smoking. I prayed the prayer then forgot all about it.

About three months later I got a phone call from my very happy dad who told me that he had finally managed to stop. I asked him how he had managed it and he told me that he recently had a nasty taste in his mouth when he was smoking and this had helped him to kick the habit. He hasn't smoked since then and that was almost twenty years ago. He was in his late fifties at the time and had been smoking since he was nine years old! Not that I am against anyone that smokes but it was affecting his health. It was the Holy Spirit that did all these things, not me. Remember also that the Holy Spirit has the same nature as Jesus and the same nature as our heavenly Father. He only wants the very best for us. He doesn't want to destroy us.

In saying that, there are obviously those who are called to martyrdom, those who lay their life down so that others might be saved, however it would be extremely unusual for Him to ask us to do anything that would be recklessly dangerous or expected to cause us or others harm. There are obvious exceptions such as, armed forces, rescue services, police service and the like. So that's not to say He won't ask us to go to dangerous places but He will always provide confirmation that we are supposed to be there, the most obvious being that we are there to save other people's lives.

When we know the Holy Spirit, it is much easier to understand His ways and there is so much more we receive from Him that provides us with hope.

We can hope for the Baptism of the Holy Spirit.

> Now as the people were in expectation, and all reasoned in their hearts about John, whether he was the Christ or not, John answered, saying to all, 'I indeed baptize you with water; but One mightier than I is coming, whose sandal strap I am not worthy to loose. He will baptize you with the Holy Spirit and fire. His winnowing fan is in His hand, and He will thoroughly clean out His threshing floor, and gather the wheat into His barn; but the chaff He will burn with unquenchable fire.'
> (Luke 3 verses 15 to 17)

> Then Peter said to them, "Repent, and let every one of you be baptized in the name of Jesus Christ for the remission of sins; and you shall receive the gift of the Holy Spirit. For the promise is to you and to your children, and to all who are afar off, as many as the Lord our God will call."
> (Acts 2 verses 38 to 39)

We can hope for the gifts of the Holy Spirit.

> Now about the spiritual gifts (the special endowments of supernatural energy), brethren, I do not want you to be misinformed. You know that when you were heathen, you were led off after idols that could not speak [habitually] as impulse directed *and* whenever the occasion might arise. Therefore I want you to understand that no one speaking under the power *and* influence of the [Holy] Spirit of God can [ever] say, Jesus be cursed! And no one can [really] say, Jesus is [my] Lord, except by *and* under the power *and* influence of the Holy Spirit. Now there are distinctive varieties *and* distributions of endowments (gifts, [a]extraordinary powers distinguishing certain Christians, due to the power of divine grace operating in their souls by the Holy Spirit) and they vary, but the [Holy] Spirit remains the same. And there are distinctive varieties of service *and* ministration, but it is the same Lord [Who is served]. And there are distinctive varieties of operation [of working to accomplish things], but it is the same God Who inspires *and* energizes them all in all. But to each one is given the manifestation of the [Holy] Spirit [the evidence, the spiritual illumination of the Spirit] for good *and* profit. To one is given in *and* through the [Holy] Spirit [the power to speak] a message

of wisdom, and to another [the power to express] a word of knowledge *and* understanding according to the same [Holy] Spirit;

To another [[b]wonder-working] faith by the same [Holy] Spirit, to another the extraordinary powers of healing by the one Spirit;   To another the working of miracles, to another prophetic insight, the gift of interpreting the divine will and purpose); to another the ability to discern *and* distinguish between [the utterances of true] spirits [and false ones], to another various kinds of [unknown] tongues, to another the ability to interpret [such] tongues.   All these [gifts, achievements, abilities] are inspired *and* brought to pass by one and the same [Holy] Spirit, Who apportions to each person individually [exactly] as He chooses.

(1 Corinthians 12 verses 1 to 11 the Amplified Bible)

We can hope for the fruits of the Spirit.

But the fruit of the [Holy] Spirit [the work which His presence within accomplishes] is love, joy (gladness), peace, patience (an even temper, forbearance), kindness, goodness (benevolence), faithfulness, gentleness (meekness, humility), self-control (self-restraint, continence). Against such things there is no law [[f]that can bring a charge]. And those who belong to Christ Jesus (the Messiah) have crucified the flesh (the godless human nature) with its passions and appetites *and* desires.

(Galatians 5 verses 22 to 24 the Amplified Bible)

The Holy Spirit seals our salvation in Christ and guarantees our divine inheritance.

In Him you also trusted, after you heard the word of truth, the gospel of your salvation; in whom also, having believed, you were sealed with the Holy Spirit of promise, who is the guarantee of our inheritance until the redemption of the purchased possession, to the praise of His glory.

(Ephesians 1 verses 13 to 14)

Wherever the grace of God is being poured out is where the kingdom of heaven is being established and there you will also find the fruits and gifts of the spirit and the spiritual prophets, priests and kings of our generation.

This is definitely something that should give us hope for our future.

SUMMARY

1. The Holy Spirit is our guide and our helper.

2. The Holy Spirit has the same nature and character as God the Father and His son Jesus Christ.

3. Jesus was led by the Holy Spirit.

4. Believers have two natures one that is natural, the flesh and the other that is spiritual, the spirit man.

5. The flesh (human nature) is hostile to God and cannot be converted.

6. We can renew our minds to listen to the spirit man rather than listening to the flesh.

7. The spirit man is led by the Holy Spirit.

8. The spirit man has the same nature as Jesus.

9. We can hope for the baptism of the Holy Spirit.

10. We can hope for the gifts of the Spirit.

11. We can hope for the fruits of the Spirit.

CHAPTER 8
HOPE IN YOUR CALLING

'Your profession is not what brings home your weekly paycheck, your profession is what you're put here on earth to do, with such passion and such intensity that it becomes spiritual in calling.'
— Vincent van Gogh

It always seems strange to me that when people speak of someone having a calling in Christ, they invariably think about those that are pastors or missionaries or some other role directly related to looking after people or seeking their conversion.

However, I have heard people speaking about having a calling who have no experience of biblical teaching whatsoever. Many times, when speaking to teachers, doctors, nurses, police officers and similar vocational careers I have heard people speak of having this feeling that they were called into their profession.

Interesting isn't it? People were speaking about something deep inside of them that led them to choose their career?

I believe they had experienced hearing the voice of the Holy Spirit speaking to them. Not everyone can be the pastor, not everyone can be a mighty evangelist or praise leader.

The bible speaks about those called into specific ministry gifting in Paul's letter to the Ephesians:

> And He Himself gave some to be apostles, some prophets, some evangelists, and some pastors and teachers, for the equipping of the saints for the work of ministry, for the edifying of the body of Christ,

till we all come to the unity of the faith and of the knowledge of the Son of God, to a perfect man, to the measure of the stature of the fullness of Christ; that we should no longer be children, tossed to and fro and carried about with every wind of doctrine, by the trickery of men, in the cunning craftiness of deceitful plotting, but, speaking the truth in love, may grow up in all things into Him who is the head—Christ— from whom the whole body, joined and knit together by what every joint supplies, according to the effective working by which every part does its share, causes growth of the body for the edifying of itself in love.
(Ephesians 4 verses 11 to 16)

Notice though that it is not the apostles, prophets, pastors, evangelists and teachers that Paul expected to do the work of the ministry but the 'saints'. When Paul speaks about saints, he isn't talking about those that have been canonized by the Catholic Church. He is meaning ordinary believers causing the growth of the body, which is speaking of the church.

However, it is important to realise that when Jesus and the apostles were speaking about building up the body, equipping of the saints and the growth of the church, they were speaking about the Kingdom of Heaven and not simply about getting a congregation to grow. Look at what Jesus said the first time he mentioned the word 'church'.

Now when Jesus went into the region of Caesarea Philippi, He asked His disciples, Who do people say that the Son of Man is? And they answered, Some say John the Baptist; others say Elijah; and others Jeremiah or one of the prophets. He said to them, But who do you [yourselves] say that I am? Simon Peter replied, You are the Christ, the Son of the living God. Then Jesus answered him, Blessed (happy, fortunate, and to be envied) are you, Simon Bar-Jonah. For flesh and blood [men] have not revealed this to you, but My Father Who is in heaven. And I tell you, you are Peter [Greek, *Petros*—a large piece of rock], and on this rock [Greek,*petra*—a huge rock like Gibraltar] I will build My church, and the gates of Hades (the powers of the[g]infernal region) shall not overpower it [or be strong to its detriment or hold out against it]. I will give you the keys of the kingdom of heaven; and whatever you bind (declare to be improper and unlawful) on earth [i]must be what is already bound in heaven; and whatever you loose (declare lawful) on earth must be what is already loosed in heaven.
(Matthew 16 verses 13 to 19 the Amplified bible)

Jesus says, 'I will build my church and the gates of Hades (hell) will not prevail against it'. He then goes on to say 'And I will give you the keys of the kingdom of heaven'.

So, the building up of the church is directly related to the kingdom of heaven. Moreover, the word church referred to in this passage of scripture is the Greek word 'ecclesia' (Strongs 1577) which relates to people being called out, to community, to an assembly, those that have been called out or chosen.

The apostle Paul, when writing to the church in Ephesus, is speaking to these called out ones. The emphasis added is mine.

> Therefore I also, after I heard of your faith in the Lord Jesus and your love for all the saints, do not cease to give thanks for you, making mention of you in my prayers: that the God of our Lord Jesus Christ, the Father of glory, may give to you the spirit of wisdom and revelation in the knowledge of Him, the eyes of your understanding being enlightened; that you may know what is the **hope of His calling**, what are the riches of the glory of His inheritance in the saints, and what is the exceeding greatness of His power toward us who believe, according to the working of His mighty power which He worked in Christ when He raised Him from the dead and seated Him at His right hand in the heavenly places, far above all principality and power and might and dominion, and every name that is named, not only in this age but also in that which is to come. And He put all things under His feet, and gave Him to be head over all things to the church, which is His body, the fullness of Him who fills all in all.
> (Ephesians 1 verses 15 to 23)

When Paul speaks of the hope of his calling, he is not merely speaking about church meetings or church missionary programmes. He is actually speaking about life in general, about His glory 'filling all in all'. Therefore the church is really the community of called out ones, those that have answered the Father's call on their lives. Every one of us therefore needs to know what his calling is for our family, church, our community and for ourselves individually. When we place our hope in the Holy Spirit, He leads us in the 'way we should go' or into the business or career that is our true destiny.

Motivated by the Holy Spirit, King Solomon wrote these words.

> Train up a child in the way he should go, and when he is old he will not depart from it.
> (Proverbs 22 verse 6)

He is obviously speaking to parents here but it holds equally true for our heavenly Father. He has a plan and a desire for each of our lives and, unlike our earthly fathers, knows what is best for us. He knows our gifts and abilities and also knows our faults better than anyone. He is therefore far better placed than us to lead us in the 'way we should go', or what our particular calling should be.

This calling relates to establishing His kingdom across the whole world. This is what the church was created for, the establishment of the Kingdom of heaven upon the earth.

What often happens instead of course is that some church leaders are trying to build their own ministries so that they can be personally successful and are expecting Jesus to take care of establishing the kingdom. As a result, the church has to a large extent become totally detached from real life and become something that we relate to only on Sundays or, for a large proportion of the population, something we relate to for occasions such as weddings and funerals.

If an earthly king was seeking to establish a colony of his kingdom, he wouldn't only focus on government structure but on every aspect of society so that the whole colony represented his kingdom and the way things are done in that kingdom.

This 'calling' is therefore speaking about every walk of life. In every facet of society there should be people who's calling in Christ is to be a representative of Christ in that particular area.

When Jesus taught His disciples to pray he showed them that they should pray for the coming of His Father's kingdom on the earth:

> In this manner, therefore, pray:
> Our Father in heaven,
> Hallowed be Your name.
> Your kingdom come.
> Your will be done
> On earth as it is in heaven.
> Give us this day our daily bread.
> And forgive us our debts,
> As we forgive our debtors.
> And do not lead us into temptation,
> But deliver us from the evil one.
> For Yours is the kingdom and the power and the glory forever.
> Amen.
> (Matthew 6 verses 9 to 13)

Notice that for the kingdom to be established, God's will needs to be done on the earth. It also says, 'on earth as it is in heaven' not, 'in the church meeting on a Sunday'.

The earth includes every area of life, not just church meetings. It's therefore clear that people can be called by God to establish His kingdom in many different areas of life. For example:

1. Government – both local and national
2. Economics
3. Business
4. Science and technology
5. Education
6. Communication
7. Entertainment and the arts
8. Family
9. Sport and leisure
10. Social issues
11. Environment
12. Church

The list is actually endless. It's about spreading the influence of the king and establishing the kingdom on the earth. When talking about the, 'hope of his calling', Paul is speaking about a glorious church which is impacting every area of life. This releases church members from unnecessary pressure to be a 'Holy Joe' or from having a 'ministry'.

It's such a shame but there are many Christians who feel unworthy or unaccepted in their church. They do have a calling in Christ as every Christian has a calling and a ministry they are destined to walk in. However they perceive His calling to relate to something to do with church meetings or missionary programmes.

There is then a danger that they might receive a word from a visiting minister or have a dream where they are told they will become a mighty missionary or a great worship leader etc. While sometimes these words and dreams are from God, we do need to check them out with the right people to ensure we are hearing properly. It may be a huge mistake for someone who has a calling to be a teacher to believe that they are destined to be the Pastor in their church, especially when there is already someone in place fulfilling that role. I say may be, because occasionally through circumstances, a person may need to fulfil a role that doesn't really fit until a person with that particular calling is raised up to take that place in a church.

This pressure to have a 'ministry' or to be doing something that fits in with their perceptions of what a Christian should be doing has caused many people to miss their destiny. They end up miserable, performing a duty in an area that they were never called into. They may even end up causing conflict by being jealous of those God is blessing in that area of service. The Apostle Paul actually speaks about this in his letter to the Corinthians, where he determines only to minister within the sphere of influence he has been given by the Father.

> For we dare not class ourselves or compare ourselves with those who commend themselves. But they, measuring themselves by themselves, and comparing themselves among themselves, are not wise. We, however, will not boast beyond measure, but within the limits of the sphere which God appointed us—a sphere which especially includes you. For we are not overextending ourselves (as though our authority did not extend to you), for it was to you that we came with the gospel of Christ; not boasting of things beyond measure, that is, in other men's labours, but having hope, that as your faith is increased, we shall be greatly enlarged by you in our sphere, to preach the gospel in the regions beyond you, and not to boast in another man's sphere of accomplishment. But "he who glories, let him glory in the LORD." For not he who commends himself is approved, but whom the Lord commends.
> (2 Corinthians 10 verses 12 to18)

We need to be moving in the 'sphere of influence' that God has given us. Otherwise we could end up living our lives where our whole Christian walk relates to trying to fulfil a fantasy, presuming we are called to serve in an area the Lord has not in fact called us into. Those who know us best are most often the ones that the Lord uses to guide us in our calling in Him. We should really be seeking confirmation from them before stepping out on any new path.

Presumption is a very dangerous thing. It can cause people to spend years trying desperately to fulfil a calling they believe God has given them, when in fact He has opened doors into other walks of life that they either haven't seen or have deliberately chosen not to enter.

There are countless opportunities available to serve the King of Kings. You don't have to be a pastor or a missionary to fulfil His calling, you just need to be who you are and follow Him. His calling is more about being who you are and becoming more like Jesus than it is about what you do. When God opens the door, we simply walk into the sphere of influence he has for us. We are released to simply be ourselves. It's not difficult when our hope is in the Lord.

A good example of calling is found in Acts Chapter 6

> Now about this time, when the number of the disciples was greatly increasing, complaint was made by the Hellenists (the Greek-

speaking Jews) against the [native] Hebrews because their widows were being overlooked *and* neglected in the daily ministration (distribution of relief). So the Twelve [apostles] convened the multitude of the disciples and said, 'It is not seemly *or* desirable *or* right that we should have to give up *or* neglect [preaching] the Word of God in order to attend to serving at tables *and* superintending the distribution of food. Therefore select out from among yourselves, brethren, seven men of good *and* attested character *and* repute, full of the [Holy] Spirit and wisdom, whom we may assign to look after this business *and* duty. But we will continue to devote ourselves steadfastly to prayer and the ministry of the Word.' And the suggestion pleased the whole assembly, and they selected Stephen, a man full of faith (a strong and welcome belief that Jesus is the Messiah) and full of *and* controlled by the Holy Spirit, and Philip, and Prochorus, and Nicanor, and Timon, and Parmenas, and Nicolaus, a proselyte (convert) from Antioch. These they presented to the apostles, who after prayer laid their hands on them. And the message of God kept on spreading, and the number of disciples multiplied greatly in Jerusalem; and [besides] a large number of the priests were obedient to the faith [in Jesus as the Messiah, through Whom is obtained eternal salvation in the kingdom of God].
(Acts 6 verses 1 to 7 the Amplified bible)

What was actually happening here was that seven men were appointed by God to run the church catering business. They could have taken offence and refused to carry out what some people might have considered to be a menial task but they were obviously enthusiastic about the task they had been given.

And Stephen, full of faith and power, did great wonders and signs among the people. (Acts 6 verse 8)

Stephen was enthusiastic about his calling and served the King willingly in the area he was called to (in his sphere of influence) and wonders and signs were released among the people.

When we serve Him in our sphere of influence and calling, the Lord steps in and helps us establish His kingdom. When we try to do it in our own strength and in an area he has not in fact called us into, there are no signs and wonders and the power and glory of the kingdom is not being established.

Now you are the body of Christ, and members individually. And

God has appointed these in the church: first apostles, second prophets, third teachers, after that miracles, then gifts of healings, helps, administrations, varieties of tongues.
(1 Corinthians 12 verses 27 to 28)

When we look at this passage of scripture from a kingdom perspective we see that the ministries mentioned by Paul relates to the whole kingdom of heaven. Someone can therefore be an apostle or prophet in the business world serving the King of Glory. Another can serve the King as a school administrator or teacher. Someone else might 'help' run a scout troop or day care centre.

Our calling may seem to us to be quite small compared to what we see being experienced by others but God isn't impressed by what we see as success. He is far more interested in how we treat our families and how we relate to other people. The opportunities to serve the King of Kings are truly endless. If we allow the Lord to open the doors for us and function in the area He has chosen, we will be absolutely amazed by what he can do through us.

Isn't that something to hope for?

SUMMARY

1. Having a calling in Christ relates to more than church meetings or missionary work .

2. Calling relaters to establishing God's kingdom upon the earth.

3. It covers every aspect of life and many different professions.

4. It relates to your sphere of influence.

5. Moving in your sphere of influence is one of the keys to finding your proper calling.

Gordon C Methven

CHAPTER 9
WARFARE AGAINST HOPE

'All warfare is based on deception.' - Sun Tzu

I've spent the last few chapters telling you about many different things in God's word that gives us hope. Why is it then that we can often feel so hopeless? What causes that unreasoning despair that sometimes comes into our minds for no apparent cause?

In his letter to the Ephesians Paul tells them that we are not wrestling against flesh and blood but against principalities and powers in heavenly places.

> For we do not wrestle against flesh and blood, but against principalities, against powers, against the rulers of the darkness of this age, against spiritual hosts of wickedness in the heavenly places. (Ephesians 6 verse 12)

According to the bible, the spiritual realm is as real as the natural one and directly affects events on Earth. There are wicked beings in this realm that hate mankind and seek to destroy us. Thankfully, the grace of God is also constantly in operation as He seeks to establish the Kingdom of God here on Earth. That's why Jesus taught us to pray, 'Your Kingdom come, your will be done on earth as it is in Heaven' (Matthew 6 verse 10).

There has been a battle raging in the spirit realm, over who rules planet earth since the fall of Adam and Eve. You can read the book of Genesis for yourself but when God created Adam and Eve He gave them dominion over planet earth. When Adam disobeyed God and bit into the fruit presented to him by his wife, they lost dominion. They lost the rule of the kingdom and it passed into the control of satan. The earth then came under the control of the kingdom of darkness.

This meant that our Father God could only act if he was given the authority to do so by mankind. Yet mankind was under the control of the Kingdom of darkness. It took Abraham entering into a covenant with God to break that stranglehold and allow a measure of God's kingdom rule back onto the earth through the nation of Israel. Yet sin still had dominion across the earth.

When Jesus sacrificed Himself on the cross, He paid the penalty for the sins of mankind once and for all and opened the way into the Kingdom of Heaven for all of us.

> And you [He made alive], when you were dead (slain) by [your] trespasses and sins. In which at one time you walked [habitually]. You were following the course *and* fashion of this world [were under the sway of the tendency of this present age], following the prince of the power of the air. [You were obedient to and under the control of] the [demon] spirit that still constantly works in the sons of disobedience [the careless, the rebellious, and the unbelieving, who go against the purposes of God]. Among these we as well as you once lived *and* conducted ourselves in the passions of our flesh [our behavior governed by our corrupt and sensual nature], obeying the impulses of the flesh and the thoughts of the mind [our cravings dictated by our senses and our dark imaginings]. We were then by nature children of [God's] wrath *and* heirs of [His] indignation, like the rest of mankind. But God—so rich is He in His mercy! Because of *and* in order to satisfy the great *and* wonderful *and* intense love with which He loved us, even when we were dead (slain) by [our own] shortcomings *and* trespasses, He made us alive together in fellowship *and* in union with Christ; [He gave us the very life of Christ Himself, the same new life with which He quickened Him, for] it is by grace (His favor and mercy which you did not deserve) that you are saved (delivered from judgment and made partakers of Christ's salvation). And He raised us up together with Him and made us sit down together [giving us joint seating with Him] in the heavenly sphere [by virtue of our being] in Christ Jesus (the Messiah, the Anointed One). He did this that He might clearly demonstrate through the ages to come the immeasurable (limitless, surpassing) riches of His free grace (His unmerited favor) in [His] kindness *and* goodness of heart toward us in Christ Jesus. For it is by free grace (God's unmerited favor) that you are saved (delivered from judgment *and* made partakers of Christ's salvation) through

[your] faith. And this [salvation] is not of yourselves [of your own doing, it came not through your own striving], but it is the gift of God; not because of works [not the fulfillment of the Law's demands], lest any man should boast. [It is not the result of what anyone can possibly do, so no one can pride himself in it or take glory to himself.] For we are God's [own] handiwork (His workmanship), recreated in Christ Jesus, [born anew] that we may do those good works which God predestined (planned beforehand) for us [taking paths which He prepared ahead of time], that we should walk in them [living the good life which He prearranged and made ready for us to live].
(Ephesians 2 verses 1 to 10 the Amplified bible)

By His sacrifice on the cross Jesus gave mankind back authority in the Kingdom of Heaven. However, there is still a battle raging in the spirit realm over who has dominion over planet earth. Our Father has given us back the authority through Christ to establish His kingdom here on earth but the forces of darkness certainly don't want to give it up.

We have the authority on planet earth to release God's kingdom. As we carry out the good works He has pre-ordained for us in the area in which we have been called and as we pray according to the word of God it releases His grace into the earth in the form of faith, hope and love.

The thing that these evil princes hate more than anything else is the grace of God so they will use every means within their power to lessen God's holy influence. Those that are called into the Kingdom of Heaven are the greatest threat to them so it is against them that the forces of darkness are arrayed. This is not to cause any of us to fear however, because as it says in 2 Kings, there are more spiritual forces on our side than are against us.

So he answered, 'Do not fear, for those who are with us are more than those who are with them.' And Elisha prayed, and said, 'LORD, I pray, open his eyes that he may see.' Then the LORD opened the eyes of the young man, and he saw. And behold, the mountain was full of horses and chariots of fire all around Elisha. So when the Syrians came down to him, Elisha prayed to the LORD, and said, 'Strike this people, I pray, with blindness.' And He struck them with blindness according to the word of Elisha.
(2 Kings 6 verses 16 to 18)

The warfare in the spirit is primarily against the grace of God. As I have already mentioned, this grace produces the fruits of the spirit in our lives. So it is in these areas that we will notice the warfare coming against us.

When we feel our peace and joy being affected it is a sure sign of spiritual warfare. This may be as a direct result of a tragedy, illness or a serious situation in our lives or in the lives of those we love, or when we are facing confrontation. At such times it is easier to recognize we are in a battle.

However there are other times when the enemy uses more subtle approaches to try and upset us. Anytime you feel your peace and joy or your patience being affected, when there seems to be no valid reason for it, then it is a sure sign that there is spiritual warfare on the go. The key for breakthrough is to immediately take it to the Lord in prayer.

The opposite of hope is despair. It is often the case that what people think of as hope is simply a desire that what they fear will not happen to them. The opposite of faith is doubt and unbelief and the opposite of love is hate. These forces of the kingdom of darkness will try to influence people in such a way that they hate others, doubt that anything good will ever happen to them and fear for their future.

The way of the Kingdom is completely different. Jesus teaches us to love our enemies forgive those who hurt us, always focus on the good and have hope for the future.

Spiritual warfare comes against people in a variety of ways. Evil principalities may try to corrupt our love and turn it into lust causing us to get involved in sins of the flesh. They may try come against our faith and bring deception into our lives. However I believe that the main area of warfare comes against our hope, because hope is the anchor of the soul and most of spiritual warfare happens in the soul, which consists of our mind will and emotions.

When we enter into covenant relationship with Jesus Christ, our Father in Heaven adopts us as his own children. This is confirmed by the sign of the covenant which is baptism in water.

> Are you ignorant of the fact that all of us who have been baptized into Christ Jesus were baptized into His death? We were buried therefore with Him by the baptism into death, so that just as Christ was raised from the dead by the glorious [power] of the Father, so we too might [habitually] live *and* behave in newness of life. For if we have become one with Him by sharing a death like His, we shall also be [one with Him in sharing] His resurrection [by a new life lived for God].
> (Romans 6 verses 3 to 5 the Amplified Bible)

> In Him also you were circumcised with a circumcision not made with hands, but in a [spiritual] circumcision [performed by] Christ by stripping off the body of the flesh (the whole corrupt, carnal nature

with its passions and lusts). [Thus you were circumcised when] you were buried with Him in [your] baptism, in which you were also raised with Him [to a new life] through [your] faith in the working of God [as displayed] when He raised Him up from the dead. And you who were dead in trespasses and in the uncircumcision of your flesh (your sensuality, your sinful carnal nature), [God] brought to life together with [Christ], having [freely] forgiven us all our transgressions.
(2 Corinthians verses 11 to 13 the Amplified Bible)

Those who enter into baptism are confirming whose kingdom they belong to. This increases the warfare against them but also increases the protection from the forces of light which, as I've already said previously are greater than the forces of darkness.

Our Father in heaven wants the very best for us. When I'm reading the bible I see lots of mention of the word, 'blessing' which, simply speaking is the word used to convey the Lord's favour acting upon our lives. The forces of darkness will always try to corrupt the blessing and turn it into a curse.

As the corrupt version of a blessing is a curse, there are also corrupt versions of the three graces.

The corruption of love is called lust - the desire to benefit self at the expense of others.

The corruption of faith is deception where people believe a lie to be the truth.

The corruption of biblical hope is religious fantasy. A religious fantasy is where people have a form of hope that is based on deception. Such hope only leads to disappointment and failure because it isn't grounded in reality.

True grace	Counterfeit version
Faith	Deception
Hope	Religious Fantasy
Love	Lust

Whether we are operating in faith, hope and love or in the counterfeit versions of deception, religious fantasy and lust, the bible tells us that there will be consequences in our lives. Those who are led by the spirit will manifest faith, hope and love while those who are led by the flesh may well manifest deception, religious fantasy and lust

But I say, walk and live [habitually] in the [Holy] Spirit [responsive to and controlled and guided by the Spirit]; then you will certainly not gratify the cravings and desires of the flesh (of human nature without

89

God). For the desires of the flesh are opposed to the [Holy] Spirit, and the [desires of the] Spirit are opposed to the flesh (godless human nature); for these are antagonistic to each other [continually withstanding and in conflict with each other], so that you are not free but are prevented from doing what you desire to do. But if you are guided (led) by the [Holy] Spirit, you are not subject to the Law. Now the doings (practices) of the flesh are clear (obvious): they are immorality, impurity, indecency, Idolatry, sorcery, enmity, strife, jealousy, anger (ill temper), selfishness, divisions (dissensions), party spirit (factions, sects with peculiar opinions, heresies), Envy, drunkenness, carousing, and the like. I warn you beforehand, just as I did previously, that those who do such things shall not inherit the kingdom of God. But the fruit of the [Holy] Spirit [the work which His presence within accomplishes] is love, joy (gladness), peace, patience (an even temper, forbearance), kindness, goodness (benevolence), faithfulness, gentleness (meekness, humility), self-control (self-restraint, continence). Against such things there is no law that can bring a charge]. And those who belong to Christ Jesus (the Messiah) have crucified the flesh (the godless human nature) with its passions and appetites and desires. If we live by the [Holy] Spirit, let us also walk by the Spirit. [If by the Holy Spirit we have our life in God, let us go forward walking in line, our conduct controlled by the Spirit.] Let us not become vainglorious and self-conceited, competitive and challenging and provoking and irritating to one another, envying and being jealous of one another.
(Galatians 5 verses 16 to 26 the Amplified Bible)

When I examine these fruits it seems obvious to me where the root came from. There are clearly elements of each that may lead to the other fruits manifesting in people's lives but you will get the general idea.

Fruits of the Spirit
Love	love, kindness, goodness, gentleness
Faith	faithfulness, self control
Hope	joy, peace, patience

Fruits of the Flesh
Lust	selfishness, immorality, impurity, indecency
Deception	idolatry, sorcery, party spirit (factions, sects with peculiar opinions, heresies), divisions dissensions)
Religious Fantasy	anger, jealousy, envy, enmity, strife

Hope, faith and love obviously flow together and all of the fruits of the Spirit can come from different aspects of the three graces. However the main thing we get; our joy, peace and patience from is hope.

Similarly, the fruits of the flesh are interconnected and flow out from the counterfeit version of the three graces.

The way to avoid the fruits of the flesh is to be led and controlled by the Holy Spirit but how do we know we are being spirit led and not being deceived?

The answer is of course that we will know by the fruits that operate in our lives. There is no quick fix. It's all about walking in faith with the Prince of Peace and gradually seeing the fruits of the spirit manifesting themselves more often in our lives as we recognize His voice and learn to live in His ways.

The Holy Spirit promotes the Kingdom of God. If we seek first the Kingdom and His righteousness then all things will be given to us, including knowing how to flow in faith, hope and love. After all, the bible tells us that the Kingdom of God is righteousness, peace and joy in the Holy Spirit.

> Therefore do not let your good be spoken of as evil; for the kingdom of God is not eating and drinking, but righteousness and peace and joy in the Holy Spirit. For he who serves Christ in these things is acceptable to God and approved by men.
> (Romans 14 verses 16 to 18)

Sometimes we get these thoughts coming into our minds that we are not as important to God as other people are. Our own calling seems unimportant and even dull and boring compared to that which we see being enjoyed by other people.

It's important to remember at such times that that God loves each of us individually. It matters not a jot to him what our calling is. He doesn't love the pastor more than you! He is far more interested in who you are than in what you can do for Him.

Each of us has the same opportunity to experience the 'hope of glory'. His greatest joy is in seeing us become more like Jesus. The Parable of the Workers in the Vineyard explains this aspect of the Kingdom:

> For the kingdom of heaven is like the owner of an estate who went out in the morning [a]along with the dawn to hire workmen for his vineyard. After agreeing with the laborers for a denarius a day, he sent them into his vineyard. And going out about the third hour (nine o'clock), he saw others standing idle in the marketplace; and he said to them, You go also into the vineyard, and whatever is right I

will pay you. And they went. He went out again about the sixth hour (noon), and the ninth hour (three o'clock) he did the same. And about the eleventh hour (five o'clock) he went out and found still others standing around, and said to them, Why do you stand here idle all day? They answered him, Because nobody has hired us. He told them, You go out into the vineyard also and you will get whatever is just and fair. When evening came, the owner of the vineyard said to his manager, 'Call the workmen and pay them their wages, beginning with the last and ending with the first.' And those who had been hired at the eleventh hour (five o'clock) came and received a denarius each. Now when the first came, they supposed they would get more, but each of them also received a denarius. And when they received it, they grumbled at the owner of the estate, saying, 'These [men] who came last worked no more than an hour, and yet you have made them rank with us who have borne the burden and the [ ]scorching heat of the day.' But he answered one of them, 'Friend, I am doing you no injustice. Did you not agree with me for a denarius? Take what belongs to you and go. I choose to give to this man hired last the same as I give to you. Am I not permitted to do what I choose with what is mine? [Or do you begrudge my being generous?] Is your eye evil because I am good? So those who [now] are last will be first [then], and those who [now] are first will be last [then]. For many are called, but few chosen. (Matthew 20 verses 1 to 16 the Amplified Bible)

When we get to heaven there will be some who were first that will be last and some who were last will be first.

So never despise your calling but use it to become more like Jesus. There are those with huge ministries that will be last in heaven because they haven't used their time on earth to become more like Jesus. Even though they had a large ministry in life they may well find that someone who served them as a clerk will be higher than them when they enter heaven because the clerk was more Christ-like.

Our calling makes no difference to the Father. Those who do much work get the same reward as those who do little. It's not about how much work we do for Jesus but more about how much like him we become.

That helps take off the pressure to become somebody important in church spheres. Our Father knows which calling is most likely to make us become more like Jesus. If we walk in the calling he has chosen for us then we will become more like Jesus and that is what it is really all about.

To sum up I'll quote from the teaching of the Scottish theologian Andrew Murray when describing the true nature of religion. When he speaks of religion he is referring to faith:

'Here we see once and for all what the true nature of religion is. Its work and effect is within; its glory, its life and its perfection are all within. It is solely the raising of a new life, new love and new birth in the inward spirit of our hearts. This was the spiritual nature of religion in its beginning and this alone is its whole nature until the end of time. It is nothing else but the power, life and Spirit of God, as Father, Son and Holy Spirit, working, creating and reviving life in the fallen soul and driving all its evil out of it. Religion is no true divine service, no proper worship of God, has no good in it, can do no good to man, can remove no evil out of him, can raise no divine life in him but insofar as it serves, worships, conforms to and gives itself up to this operation of the holy, triune God as living and dwelling in the soul. Keep close to this idea of religion as an inward spiritual life in the soul. Observe all its works within you, the death and life that are found there. Seek no good, no comfort but in the inward awakening of all that is holy and heavenly in your heart. And then, in-as much as you have this inward religion, so much you have of a real salvation. For salvation is nothing but a victory over nature. Insofar as you resist your own vain, selfish and earthly nature; insofar as you overcome all your own natural inclinations of the old man; insofar as God enters into, lives in and operates in you, he will be the light, the life and the spirit of your soul and you will be in Him the new creature that worships Him in spirit and in truth. All scripture brings us to the conclusion that all religion is but a dead work unless it is the work of the Spirit of God. All our sacraments, prayers, singing, preaching and hearing are only so many ways of being fervent in the spirit and of giving up ourselves more and more to the inward working, enlightening, quickening, sanctifying Spirit of God within us – all so that a true, real, Christlike nature may be formed in us by the Spirit."

As I have already quoted in previous chapters:

The mystery which has been hidden from ages and from generations, but now has been revealed to His saints. To them God willed to make known what are the riches of the glory of this mystery among the Gentiles: which is Christ in you, the hope of glory.
(1 Colossians verses 26 to 27)

It is by holding fast to this hope that we deal with the warfare that comes against us.

SUMMARY

1. There is a battle raging in the spirit realm regarding who rules mankind, the kingdom of heaven or the kingdom of darkness.

2. Faith, hope and love are aspects of the kingdom of heaven and are poured into the earth by the grace of God.

3. Christians have authority to release the kingdom of heaven on the earth through faith, hope and love under the leading of the Holy Spirit.

4. The warfare in the spirit realm is to stop grace flowing on the earth and thereby prevent faith, hope and love and the gifts and fruits of the spirit from manifesting.

5. Much of the warfare is against our hope because if we give in to despair the forces of darkness are victorious.

6. We should not fear because the armies of heaven are on our side. They outnumber the forces of darkness.

7. The counterfeit versions of the three graces, faith, hope and love. are deception, religious fantasy and lust.

8. We know the leading of the spirit by the fruit it produces in our lives. It is the same with the fruits of the flesh.

9. True faith produces godly character in our lives through the leading of the Holy Spirit, which helps establish God's kingdom on the earth.

CHAPTER 10
HOPE, THE ANCHOR OF OUR SOULS

'While there's life, there's hope.' - Cicero

Tragedy can affect people in such a way that they need to find someone to blame. It's easy to blame God in such situations but the truth is God loves you and wouldn't hurt you in any way.

Lesley and I experienced another family crisis when our girls were still at Primary School when a close family relative committed suicide. You can imagine how difficult it was to come to terms with the situation. How could it have happened? Why didn't God stop it from happening? What about their salvation? So many times I have heard people ask these questions, 'Why didn't God intervene?' 'Doesn't He love us anymore?' The answers to these questions provoke much argument but we have found the following to be of help during this and other 'storms of life'.

1. Just because a tragedy has happened does not mean that God has stopped loving us.

The Bible has many examples where tragedy affected people. Some examples to look at are Job, Joseph and King David. However they never stopped believing that God loved them and only wanted the best for them.

2. The bible tells us that we are in a spiritual war.

For we do not wrestle against flesh and blood, but against principalities, against powers, against the rulers of the darkness of this age, against spiritual hosts of wickedness in the heavenly places. (Ephesians 6 verse 12)

There are wicked beings in the spiritual realm that seek to destroy mankind. How else can people of faith explain the terrible things that go on the world? I believe that the holocaust, murder, rape, needless suicide and other horrible things that have happened and continue to happen to mankind can be explained by this passage of scripture. We are in a war and in a war there are casualties.

It is surely not the will of the Father for such things to happen yet they do. That is why Jesus encourages us to pray, 'your will be done on earth as it is in heaven'.

> Pray, therefore, like this: Our Father Who is in heaven, hallowed (kept holy) be Your name. Your kingdom come, Your will be done on earth as it is in heaven. Give us this day our daily bread. And forgive us our debts, as we also have forgiven (left, remitted, and let go of the debts, and have given up resentment against) our debtors. And lead (bring) us not into temptation, but deliver us from the evil one. For Yours is the kingdom and the power and the glory forever. Amen.
> (Matthew 6 verses 9 to 13 the Amplified Bible)

The whole bible is about establishing God's Kingdom on earth. If it were already established, there would be no need for the church. The church is the vessel that God intended to use to build the Kingdom of Heaven and bring about His will on the earth.

There are two kingdoms each vying over the rule of the earth. One is the kingdom of light, the other is the kingdom of darkness.

This is the reason why tragedy's and disasters happen. It is not God's will but a consequence of the spiritual war, that still rages in the heavenly sphere.

3. The bible tells us that there is a time to die and also a time to mourn.

> To everything there is a season, and a time for every matter *or* purpose under heaven:
> A time to be born and a time to die, a time to plant and a time to pluck up what is planted,
> A time to kill and a time to heal, a time to break down and a time to build up,

A time to weep and a time to laugh, a time to mourn and a time to dance,

A time to cast away stones and a time to gather stones together, a time to embrace and a time to refrain from embracing,

A time to get and a time to lose, a time to keep and a time to cast away,

A time to rend and a time to sew, a time to keep silence and a time to speak,

A time to love and a time to hate, a time for war and a time for peace.

(Ephesians 3 verses 1 to 8 the Amplified Bible)

It's awful when we lose someone dear to us but there is a time to die and maybe it was that person's time.

4. God is eternal and thinks eternally.

Our life here on earth is temporary but our God is eternal. He is thinking of what is best for us eternally and sees what may happen in the future. That is why he may sometimes allow people to die or be killed because he is thinking of our eternal lives.

It is amazing how many great works and charities have been founded because someone was positively affected by the death of a loved one resulting in thousands of lives being saved.

5. God is actually intervening all the time.

How many times have you been about to step into a busy street in front of an unseen motor vehicle and something made you stop? How often do the brakes fail, or the wheel comes off a car when a person is going at low speeds on a quiet road instead of at a busy junction? How often have you had a feeling or an emotional check that something wasn't quite right which prevented you making a horrendous mistake or prevented a tragedy occurring?

Some years ago my sister was standing outside a church building in Dundee, Scotland. She heard someone telling her to go over to a nearby shop as there was something in the window. She walked over to the window then realised that she hadn't a clue why she was there. Just then a large chimney stack fell from the roof of the building and struck the pavement where she had been standing. She then realised that there was no-one else there. Who was it that had spoken to her? Susan now believes absolutely in divine intervention.

It is actually unusual for God not to intervene. My own belief is that

God is intervening in human affairs and preventing tragedies all the time but we only notice the disasters. I mean; if, as the bible says, there are all these wicked spirits trying to destroy us, then it is amazing that there aren't far more disasters and tragedies taking place than there actually are. The times when God intervenes to prevent a tragedy are often simply written off as coincidence.

I have often heard people say, 'If there is a God then why do so many horrible things happen all the time?' I turn that one around and say, 'If there isn't a God why aren't these horrible things happening more often?'

We also hear about disasters all over the world instantly by means of the media and internet. Our ancestors were far more insulated against things like that than we are.

6. Something has affected the prayer cover, thereby allowing the wicked spirits in heavenly places to influence earthly events.

The bible is full of examples of where God intervened in human affairs because of the prayers of His people. However there are also examples in the bible where He did not intervene.

We cannot allow tragedies and disasters to influence our thinking into believing that God doesn't exist or that he doesn't love us. Either of these points of view can make a person miserable and cause hope to fade.

7. The bible does not say that suicide victims will go to hell.

I have known relatives, friends and acquaintances that have killed themselves and experienced the torture of thinking that they have gone to hell. There is nothing in the bible however that says a person that commits suicide will go to hell. This belief is based upon religious teaching from the middle ages from the likes of Augustine and Thomas Aquinas and their interpretation of the commandment, 'Thou shalt not kill', that could be better translated as, 'Thou shalt not commit murder'.

The killing of another human being can be justified in certain situations and it is not necessarily a sin to kill someone, for example, killing a maniac with a machine gun who is firing into a crowd of people. Similarly, there are situations where suicide has been regarded as admirable such as a spy killing himself in wartime to prevent vital information falling into the hands of the enemy and thereby saving thousands of lives. A soldier throwing himself on top of a grenade to prevent the shrapnel hitting his colleagues is a hero however suicidal his actions.

The bible is actually silent on the subject of whether suicide is a sin. I am not an advocate of throwing away God's greatest gift but in my opinion there is no biblical basis to the assertion that someone who does so will automatically go to hell. Take Samson for example, who killed himself and thousands of Philistines by pushing against the pillars of the temple causing the roof to collapse upon them (see Judges Chapter 16). He is mentioned in Hebrews Chapter 11 as one of the heroes of faith.

8. People having illness, disability and disease is not a sign that God is angry with them.

Jesus spent a lot of His time healing people.

> Then Jesus went about all the cities and villages, teaching in their synagogues, preaching the gospel of the kingdom, and healing every sickness and every disease among the people.
> (Matthew 9 verse 35)

> How God anointed Jesus of Nazareth with the Holy Spirit and with power, who went about doing good and healing all who were oppressed by the devil, for God was with Him.
> (Acts 10 verse 38)

Jesus commissioned His disciples to heal people.

> And He said to them, 'Go into all the world and preach the gospel to every creature. He who believes and is baptized will be saved; but he who does not believe will be condemned. And these signs will follow those who believe: In My name they will cast out demons; they will speak with new tongues; they will take up serpents; and if they drink anything deadly, it will by no means hurt them; they will lay hands on the sick, and they will recover.'
> (Mark 16 verses 15 to 18)

Those who say that God is punishing people for their sin, when disaster, illness, disability and disease come upon them are therefore mistaken.

These things are signs that the kingdom of darkness is operating in an area. However, when you see people getting healed then it is a sign that the kingdom of heaven is expanding. People who are, or have children who are disabled or ill aren't any more sinful than anyone else.

When we know the true nature of our Father in heaven and His son Jesus Christ such negative thoughts no longer have the same power to cause despair. In place of misery we have a hope that reaches right into the presence of God Himself and uplifts us through the power of the Holy Spirit. As it says in Hebrews:

This was so that, by two unchangeable things [His promise and His oath] in which it is impossible for God ever to prove false *or* deceive us, we who have fled [to Him] for refuge might have mighty indwelling strength *and* strong encouragement to grasp *and* hold fast the hope appointed for us *and* set before [us]. [Now] we have this [hope] as a sure and steadfast anchor of the soul [it cannot slip and it cannot break down under whoever steps out upon it—a hope] that reaches farther *and* enters into [the very certainty of the Presence] within the veil, where Jesus has entered in for us [in advance], a Forerunner having become a High Priest forever after the order (with the rank) of Melchizedek.
(Hebrews 6 verses 18 to 20 the Amplified Bible)

It is hope that helps us overcome these and other trials or storms of life. It truly is the 'anchor of our soul'.

<u>SUMMARY</u>

1. Just because a tragedy has happened does not mean that God has stopped loving us.

2. The bible tells us that we are in a spiritual war.

3. The bible tells us that there is a time to die and also a time to mourn.

4. God is eternal and thinks eternally.

5. God is actually intervening all the time.

6. When tragedy occurs something may have affected the prayer cover, thereby allowing the wicked spirits in heavenly places to influence earthly events.

7. The bible does not say that suicide victims will go to hell.

8. People having illness, disability and disease is not a sign that God is angry with them.

Gordon C Methven

CHAPTER 11
HOPE IN HEAVEN

'The best moment of a Christian's life is his last one, because it is the one that is nearest heaven. And then it is that he begins to strike the keynote of the song which he shall sing to all eternity.' - Charles Spurgeon

Another aspect of my faith that gives me hope for eternal life is that when I die, the Lord will call me home to heaven. Not that I make it the main focus of my life though. I believe that the most important thing about my faith is that it gives me hope for my life and family. However, it is good to know that when my life's work is done, my Father will call me home to spend eternity with Him.

How do I know that this is true? The answer is that the bible makes numerous references to heaven.

> So He said to them, "When you pray, say: Our Father in heaven, Hallowed be Your name. Your kingdom come. Your will be done on earth as it is in heaven.
> (Luke 11 verse 2)

Jesus clearly speaks of heaven being a separate place to earth. That's good enough for me!

> Rejoice in that day and leap for joy! For indeed your reward is great in heaven, For in like manner their fathers did to the prophets.
> (Luke 6 verse 23)

Jesus speaks of there being a reward in heaven. That means that heaven exists.

> So when Jesus heard these things, He said to him, 'You still lack one thing. Sell all that you have and distribute to the poor, and you will have treasure in heaven; and come, follow Me.'
> (Luke 18 verse 22)

Jesus speaks of there being treasure in heaven for those that give to the poor.

> For God so loved the world that He gave His only begotten Son, that whoever believes in Him should not perish but have everlasting life.
> (John 3 verse 16)

It's clear that our mortal bodies perish because everyone dies eventually. However Jesus must have been speaking about something else when he says that whoever believes in Him will not perish but have everlasting life. Surely this eternal life must refer to the spirit realm.

> The sheep that are My own hear *and* are listening to My voice; and I know them, and they follow Me. And I give them eternal life, and they shall never lose it *or* perish throughout the ages. [To all eternity they shall never by any means be destroyed.] And no one is able to snatch them out of My hand. My Father, Who has given them to Me, is greater *and* mightier than all [else]; and no one is able to snatch [them] out of the Father's hand.
> (John 10 verses 27 to 29 the Amplified Bible)

> Paul, a bond servant of God and an apostle (a special messenger) of Jesus Christ (the Messiah) to stimulate and promote the faith of God's chosen ones and to lead them on to accurate discernment and recognition of and acquaintance with the Truth which belongs to and harmonizes with and tends to godliness, [Resting] in the hope of eternal life, [life] which the ever truthful God Who cannot deceive promised before the world or the ages of time began. And [now] in His own appointed time He has made manifest (made known) His Word and revealed it as His message through the preaching entrusted to me by command of God our Savior;
> (Titus 1 verses 1 to 3 the Amplified Bible)

It is this eternal life in the spirit that the bible speaks of when it makes reference to heaven. I believe though that focusing on going to heaven has caused the gospel to be misrepresented by generations of preachers and teachers. The gospel isn't primarily a message about what happens to you after you die but more importantly about having the life of God within your heart when you are living here on the earth.

There is a passage of scripture where Jesus makes an interesting answer to Sadduces who are seeking to ridicule belief in the resurrection. The Sadduces were a group of Jewish believers that maintained there was no life after death.

> Also there came to Him some Sadducees, those who say that there is no resurrection. And they asked Him a question, saying, 'Teacher, Moses wrote for us [a law] that if a man's brother dies, leaving a wife and no children, the man shall take the woman and raise up offspring for his brother. Now there were seven brothers; and the first took a wife and died without [having any] children. And the second. And then the third took her, and in like manner all seven, and they died, leaving no children. Last of all, the woman died also. Now in the resurrection whose wife will the woman be? For the seven married her.' And Jesus said to them, 'The people of this world *and* present age marry and are given in marriage; but those who are considered worthy to gain that other world *and* that future age and to attain to the resurrection from the dead neither marry nor are given in marriage; for they cannot die again, but they are angel-like *and* equal to angels. And being sons of *and* sharers in the resurrection, they are sons of God. But that the dead are raised [from death]—even Moses made known *and* showed in the passage concerning the [burning] bush, where he calls the Lord, The God of Abraham, the God of Isaac, and the God of Jacob. Now He is not the God of the dead, but of the living, for to Him all men are alive [whether in the body or out of it] *and* they are alive [not dead] unto Him [in definite relationship to Him]. And some of the scribes replied, Teacher, you have spoken well *and* expertly [so that there is no room for blame]. For they did not dare to question Him further.
> (Luke 20 verses 27 to 40 the Amplified Bible)

Jesus clearly states His belief in eternal life and in the resurrection from the dead. In the gospel of John He speaks of preparing a place in His Father's house for His disciples.

> Do not let your hearts be troubled (distressed, agitated). You believe in *and* adhere to *and* trust in *and* rely on God; believe in *and* adhere

to *and* trust in *and* rely also on Me. In My Father's house there are many dwelling places (homes). If it were not so, I would have told you; for I am going away to prepare a place for you. And when (if) I go and make ready a place for you, I will come back again and will take you to Myself, that where I am you may be also.
(John 14 verses 1 to 3 the Amplified Bible)

Jesus mentions dwelling places, that literally means places to live.

King David wrote a psalm about the Lord being a shepherd that guided him through all the days of his life. He finishes the psalm with a line that can only refer to eternal life for if death was something that ended that relationship he wouldn't have used the word 'forever'.

The Lord is my Shepherd [to feed, guide, and shield me], I shall not lack. He makes me lie down in [fresh, tender] green pastures; He leads me beside the still *and* restful waters. He refreshes *and* restores my life (my self); He leads me in the paths of righteousness [uprightness and right standing with Him—not for my earning it, but] for His name's sake. Yes, though I walk through the [deep, sunless] valley of the shadow of death, I will fear *or* dread no evil, for You are with me; Your rod [to protect] and Your staff [to guide], they comfort me. You prepare a table before me in the presence of my enemies. You anoint my head with oil; my [brimming] cup runs over. Surely *or* only goodness, mercy, *and* unfailing love shall follow me all the days of my life, and through the length of my days the house of the Lord [and His presence] shall be my dwelling place.
(Psalm 23 the Amplified Bible)

The gospel of Matthew also gives a clear indication of eternal life when the Old Testament prophets Elijah and Moses, appeared to Jesus on a mountain and spoke with Him.

And six days after this, Jesus took with Him Peter and James and John his brother, and led them up on a high mountain by themselves. And His appearance underwent a change in their presence; and His face shone clear and bright like the sun, and His clothing became as white as light. And behold, there appeared to them Moses and Elijah, who kept talking with Him. Then Peter began to speak and said to Jesus, Lord, it is good and delightful that we are here; if You approve, I will put up three booths here—one for You and one for Moses and one for Elijah. While he was still speaking, behold, a shining cloud [composed of light] overshadowed

them, and a voice from the cloud said, This is My Son, My Beloved, with Whom I am [and have always been] delighted. Listen to Him! When the disciples heard it, they fell on their faces and were seized with alarm and struck with fear. But Jesus came and touched them and said, Get up, and do not be afraid. And when they raised their eyes, they saw no one but Jesus only.
(Matthew 17 verses 1 to 8 the Amplified Bible)

The Apostle Peter also spoke of an inheritance reserved in heaven for God's people.

Blessed be the God and Father of our Lord Jesus Christ, who according to His abundant mercy has begotten us again to a living hope through the resurrection of Jesus Christ from the dead, to an inheritance incorruptible and undefiled and that does not fade away, reserved in heaven for you.
(I Peter 4 verses 3 to 4)

The Hope of Glory is that we will become like Jesus. This includes spending life in eternity with our Father in Heaven.

SUMMARY

1. The bible makes numerous references to heaven as being a real place.

2. There are rewards reserved in heaven for those who do God's will.

3. Heaven is the eternal home of those who walk with Jesus.

4. Jesus believed in heaven and also in eternal life.

5. Jesus was transfigured and talked with Moses and Elijah in front of three witnesses.

CONCLUSION

There is so much written in the bible that gives me cause to hope. I have often heard people say that there are too many inconsistencies and contradictions in the bible for them to believe in it.

However I have read it cover to cover and found that any inconsistencies merely cause me to believe more in its authenticity. As in a court of law, where the evidence given is remarkably similar it sometimes tends to point towards people having made something up rather than what they are saying being true. However, where people are telling the truth there will always be inconsistencies as they see things slightly differently but generally they will all be saying the same thing.

Moreover, where there are contradictions it often tends to mean that people are reading a passage of scripture out of context. For example because they believe in an angry God, they interpret promises as commandments. "If you love me you will obey me" is to me a promise but it could easily be interpreted otherwise.

The bible is a message of faith, hope and love to the world. It should always be read and interpreted in that context.

I can think of no better way of concluding a book about the hope of glory than by including my favourite hymn, the stirring Boy's Brigade anthem, 'Will your anchor hold'. It has been a constant in my life and something that has given me hope when I needed it.

Words by Priscilla J. Owens and music by William James Kirkpatrick, my thanks to them both who are no doubt now part of the heavenly host that are cheering us on.

Will your anchor hold in the storms of life
When the clouds unfold their wings of strife?
When the strong tides lift and the cables strain
Will your anchor drift, or firm remain?

Chorus:
We have an anchor that keeps the soul
Steadfast and sure while the billows roll
Fastened to the Rock which cannot move
Grounded firm and deep in the Saviour's love

It is safely moored, 'twill the storm withstand
For 'tis well secured by the Saviour's hand
Though the tempest rage and the wild winds blow
Not an angry wave shall our bark o'erflow

* It will firmly hold in the Floods of Death
When the waters cold chill our latest breath
On the rising tide it can never fail
While our hopes abide within the veil

When our eyes behold through the gath'ring night
The city of gold, our harbour bright
We shall anchor fast by the heav'nly shore
With the storms all past forevermore

*Alternate verse:
It will surely hold in the Straits of Fear
When the breakers tell that the reef is near
Though the tempest rave and the wild winds blow
Not an angry wave shall our bark o'erflow

May <u>your</u> anchor hold. Thanks for reading.

ABOUT THE AUTHOR

Gordon Methven was a police officer in the North of Scotland for twenty five years where he had a passion for helping resolve social issues and neighbour-hood troubles. He is a qualified mediator and counselor who has helped many people turn their lives around with his friendly, common sense approach to their problems. He has been a Christian lay preacher and teacher for over twenty years and is also a church deacon. He is currently a freelance writer and represents the city of Elgin as a community councilor. He is married with two grown up daughters.

Printed in Great Britain
by Amazon